MARTIN

BEST-SELLIN

CW00525129

TOP STOCKS

TWENTY-EIGHTH EDITION

2022

A SHAREBUYER'S GUIDE TO

LEADING AUSTRALIAN COMPANIES

WILEY

The author and publisher would like to thank Alan Hull (author of *Active Investing*, Revised Edition, *Trade My Way* and *Invest My Way*; www.alanhull.com) for generating the five-year share-price charts.

This twenty-eighth edition first published in 2022 by Wrightbooks an imprint of John Wiley & Sons Australia, Ltd

42 McDougall Street, Milton Qld 4064

Office also in Melbourne

Typeset in Adobe Garamond Pro Regular by 10/12 pt

First edition published as *Top Stocks* by Wrightbooks in 1995

New edition published annually

© Martin Roth 2022

The moral rights of the author have been asserted

ISBN: 978-0-730-39146-3

A catalogue record for this
book is available from the
National Library of Australia

Cover design: Wiley
Cover image: Graph © FrankRamspott/Getty Images

Charts provided by MetaStock

Disclaimer

Printed in Singapore
M115214_280921

Contents

PART I: the companies

PART II: the tables

Preface

Economic uncertainty, political instability, trade wars and of course the COVID-19 pandemic are exerting a tenacious influence on global financial markets. Yet, in the midst of this environment, numerous fine companies continue to emerge in Australia, with great potential for investors.

During 2020 Australia entered its first recession in 29 years as the pandemic hurt many businesses. Some may not even survive. As the old stock market adage warns us, it is when the tide goes out that we learn who has been swimming naked.

But in fact, when the economic tide went out in 2020 it also revealed something else, something of importance — that Australia boasts many companies of very high quality. We saw this particularly in August 2021 as company after company announced some quite wonderful financial results.

Many of these are companies that make solid profits year after year, that have just moderate levels of debt and that pay regular dividends to their shareholders. Most importantly for readers of this book, they are exactly the kinds of companies that are found in *Top Stocks*.

In *Top Stocks 2022* are 23 new companies, including nine that have never appeared in any previous edition of the book. This is the third-highest number of new companies in the 28-year history of the book.

They are often smaller to medium-sized corporations. Some will be unfamiliar to investors. But all meet the stringent *Top Stocks* criteria, including solid profits and moderate debt levels.

Guiding investors towards value stocks has been one of the paramount aims of the book from the very first edition. Indeed, one of the rationales for the book has always been to highlight the truth that Australia boasts many excellent companies that continue to make good profits year after year regardless of the direction of the financial markets. Despite the title, *Top Stocks* is actually a book about companies.

Right from the start it has been an attempt to help investors find the best public companies in Australia, using strict criteria. These criteria are explained fully later. But, in essence, all companies in the book must have been publicly listed for at least five years and must have been making a profit and paying a dividend for each of those five years. They must also meet tough benchmarks of profitability and debt levels. It is completely objective. My own personal views count for nothing. In addition, share prices have never been relevant.

Of course, such stocks could not withstand the tidal wave of a substantial market sell-off. They too would be affected. But they should be affected less. And if they are good companies they will continue to thrive and to pay dividends. And they will bounce back faster than many others.

Of the 91 companies in *Top Stocks 2022* — one more than in last year's edition — fully 71 reported a higher after-tax profit in their latest full financial year (June 2021 for most of them). In addition, 70 recorded higher earnings per share and 69 paid a higher dividend.

And though, as I write above, share prices are not relevant for selection to *Top Stocks*, 61 of the companies in the book have provided investor returns — share price appreciation plus dividends — of an average of at least 10 per cent per year over a five-year period.

Green and ethical investing

Each year I try to identify trends among the companies of *Top Stocks*. Many investors have in recent years become aware of a new buzz-phrase in the investment world — Environmental, Social and Governance (ESG) analysis and investing. It refers to a growing trend towards rating companies according to their adherence to a set of non-financial ethical standards.

In this case, it means:

1. Environmental. How does the company address issues such as climate change, renewable energy, sustainability and green technology?
2. Social. How does the company treat its employees, customers, suppliers and community?
3. Governance. How does the company treat such issues as executive compensation, ethical business practices, corporate diversity and the relationship with shareholders?

Of course, there are no set rules about how to analyse a company for its ESG practices. Much is subjective. What is socially responsible for one investor may not be for another. For example, big banks are included in the portfolios of some ethical funds, but are excluded from others.

Another example: the resources sector has helped Australia become wealthy. Our coal and iron ore exports have helped bring electricity and industry to countries like China, contributing to the raising of hundreds of millions from poverty. Yet you are unlikely to find ethical investors buying shares in coal-mining companies.

The *Australian Financial Review* wrote in September 2021 in a report on this trend: 'A growing chorus in the investment community is warning that investors need to climate-proof their portfolios or risk missing out on potentially overlooked returns offered by the global transition to a zero-carbon economy.'

It quoted a portfolio manager arguing that climate change was the next mega-trend and the biggest investment opportunity since the internet.

Look at BHP. In August 2021 it announced that it was selling its oil and gas businesses — it was already in the process of getting rid of its thermal coal interests — in order 'to grow value through producing the commodities the world needs for economic growth and decarbonisation'.

BHP CEO Mike Henry said in a company press release: 'The world will need more copper and nickel for electrification, renewable power and electric vehicles, iron ore and high-quality metallurgical coal to produce the steel for infrastructure, including that required for decarbonisation, and the potash required for sustainable global food production. We are actively positioning BHP to meet the world's needs.'

One of the companies in this book, Australian Ethical Investment, is at the heart of this movement. It offers a series of socially responsible funds and in 2020 was named by Morningstar, the financial information service, as one of the six leading asset managers in the field of ethical investing, selected from 40 managers around the world. (Though investors might have done better investing in the shares of the company itself, rather than in its funds. Over the five years to September 2021 it was the top stock market performer of all 91 companies in this book.)

The company's website (www.australianethical.com.au) contains a considerable amount of information about its investment process.

Here are some companies from *Top Stocks 2022* with a connection to the ethical investing and green energy trends:

- ALS is one of the world's largest providers of laboratory analysis services. It sees particular potential in its Life Sciences division, which provides testing services for the environmental, food and pharmaceutical sectors. This division already contributes more than half of company income.
- Australian Ethical Investment, cited above, is a wealth management company that specialises in investments in corporations that meet a set of ethical criteria.
- BHP Group has declared that it sees its greatest potential in 'future-facing' commodities, such as copper and nickel for electrification, renewable power and electric vehicles, and potash for fertiliser. It is ending its exposure to thermal coal and petroleum.
- Fortescue Metals has launched Fortescue Future Industries, a global green energy business, with a particular focus on green hydrogen, which the company predicts could become a US$12 trillion market by 2050.
- GWA Group, a leading producer of bathroom products, is seeing growing sales for its Caroma Smart Command intelligent bathroom system, which enables the monitoring and management of water usage in commercial buildings, helping reduce water wastage.

- Magellan Financial Group runs the Magellan Sustainable Fund, which it describes as 'an actively constructed, systematically managed and continuously monitored ESG-focused portfolio of 70–90 of the world's best businesses'.
- Mineral Resources has a substantial exposure to lithium, through its holdings in the Wodgina lithium mine and the Mount Marion lithium project.
- Pendal Group is a funds management company. Its subsidiary Regnan, an ESG specialist, plans a series of socially responsible funds and products that are aligned with the 17 sustainable development goals of the United Nations.
- Perpetual has acquired the American investment firm Trillium Asset Management, which has a speciality in ESG funds, and it plans to launch ESG funds in Australia.
- Pinnacle Investment Management is working to expand into specialist ethical funds.
- Platinum Asset Management has recruited a dedicated ESG analyst to help integrate ethical concerns into the company's investment analysis.
- PWR is an engineering company with a specialty in cooling systems. It is actively working with developers of electric vehicles, alternative energy storage systems and hydrogen fuel-cell technology.
- Rio Tinto has earmarked US$2.4 billion for the Jadar lithium project in Serbia, aiming to become Europe's largest source of lithium for electric vehicle batteries.
- Sandfire Resources expects a rapid rise in demand for its copper from the electric vehicle and the wind and solar energy industries. Its forecast is that global copper demand from clean energy sources will rise from 1 million tonnes in 2020 to 5.4 million tonnes in 2030.

Health care companies

Some investors are not aware that Australia boasts a dynamic health care industry. In fact, Healthcare is the third largest major sector on the ASX, after Financials and Materials. Many of these companies are showing excellent growth, although dividend yields are generally small. Here are health care companies in this edition of *Top Stocks*.

Health care companies

	Year-on-year after-tax profit growth (2021) (%)	Dividend yield (%)
Ansell	41.8	2.8
Cochlear	53.9	1.1
CSL	2.6	1.0
Integral Diagnostics	35.8	2.8
Pacific Smiles	73.1	1.0
Pro Medicus	33.7	0.2
Sonic Healthcare	149.2	2.1
Virtus Health	138.8	3.7

Small companies with high dividend yields

With interest rates remaining low, many investors are seeking stocks with relatively high dividend yields. Several times in *Top Stocks* I have published a list of smaller companies with good dividend yields.

The following table shows companies from the book with a market capitalisation of below $700 million and with dividend yields of at least 4 per cent.

Dividend yield: small companies

	Dividend yield (%)
Adairs	5.9
Michael Hill	5.4
Servcorp	5.3
Grange Resources	5.1
Austal	4.2
Beacon Lighting	4.2
Schaffer	4.1

Gold

The gold price has been in the spotlight for several years. Many investors believe it is set to rise. Here are some gold-related companies from this edition of *Top Stocks*.

- Codan is a world leader in the production of gold detectors for small-scale miners.
- Evolution Mining produced 680 788 ounces of gold in the June 2021 year, with a forecast of 700 000 ounces to 760 000 ounces for the June 2022 year.
- Michael Hill International, a jewellery business, is a retailer of gold items.
- Newcrest Mining is Australia's leading gold miner, with production of 2 093 322 ounces in the June 2021 year. It expects to produce 1.8 million ounces to 2 million ounces in the June 2022 year. It maintains an extensive exploration program aimed at raising this in future years.
- Orica is a supplier of commercial explosives and sodium cyanide, with the gold sector representing around 20 per cent of sales.
- Regis Resources, a smaller gold production company, produced 372 870 ounces of gold in the June 2021 year, with a forecast of 460 000 ounces to 515 000 ounces in the June 2022 year.
- Sandfire Resources is predominantly a copper miner, but in the June 2021 year it also produced 39 459 ounces of gold, with a forecast of 30 000 ounces to 34 000 ounces in the June 2022 year.

Who is *Top Stocks* written for?

Top Stocks is written for all those investors wishing to exercise a degree of control over their portfolios. It is for those just starting out, as well as for those with plenty of experience but who still feel the need for some guidance through the thickets of more than 2000 listed stocks.

It is not a how-to book. It does not give step-by-step instructions to 'winning' in the stock market. Rather, it is an independent and objective evaluation of leading companies, based on rigid criteria, with the intention of yielding a large selection of stocks that can become the starting point for investors wishing to do their own research.

A large amount of information is presented on each company, and another key feature of the book is that the data is presented in a common format, to allow readers to make easy comparisons between companies.

It is necessarily a conservative book. All stocks must have been listed for five years even to be considered for inclusion. It is especially suited to those seeking out value stocks for longer-term investment.

Yet, perhaps ironically, the book is also being used by short-term traders seeking a good selection of financially sound and reliable companies whose shares they can trade.

In addition, there are many regular readers who buy the book each year, and to them in particular I express my thanks.

What are the entry criteria?

The criteria for inclusion in *Top Stocks* are strict:

- All companies must be included in the All Ordinaries Index, which comprises Australia's 500 largest stocks (out of more than 2000). The reason for excluding smaller companies is that there is often little investor information available on them and some are so thinly traded as to be almost illiquid. In fact, the 500 All Ordinaries companies comprise, by market capitalisation, more than 95 per cent of the entire market.
- It is necessary that all companies be publicly listed since at least the end of 2016, and have a five-year record of profits and dividend payments, each year.
- All companies are required to post a return-on-equity ratio of at least 10 per cent in their latest financial year.
- No company should have a debt-to-equity ratio of more than 70 per cent.
- It must be stressed that share price performance is NOT one of the criteria for inclusion in this book. The purpose is to select companies with good profits and a strong balance sheet. These may not offer the spectacular share-price returns of a high-tech start-up or a promising lithium miner, but they should also present far less risk.

- There are several notable exclusions. Listed managed investments are out, as these mainly buy other shares or investments. Examples are Australian Foundation Investment Company and all the real estate investment trusts.
- A further exclusion are the foreign-registered stocks listed on the ASX. There is sometimes a lack of information available about such companies. In addition, their stock prices tend to move on events and trends in their home countries, making it difficult at times for local investors to follow them.

It is surely a tribute to the strength and resilience of Australian corporations that, once again, despite the volatility of recent years, so many companies have qualified for the book.

Changes to this edition

A total of 22 companies from *Top Stocks 2021* have been omitted from this new edition.

Two companies, 1300SMILES and Vita Group, were dropped from the All Ordinaries Index, so no longer met one of the requirements for inclusion in the book.

Two corporations, DWS and Mortgage Choice, were acquired during the year.

Two companies saw their debt-to-equity ratio rise above the 70 per cent limit for this book. One of these, Ramsay Health Care, expanded its borrowings. The other, Woolworths Group, sharply reduced its shareholders' equity.

The remaining 16 excluded companies had return-on-equity ratios that fell below the required 10 per cent:

Adbri
Alumina
ANZ Banking Group
Australian Pharmaceutical Industries
Brickworks
Class
Integrated Research
InvoCare
Lifestyle Communities
McPherson's
MNF Group
Northern Star Resources
SeaLink Travel Group
Select Harvests
Service Stream
Westpac Banking

There are 23 new companies in this book (although 14 of them have appeared in earlier editions of the book, but were not in *Top Stocks 2021*).

The new companies in this book are:

ALS
Austal
BlueScope Steel
Bravura Solutions*
Carsales.com
CIMIC Group
Costa Group*
CSL
Elders*
Grange Resources*
McMillan Shakespeare
Metcash
Michael Hill International*
Monadelphous Group
Newcrest Mining
Orora
Premier Investments*
Reece
Reliance Worldwide*
Seven Group Holdings*
Sonic Healthcare
Steadfast Group*
Virtus Health

* Companies that have not appeared in any previous edition of *Top Stocks*.

Companies in every edition of *Top Stocks*

This is the 28th edition of *Top Stocks*. With the elimination of ANZ Banking and Westpac Banking — the return on equity figures for both banks fell below the required 10 per cent for this edition of the book — just one company has appeared in every edition: Commonwealth Bank of Australia.

Once again it is my hope that *Top Stocks* will serve you well.

Martin Roth
Melbourne
September 2021

Introduction

The 91 companies in this book have been placed as much as possible into a common format, for ease of comparison. Please study the following explanations in order to get as much as possible from the large amount of data.

The tables have been made as concise as possible, though they repay careful study, as they contain large amounts of information.

Note that the tables for the banks have been arranged a little differently from the others. Details of these are outlined later in this Introduction.

Head

At the head of each entry is the company name, with its three-letter ASX code and the website address.

Share-price chart

Under the company name is a long-term share-price chart, to September 2021, provided by Alan Hull (www.alanhull.com), author of *Invest My Way*, *Trade My Way* and *Active Investing*.

Small table

Under the share-price chart is a small table with the following data.

Sector

This is the company's sector as designated by the ASX. These sectors are based on the Global Industry Classification Standard — developed by S&P Dow Jones Indices and Morgan Stanley Capital International — which was aimed at standardising global industry sectors. You can learn more about these on the ASX website.

Share price

This is the closing price on 2 September 2021. Also included are the 12-month high and low prices, as of the same date.

Market capitalisation

This is the size of the company, as determined by the stock market. It is the share price multiplied by the number of shares in issue. All companies in this book must be in the All Ordinaries Index, which comprises Australia's 500 largest stocks, as measured by market capitalisation.

Price-to-NTA-per-share ratio

The NTA-per-share figure expresses the worth of a company's net tangible assets — that is, its assets minus its liabilities and intangible assets — for each share of the company. The price-to-NTA-per-share ratio relates this figure to the share price.

A ratio of one means that the company is valued exactly according to the value of its assets. A ratio below one suggests that the shares are a bargain, though usually there is a good reason for this. Profits are more important than assets.

Some companies in this book have a negative NTA-per-share figure — as a result of having intangible assets valued at more than their net assets — and a price-to-NTA-per-share ratio cannot be calculated.

See Table M, in the second part of this book, for a little more detail on this ratio.

Five-year share price return

This is the approximate total return you could have received from the stock in the five years to September 2021. It is based on the share price appreciation or depreciation plus dividends, and is expressed as a compounded annual rate of return.

Dividend reinvestment plan

A dividend reinvestment plan (DRP) allows shareholders to receive additional shares in their company in place of the dividend. Usually — though not always — these shares are provided at a small discount to the prevailing price, which can make them quite attractive. And of course no broking fees apply.

Many large companies offer such plans. However, they come and go. When a company needs finance it may introduce a DRP. When its financing requirements become less pressing it may withdraw it. Some companies that have a DRP in place may decide to deactivate it for a time.

The information in this book is based on up-to-date information from the companies. But if you are investing in a particular company in expectations of a DRP, be sure to check that it is still on offer. The company's own website will often provide this information.

Price/earnings ratio

The price/earnings ratio (PER) is one of the most popular measures of whether a share is cheap or expensive. It is calculated by dividing the share price — in this case the closing price for 2 September 2021 — by the earnings per share figure. Obviously the share price is continually changing, so the PER figures in this book are for guidance only. Many newspapers publish each morning the latest PER for every stock.

Dividend yield

This is the latest full-year dividend expressed as a percentage of the share price. Like the price/earnings ratio, it changes as the share price moves. It is a useful figure, especially for investors who are buying shares for income, as it allows you to compare this income with alternative investments, such as a bank term deposit or a rental property.

Company commentary

Each commentary begins with a brief introduction to the company and its activities. Then follow the highlights of its latest business results. For the majority of the companies these are their June 2021 results, which were issued during July and August 2021. Finally, there is a section on the outlook for the company.

Main table

Here is what you can find in the main table.

Revenues

These are the company's revenues from its business activities, generally the sale of products or services. However, it does not usually include additional income from such sources as investments, bank interest or the sale of assets. If the information is available, the revenues figure has been broken down into the major product areas.

As much as possible, the figures are for continuing businesses. When a company sells a part of its operations the financial results for the sold activities are now separated from the core results. This can mean that the previous year's results are restated — also excluding the sold business — to make year-on-year comparisons more valid.

Earnings before interest and taxation

Earnings before interest and taxation (EBIT) is the firm's profit from its operations before the payment of interest and tax. This figure is often used by analysts examining a company. The reason is that some companies have borrowed extensively to finance their activities, while others have opted for alternative means. By expressing profits before interest payments it is possible to compare more precisely the performance of these companies. The net interest figure — interest payments minus interest receipts — has been used for this calculation.

You will also find many companies using a measure called EBITDA, which is earnings before interest, taxation, depreciation and amortisation.

EBIT margin

This is the company's EBIT expressed as a percentage of its revenues. It is a gauge of a company's efficiency. A high EBIT margin suggests that a company is achieving success in keeping its costs low.

Gross margin

The gross margin is the company's gross profit as a percentage of its sales. The gross profit is the amount left over after deducting from a company's sales figure its cost of sales:

that is, its manufacturing costs or, for a retailer, the cost of purchasing the goods it sells. The cost of goods sold figure does not usually include marketing or administration costs.

As there are different ways of calculating the cost of goods sold figure, this ratio is better used for year-to-year comparisons of a single company's efficiency, rather than in comparing one company with another.

Many companies do not present a cost of goods sold figure, so a gross margin ratio is not given for every stock in this book.

The revenues for some companies include a mix of sales and services. Where a breakdown is possible, the gross profit figure will relate to sales only.

Profit before tax/profit after tax
The profit before tax figure is simply the EBIT figure minus net interest payments. The profit after tax figure is, of course, the company's profit after the payment of tax, and also after the deduction of minority interests. Minority interests are that part of a company's profit that is claimed by outside interests, usually the other shareholders in a subsidiary that is not fully owned by the company. Many companies do not have any minority interests, and for those that do it is generally a tiny figure.

As much as possible, I have adjusted the profit figures to exclude non-recurring profits and losses, which are often referred to as significant items. It is for this reason that the profit figures in *Top Stocks* sometimes differ from those in the financial media or on financial websites, where profit figures normally include significant items.

Significant items are those that have an abnormal impact on profits, even though they happen in the normal course of the company's operations. Examples are the profit from the sale of a business, or expenses of a business restructuring, the write-down of property, an inventory write-down, a bad-debt loss or a write-off for research and development expenditure.

Significant items are controversial. It is often a matter of subjective judgement as to what is included and what excluded. After analysing the accounts of hundreds of companies, while writing the various editions of this book, it is clear that different companies use varying interpretations of what is significant.

Further, when they do report a significant item there is no consistency as to whether they use pre-tax figures or after-tax figures. Some report both, making it easy to adjust the profit figures in the tables in this book. But difficulties arise when only one figure is given for significant items.

In normal circumstances most companies do not report significant items. But investors should be aware of this issue. It sometimes causes consternation for readers of *Top Stocks* to find that a particular profit figure in this book is substantially different from that given by some other source. My publisher occasionally receives emails from readers enquiring why a profit figure in this book is so different from that reported elsewhere. In virtually all cases the reason is that I have stripped out a significant item.

It is also worth noting my observation that a growing number of companies present what they call an underlying profit (called a cash profit for the banks), in addition to their reported (statutory) profit. This underlying profit will exclude not only significant items but also discontinued businesses and sometimes other related items. Where all the relevant figures are available, I have used these underlying figures for the tables in this book.

It should also be noted that when a company sells or terminates a significant business it will now usually report the profit or loss of that business as a separate item. It will also usually backdate its previous year's accounts to exclude that business, so that worthwhile comparisons can be made of continuing businesses.

The tables in this book usually refer to continuing businesses only.

Earnings per share

Earnings per share is the after-tax profit divided by the number of shares. Because the profit figure is for a 12-month period the number of shares used is a weighted average of those on issue during the year. This number is provided by the company in its annual report and its results announcements.

Cashflow per share

The cashflow per share ratio tells — in theory — how much actual cash the company has generated from its operations.

In fact, the ratio in this book is not exactly a true measure of cashflow. It is simply the company's depreciation and amortisation figures for the year added to the after-tax profit, and then divided by a weighted average of the number of shares. Depreciation and amortisation are expenses that do not actually utilise cash, so can be added back to after-tax profit to give a kind of indication of the company's cashflow.

By contrast, a true cashflow — including such items as newly raised capital and money received from the sale of assets — would require quite complex calculations based on the company's statement of cashflows.

However, many investors use the ratio as I present it, because it is easy to calculate, and it is certainly a useful guide to approximately how much funding the company has available from its operations.

Dividend

The dividend figure is the total for the year, interim and final. It does not include special dividends. The level of franking is also provided.

Net tangible assets per share

The NTA per share figure tells the theoretical value of the company — per share — if all assets were sold and then all liabilities paid. It is very much a theoretical figure, as there is no guarantee that corporate assets are really worth the price put on them in the balance sheet. Intangible assets such as goodwill and patent rights are excluded because of the difficulty in putting a sales price on them, and also because they may in fact not have much value if separated from the company.

As already noted, some companies in this book have a negative NTA, due to the fact that their intangible assets are so great, and no figure can be listed for them.

Where a company's most recent financial results are the half-year figures, these are used to calculate this ratio.

Interest cover

The interest cover ratio indicates how many times a company could make its interest payments from its pre-tax profit. A rough rule of thumb says a ratio of at least three times is desirable. Below that and fast-rising interest rates could imperil profits. The ratio is derived by dividing the EBIT figure by net interest payments. Some companies have interest receipts that are higher than their interest payments, which turns the interest cover into a negative figure, and so it is not listed.

Return on equity

Return on equity is the after-tax profit expressed as a percentage of the shareholders' equity. In theory, it is the amount that the company's managers have made for you — the shareholder — on your money. The shareholders' equity figure used is an average for the year.

Debt-to-equity ratio

This ratio is one of the best-known measures of a company's debt levels. It is total borrowings minus the company's cash holdings, expressed as a percentage of the shareholders' equity. Some companies have no debt at all, or their cash position is greater than their level of debt, which results in a negative ratio, so no figure is listed for them.

Where a company's most recent financial results are the half-year figures, these are used to calculate this ratio.

Current ratio

The current ratio is simply the company's current assets divided by its current liabilities. Current assets are cash or assets that can, in theory, be converted quickly into cash. Current liabilities are normally those payable within a year. Thus, the current ratio measures the ability of a company to repay in a hurry its short-term debt, should the need arise. The surplus of current assets over current liabilities is referred to as the company's working capital.

Where a company's most recent financial results are the half-year figures, these are used to calculate this ratio.

Banks

The tables for the banks are somewhat different from those for most other companies. EBIT and debt-to-equity ratios have little relevance for them, as they have such high interest payments (to their customers). Other differences are examined below.

Operating income

Operating income is used instead of sales revenues. Operating income is the bank's net interest income — that is, its total interest income minus its interest expense — plus other income, such as bank fees, fund management fees and income from businesses such as corporate finance and insurance.

Net interest income

Banks borrow money — that is, they accept deposits from savers — and they lend it to businesses, homebuyers and other borrowers. They charge the borrowers more than they pay those who deposit money with them, and the difference is known as net interest income.

Operating expenses

These are all the costs of running the bank. Banks have high operating expenses, and one of the keys to profit growth is cutting these expenses. Add the provision for doubtful debts to operating expenses, then deduct the total from operating income, and you get the pre-tax profit.

Non-interest income to total income

Banks have traditionally made most of their income from savers and from lending out money. But they are also working to diversify into new fields, and this ratio is an indication of their success.

Cost-to-income ratio

As noted, the banks have high costs — numerous branches, expensive computer systems, many staff, and so on — and they are all striving to reduce these. The cost-to-income ratio expresses their expenses as a percentage of their operating income, and is one of the ratios most often used as a gauge of efficiency. The lower the ratio drops the better.

Return on assets

Banks have enormous assets, in sharp contrast to, say, a high-tech start-up whose main physical assets may be little more than a set of computers and other technological equipment. So the return on assets — the after-tax profit expressed as a percentage of the year's average total assets — is another measure of efficiency.

PART I
THE COMPANIES

Accent Group Limited

ASX code: AX1   www.accentgr.com.au

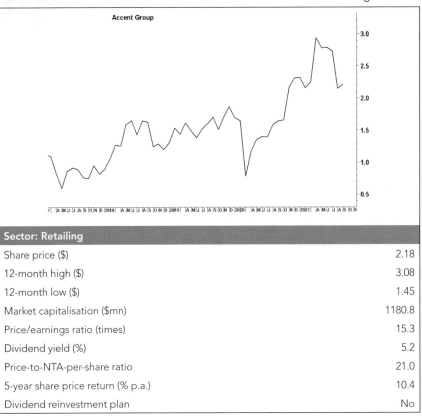

Sector: Retailing	
Share price ($)	2.18
12-month high ($)	3.08
12-month low ($)	1.45
Market capitalisation ($mn)	1180.8
Price/earnings ratio (times)	15.3
Dividend yield (%)	5.2
Price-to-NTA-per-share ratio	21.0
5-year share price return (% p.a.)	10.4
Dividend reinvestment plan	No

Sydney company Accent Group is a nationwide footwear wholesaler and retailer that has grown rapidly through a series of mergers and acquisitions. Its brands now include The Athlete's Foot — established in 1976 — Hype DC, Platypus, Podium Sports, Skechers, Merrell, CAT, Vans, Dr. Martens, Saucony, Timberland, Sperry Top-Sider, Palladium and Stance. The company's wholesale division distributes footwear and apparel. Accent also operates in New Zealand. In 2021 it acquired the Glue Store chain of youth apparel outlets.

Latest business results (June 2021, full year)

The company was again able to overcome the impact of lockdowns, with a strong rise in sales and profits. Total retail sales of $1.14 billion — including franchise stores — were up 20 per cent, with particular strength for the Hype DC, Skechers, Platypus, The Athlete's Foot, The Trybe and Subtype brands. On a same-store basis, sales rose 8 per cent. Total online sales of $210 million were up 48 per cent. Wholesale revenues grew 22 per cent to $132 million. The result also benefited from JobKeeper wage subsidies from the government and rent concessions from landlords. During the year the company opened 90 new stores and closed seven, and at June 2021 it operated a network of 638 stores, including 75 in New Zealand.

Outlook

Accent maintains its ambitious growth strategy and expects profits to continue rising, with a long-term objective of annual earnings-per-share growth of at least 10 per cent. It expects to open at least 65 new stores in the June 2022 year. It is making increasing moves into the youth apparel market, and its $13 million acquisition of the Glue Store business is part of this strategy. Glue Store operates a network of 21 outlets, and Accent plans to expand this to more than 60 stores by December 2023. It also sees the Stylerunner activewear brand that it acquired in 2019 as another key growth opportunity. It has opened the first four Stylerunner stores, and expects to increase this to 60 stores within three years. Accent believes it has seen a structural shift towards online shopping, and it plans a substantial investment in boosting this business, adding to the 31 websites it already operates. Its goal is that digital sales will eventually represent 30 per cent of total turnover, up from around 20 per cent at present. Its contactable customer database grew by 1.6 million customers in the June 2021 year to 8.4 million customers, and the company is expanding its series of loyalty programs for them.

Year to 27 June*	2020	2021
Revenues ($mn)	829.8	992.8
EBIT ($mn)	94.8	124.9
EBIT margin (%)	11.4	12.6
Profit before tax ($mn)	80.3	111.0
Profit after tax ($mn)	55.7	76.9
Earnings per share (c)	10.31	14.21
Cash flow per share (c)	29.92	35.45
Dividend (c)	9.25	11.25
Percentage franked	100	100
Net tangible assets per share ($)	0.09	0.10
Interest cover (times)	6.6	9.0
Return on equity (%)	13.7	18.4
Debt-to-equity ratio (%)	7.6	15.6
Current ratio	1.0	0.9

*28 June 2020

Adairs Limited

ASX code: ADH

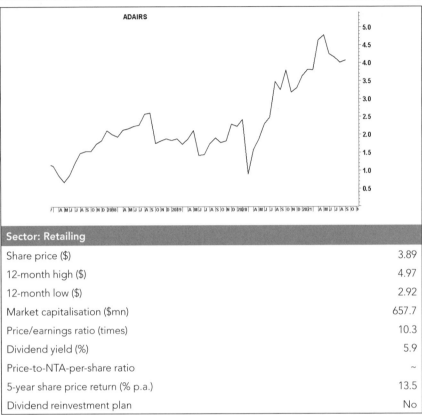

Sector: Retailing	
Share price ($)	3.89
12-month high ($)	4.97
12-month low ($)	2.92
Market capitalisation ($mn)	657.7
Price/earnings ratio (times)	10.3
Dividend yield (%)	5.9
Price-to-NTA-per-share ratio	~
5-year share price return (% p.a.)	13.5
Dividend reinvestment plan	No

Melbourne-based home furnishings specialist Adairs dates back to 1918 and the opening of a store in Chapel Street in Prahran, Melbourne. It has since grown into a nationwide chain of stores specialising in bed linen, bedding, towels, homewares, soft furnishings, children's furnishings and some bedroom furniture. It has also expanded to New Zealand, and it operates a flourishing online business. In 2019 it acquired the New Zealand–based online furniture retailer Mocka. At June 2021 it operated a total of 169 stores nationwide and in New Zealand.

Latest business results (June 2021, full year)

A booming home renovation market in the midst of the COVID-19 pandemic powered Adairs to a second consecutive double-digit gain in sales and profits. The good result came despite the disruption from store closures during the year, and was helped by a full-year contribution from Mocka, acquired in December 2019. Strong demand enabled the company to reduce discounting and raise prices, and profit margins expanded. On a like-for-like basis — excluding the impact of store closures — total revenues rose 16.5 per cent. Mocka recorded sales of $60.2 million and an underlying EBIT of $12.4 million. Total online sales of $187 million were more than 50 per cent higher than in the previous year.

Outlook

Adairs manages popular brands with high levels of customer recognition and loyalty. With an addressable Australian home furnishings market of some $12 billion it sees great scope for growth. It has become a significant beneficiary of what could be a structural trend towards online shopping — induced by the COVID-19 pandemic — and also by rising demand for homewares, as people spend more time at home. It believes its online operations could see significant further growth, and it plans to invest heavily in this business. It is fast-tracking an expansion of its warehouse facilities to support this. It is also engaged in product category expansion trials for its Mocka online business. Adairs sees particular potential in its Linen Lovers rewards program. This has grown to 950 000 members, and these accounted for more than 80 per cent of company sales in the June 2021 year. The company also continues to open new retail outlets, with an emphasis on larger stores, which generally are more profitable than smaller ones. A new national distribution centre in Melbourne is expected to generate annual cost savings of around $3.5 million from the June 2022 year. With much of its product range imported, Adairs is vulnerable to supply-chain disruptions and currency fluctuations.

Year to 27 June*	2020	2021
Revenues ($mn)	388.9	499.8
EBIT ($mn)	59.0	102.7
EBIT margin (%)	15.2	20.6
Gross margin (%)	57.1	60.7
Profit before tax ($mn)	52.8	95.3
Profit after tax ($mn)	35.3	63.7
Earnings per share (c)	21.00	37.70
Cash flow per share (c)	44.40	64.06
Dividend (c)	11	23
Percentage franked	100	100
Net tangible assets per share ($)	~	~
Interest cover (times)	9.6	13.8
Return on equity (%)	27.3	41.8
Debt-to-equity ratio (%)	0.7	~
Current ratio	0.8	0.7

*28 June 2020

ALS Limited

ASX code: ALQ

www.alsglobal.com

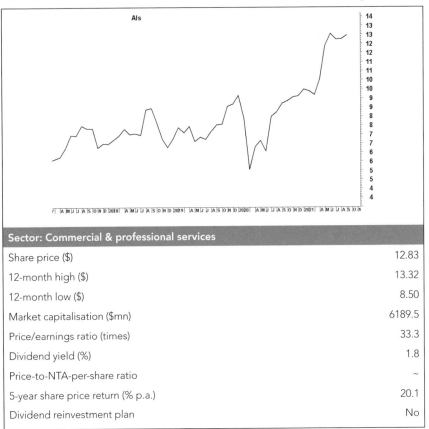

Sector: Commercial & professional services	
Share price ($)	12.83
12-month high ($)	13.32
12-month low ($)	8.50
Market capitalisation ($mn)	6189.5
Price/earnings ratio (times)	33.3
Dividend yield (%)	1.8
Price-to-NTA-per-share ratio	~
5-year share price return (% p.a.)	20.1
Dividend reinvestment plan	No

Brisbane-based ALS was established in 1863 and has become one of the world's largest providers of laboratory analysis services. It serves numerous industry sectors, and groups these into three divisions — Life Sciences (including environmental, food, pharmaceutical, consumer products and electronics), Commodities (minerals and coal) and Industrial (energy, resources, transportation, infrastructure, asset care and tribology — used oil). It processes more than 40 million samples annually at over 350 locations in 65 countries.

Latest business results (March 2021, full year)

Sales and profits edged down, though with a strong second-half recovery almost overcoming the first-half COVID-impacted decline in business. The results were hurt a little by an appreciation of the Australian dollar, though boosted by several acquisitions. The best performance came from the Commodities division, with double-digit revenue growth in the second half and an improvement in profit margins. This reflected a global recovery during the year in mining activity, with particular growth from junior explorers. However, coal-related business weakened, due to falling prices

and trade tensions between Australia and China. The Life Sciences division experiei.
a small decline in underlying revenues, but with profits edging up, and strong
performances from the Spanish food-testing business Aquimisa, acquired in 2020, and
from the Mexican pharmaceutical laboratory ARJ, which was acquired in 2019.
However, the Industrial division suffered a double-digit slump in revenues and profits,
as clients for the company's asset care operations deferred non-essential maintenance-
related inspection work.

Outlook

The global testing, inspection and certification (TIC) market was worth an estimated
US$204 billion in 2020 and ALS forecasts that it will expand to around US$244
billion by 2025. Though much TIC work is done by companies inhouse, there is a
growing trend towards outsourcing to third-party TIC providers such as ALS, due in
part to the increasing number and complexity of new regulations and standards in
many countries. A further trend is a growing middle class in developing countries
demanding high-quality standards. ALS sees particular potential for its Life Sciences
division, and plans strong organic growth in existing key markets. It is also looking for
further acquisitions, and in March 2021 acquired Investiga, a pharmaceutical testing
business with operations in both Brazil and the US. The Commodities division looks
set to remain firm, with minerals demand still at high levels. But the Industrial
division continues to experience weakness. A shortage of qualified staff has become a
problem for ALS in some regions, though the company hopes price rises will offset
higher costs.

Year to 31 March	2020	2021
Revenues ($mn)	1831.9	1761.4
Life sciences (%)	52	53
Commodities (%)	35	35
Industrial (%)	13	12
EBIT ($mn)	306.2	301.4
EBIT margin (%)	16.7	17.1
Profit before tax ($mn)	264.5	261.4
Profit after tax ($mn)	188.8	185.9
Earnings per share (c)	39.10	38.54
Cash flow per share (c)	66.93	66.02
Dividend (c)	17.6	23.1
Percentage franked	44	81
Net tangible assets per share ($)	~	~
Interest cover (times)	7.3	7.5
Return on equity (%)	17.4	17.1
Debt-to-equity ratio (%)	92.1	69.8
Current ratio	1.6	1.6

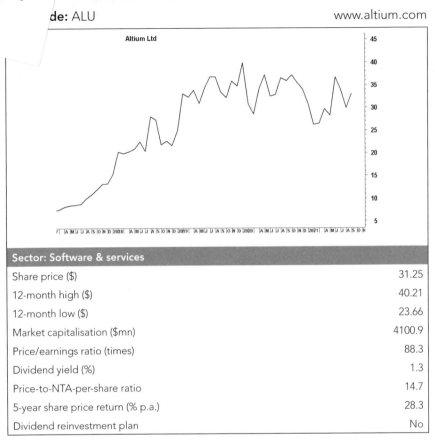

Sector: Software & services	
Share price ($)	31.25
12-month high ($)	40.21
12-month low ($)	23.66
Market capitalisation ($mn)	4100.9
Price/earnings ratio (times)	88.3
Dividend yield (%)	1.3
Price-to-NTA-per-share ratio	14.7
5-year share price return (% p.a.)	28.3
Dividend reinvestment plan	No

Sydney-based software company Altium was founded in Tasmania in 1985. It was originally named Protel. Its specialty is the provision of software that allows engineers to design printed circuit boards (PCBs). Its core product is Altium Designer. A much smaller division provides the Nexar cloud platform for connecting Altium customers with software, suppliers and manufacturers. It has sold its Tasking business. Altium has most of its operations abroad but retains its Sydney headquarters and its ASX listing.

Latest business results (June 2021, full year)

Altium's superb run of nine consecutive years of double-digit sales and profit growth came to a halt with a mixed result. The company reports its finances in US dollars, and sales rose 6 per cent, though they edged down when converted to Australian dollars. At the EBIT level profits fell 5 per cent in US dollars, but the after-tax profit recorded a double-digit gain, as a recalculation of tax assets and liabilities led to a high tax bill in the previous year. All regions reported growing sales, with a strong second half offsetting first-half weakness, including notably solid growth in China. The results have been adjusted to exclude the Tasking business, which was sold for

US$110 million in February 2021. As noted, Altium reports its finances in American dollars. All figures in this book are converted to Australian dollars using prevailing exchange rates.

Outlook

Printed circuit boards are incorporated in most electronic devices, and demand for them continues to grow. The strong rise in smart electronic connected devices is partly behind this trend. It is expensive for a customer to switch once it makes a decision to employ Altium software. The company is working to transition to a subscription-based business, and subscriptions grew 29 per cent in the June 2021 year to represent 65 per cent of total income, up from 59 per cent in the prior year. It has a strong reputation for its PCB design software, with high profit margins and a growth rate higher than the industry average. It sees particular potential for its Altium 365 product, the world's first cloud platform for PCB design and realisation. It has set itself a June 2025 target of US$500 million in total revenues, with 100 000 subscribers to its Altium Designer services, compared to more than 54 000 at June 2021. For June 2022 it forecasts revenue growth of 16 per cent to 20 per cent. At June 2021 Altium had no debt and more than US$190 million in cash holdings.

Year to 30 June	2020	2021
Revenues ($mn)	245.4	237.1
EBIT ($mn)	73.7	63.2
EBIT margin (%)	30.0	26.7
Profit before tax ($mn)	73.9	62.7
Profit after tax ($mn)	28.6	46.4
Earnings per share (c)	21.85	35.38
Cash flow per share (c)	33.92	47.33
Dividend (c)	39	40
Percentage franked	0	8
Net tangible assets per share ($)	1.49	2.12
Interest cover (times)	~	118.4
Return on equity (%)	10.8	15.3
Debt-to-equity ratio (%)	~	~
Current ratio	2.0	2.4

Ansell Limited

ASX code: ANN

www.ansell.com

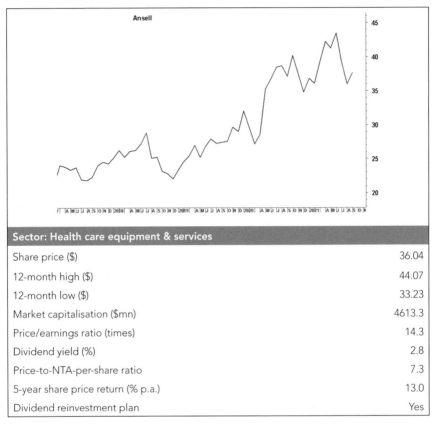

Sector: Health care equipment & services	
Share price ($)	36.04
12-month high ($)	44.07
12-month low ($)	33.23
Market capitalisation ($mn)	4613.3
Price/earnings ratio (times)	14.3
Dividend yield (%)	2.8
Price-to-NTA-per-share ratio	7.3
5-year share price return (% p.a.)	13.0
Dividend reinvestment plan	Yes

Melbourne-based Ansell has roots that stretch back to the manufacture of pneumatic bicycle tyres in the 19th century. It is today a global leader in a variety of safety and healthcare products. It makes a wide range of examination and surgical gloves for the medical profession. It also makes gloves and other hand and arm protective products for industrial applications, including for single use, along with household gloves. It has offices and production facilities in 55 countries, and more than 90 per cent of company revenues derive from abroad. Though still based in Australia, the company has its operational headquarters in the US.

Latest business results (June 2021, full year)

Ansell became a significant beneficiary of the COVID-19 pandemic, with demand soaring for its single-use gloves and personal protective equipment. The Healthcare division saw EBIT surge 66 per cent on a constant currency basis — having already risen by 35 per cent in the previous year — on a sales gain of 38 per cent. The result might have been stronger but for some supply constraints. The benefits of higher manufacturing volumes, along with some price rises, boosted profit margins. The Industrial division was also buoyant, with EBIT up 21 per cent on a constant currency basis, on sales growth of 7 per cent, and particular strength in the second half, as much of the world experienced economic recovery. For a second year the company reported strong growth in demand for chemical protection clothing. Note that Ansell reports its results in US dollars. The Australian dollar figures in this book — converted at prevailing exchange rates — are for guidance only.

Outlook

Ansell has a strong portfolio of products, which gives it a degree of pricing power. It has achieved success in its research and development efforts, with a continuing stream of innovative and high-margin products. Thanks to a major company transformation program, which still continues, it has been able to lower its manufacturing costs. It also continues to seek appropriate acquisition opportunities. However, after having greatly expanded production capability in order to meet COVID-related demand for its products, it faces the possibility of a fall in sales once the pandemic eases, though the company itself suggests the pandemic has changed society's health practices, and that demand will remain high for such items as single-use gloves. Nevertheless, it is concerned about higher shipping expenses, rising labour costs and supply constraints. Ansell's early forecast is for a June 2022 EPS of US$1.75 to US$1.95, compared to US$1.92 in June 2021.

Year to 30 June	2020	2021
Revenues ($mn)	2338.7	2667.0
Healthcare (%)	55	61
Industrial (%)	45	39
EBIT ($mn)	312.0	438.4
EBIT margin (%)	13.3	16.4
Gross margin (%)	39.2	40.0
Profit before tax ($mn)	293.2	418.6
Profit after tax ($mn)	229.0	324.6
Earnings per share (c)	175.74	252.81
Cash flow per share (c)	238.58	318.49
Dividend (c)	72.46	101.34
Percentage franked	0	0
Net tangible assets per share ($)	3.67	4.94
Interest cover (times)	16.6	22.1
Return on equity (%)	11.4	15.9
Debt-to-equity ratio (%)	7.9	13.5
Current ratio	2.4	2.1

ARB Corporation Limited

ASX code: ARB

www.arb.com.au

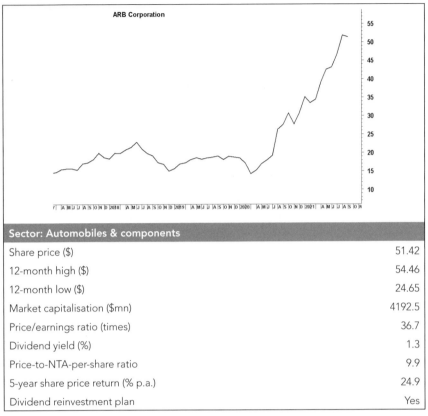

ARB Corporation

Sector: Automobiles & components	
Share price ($)	51.42
12-month high ($)	54.46
12-month low ($)	24.65
Market capitalisation ($mn)	4192.5
Price/earnings ratio (times)	36.7
Dividend yield (%)	1.3
Price-to-NTA-per-share ratio	9.9
5-year share price return (% p.a.)	24.9
Dividend reinvestment plan	Yes

Melbourne-based ARB, founded in 1975, is a prominent manufacturer of specialty automotive accessories, and an international leader in the design and production of specialised equipment for four-wheel-drive vehicles. These include its Air Locker air-operated locking differential system. It also makes and distributes a wide range of other products, including bull bars, roof racks, tow bars, canopies and the Old Man Emu range of suspension products. It operates a network of 70 ARB-brand stores throughout Australia, including 29 that are company-owned. It has established manufacturing facilities in Thailand and it exports to more than 100 countries. In 2021 it acquired the UK's Auto Styling Truckman Group.

Latest business results (June 2021, full year)

Sales and profits rocketed ahead in a superb year for the company, as strong moves towards local travel generated high demand worldwide for its products. Some 55 per cent of total income is from the Australian after-market, comprising ARB stores and other retailers, as well as vehicle dealers and fleet operators. Sales growth of 21 per cent would have been higher but for supply-chain constraints. Exports surged more than 50 per cent and now represent nearly 37 per cent of sales. A new distribution centre in New Zealand caters for steadily growing demand there. Original equip. manufacturer sales to Australian vehicle makers recorded 74 per cent growth, aft declining in the previous year, although this business is only about 8 per cent of total turnover.

Outlook

Demand remains strong globally for ARB's products, although the company is concerned that logistical and supply-chain constraints coupled with labour shortages are increasing operational costs and disrupting the timely fulfilment of sales. It regards product development as a key element in helping it maintain a competitive edge, with research and development spending of $12 million in June 2021, in line with the previous year. Recent new products include a range of accessories for the new Ford Bronco and a slide-out kitchen for four-wheel-drive vehicles incorporating benchtop, gas stove, kitchen sink and utensils drawer. It has initiated construction of a new 30 000-square-metre factory near its existing Thai operations in order to boost production capacity. Auto Styling Truckman Group is a leader in the supply of a range of vehicle utility products in the UK, and ARB expects that its £22 million acquisition of this company will help it expand its presence in European markets. Domestically it is steadily rolling out new ARB-brand stores. At June 2021 ARB had no debt and nearly $85 million in cash holdings.

Year to 30 June	2020	2021
Revenues ($mn)	465.4	623.1
EBIT ($mn)	79.8	151.9
EBIT margin (%)	17.1	24.4
Gross margin (%)	41.4	43.8
Profit before tax ($mn)	78.1	150.0
Profit after tax ($mn)	57.3	112.9
Earnings per share (c)	71.80	139.96
Cash flow per share (c)	99.03	169.11
Dividend (c)	39.5	68
Percentage franked	100	100
Net tangible assets per share ($)	4.22	5.18
Interest cover (times)	47.6	82.0
Return on equity (%)	15.9	26.3
Debt-to-equity ratio (%)	~	~
Current ratio	3.1	3.0

ocrat Leisure Limited

e: ALL   www.aristocrat.com

Sector: Consumer services	
Share price ($)	46.03
12-month high ($)	46.43
12-month low ($)	28.17
Market capitalisation ($mn)	29 392.2
Price/earnings ratio (times)	82.2
Dividend yield (%)	0.2
Price-to-NTA-per-share ratio	~
5-year share price return (% p.a.)	25.4
Dividend reinvestment plan	No

Sydney-based Aristocrat, founded in 1953, is Australia's leading developer and manufacturer of electronic machines for the gaming industry, and it is also among the world's largest. It is licensed by more than 300 gaming jurisdictions worldwide. Its products and services include gaming machines, interactive video terminal systems, electronic tables, gaming machine support services and casino management systems. It is actively bringing a large selection of its games to online and mobile devices.

Latest business results (March 2021, half year)

Aristocrat enjoyed a firm recovery after the difficulties of the September 2020 year, when COVID-19 led to the closure of many of its clients' casino operations. Revenues were down, due to a rising dollar during the period, but actually rose 11 per cent on a constant currency basis. The best result came from the company's booming digital activities, with double-digit gains in revenues and profits, to represent more than half of total company turnover. American business comprises a third of turnover, and revenues fell, but the after-tax profit was up, thanks to expanding gaming activities. The smaller Australia and New Zealand segment achieved firmer sales and profits. However, other international markets saw sales and profits sharply lower.

Outlook

Aristocrat enjoys a strong position in the global gaming industry, with high market shares in many regions. Nevertheless, this remains a competitive business, and the company is highly dependent on a continuing stream of attractive new products. To develop these it must recruit and retain large numbers of highly skilled creative specialists and technology experts, and this has been one of its key challenges. It must also spend heavily on new and enhanced products, and its design and development budget is around 11 per cent to 12 per cent of annual revenues. It expects strong growth during the September 2021 year as the COVID-19 pandemic eases and its casino clients are able fully to reopen their businesses. It has formed a new Digital Leadership Team, and it estimates that the total annual global addressable market for the digital market segment is as high as US$78 billion. It is experiencing significant growth in this market, thanks to popular games that include 'RAID: Shadow Legends', 'Lightning Link' and 'Cashman Casino'. Profit margins for digital games are also expanding rapidly, though they remain below those for the company's traditional gaming operations. With much of its income coming from outside Australia, Aristocrat's earnings are heavily influenced by currency rate trends.

Year to 30 September	2019	2020
Revenues ($mn)	4397.4	4139.1
EBIT ($mn)	1099.0	502.4
EBIT margin (%)	25.0	12.1
Profit before tax ($mn)	973.5	359.6
Profit after tax ($mn)	752.8	357.1
Earnings per share (c)	118.11	55.98
Cash flow per share (c)	182.99	126.45
Dividend (c)	56	10
Percentage franked	100	100
Interest cover (times)	8.8	3.5
Return on equity (%)	38.8	13.4
Half year to 31 March	2020	2021
Revenues ($mn)	2251.8	2229.7
Profit before tax ($mn)	403.7	480.9
Profit after tax ($mn)	305.9	362.2
Earnings per share (c)	47.90	56.79
Dividend (c)	0	15
Percentage franked	~	100
Net tangible assets per share ($)	~	~
Debt-to-equity ratio (%)	64.1	48.9
Current ratio	1.9	2.6

ASX Limited

ASX code: ASX

www.asx.com.au

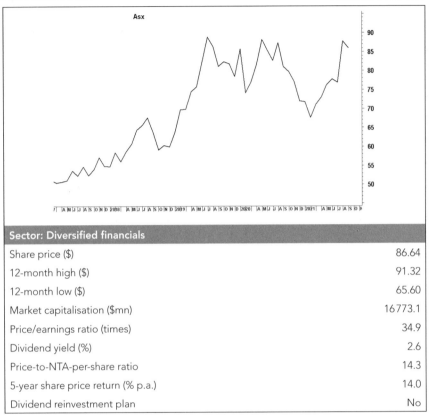

Sector: Diversified financials	
Share price ($)	86.64
12-month high ($)	91.32
12-month low ($)	65.60
Market capitalisation ($mn)	16773.1
Price/earnings ratio (times)	34.9
Dividend yield (%)	2.6
Price-to-NTA-per-share ratio	14.3
5-year share price return (% p.a.)	14.0
Dividend reinvestment plan	No

ASX (Australian Securities Exchange) was formed in 1987 through the amalgamation of six independent stock exchanges that formerly operated in the state capital cities. Each of those exchanges had a history of share trading dating back to the 19th century. Though originally a mutual organisation of stockbrokers, in 1998 ASX became a listed company, with its shares traded on its own market. It expanded in 2006 when it merged with the Sydney Futures Exchange. Today it provides primary, secondary and derivative market services, along with clearing, settlement and compliance services. It is also a provider of a range of comprehensive market data and technical services.

Latest business results (June 2021, full year)

Revenues were up again but rising expenses sent profits lower, bringing to an end 10 straight years of annual profit increases. For a second year the best result came from the smallest division, Equity Post-Trade Services, with revenues up 13 per cent, reflecting a 17 per cent rise in cash market settlement revenue and a 9 per cent increase in cash market clearing revenue. The Listings and Issuer Services division recorded a 9 per cent increase, with continuing solid growth in secondary capital raisings offsetting a decline in annual listing revenues. There were 176 new listings during the year — the highest number in 15 years — up from 83 in the previous year. The Trading Services division saw a 3 per cent rise in revenues, thanks especially to buoyant demand for the company's information services. But revenues fell 10 per cent for the largest division, Derivatives and OTC Markets, affected by low interest rates. Expenses for the year swelled 8 per cent, in part due to investments for future growth.

Outlook

ASX's profits are highly geared to levels of market activity. Nevertheless, such is the diverse variety of instruments available to investors nowadays that even market weakness does not necessarily lead to a decline in trading volumes. The company also enjoys a high degree of protection in its operations, with little effective competition for many of its businesses. It is investing heavily in a major new platform using distributed ledger technology — sometimes referred to as blockchain — to replace its CHESS equities clearing and settlement system. After a series of delays this is now in the testing phase and is due to go live in April 2023. ASX expects expenses to grow by 5 per cent to 7 per cent in the June 2022 year, including costs related to a market outage in November 2020.

Year to 30 June	2020	2021
Revenues ($mn)	949.0	962.3
Derivatives and OTC markets (%)	34	30
Trading services (%)	27	28
Listings and issuer services (%)	25	27
Equity post-trade services (%)	14	15
EBIT ($mn)	637.0	641.2
EBIT margin (%)	67.1	66.6
Profit before tax ($mn)	720.8	687.9
Profit after tax ($mn)	498.6	480.9
Earnings per share (c)	257.56	248.41
Cash flow per share (c)	284.42	277.08
Dividend (c)	238.9	223.6
Percentage franked	100	100
Net tangible assets per share ($)	6.32	6.04
Interest cover (times)	~	~
Return on equity (%)	13.1	12.9
Debt-to-equity ratio (%)	~	~
Current ratio	1.1	1.1

AUB Group Limited

ASX code: AUB

www.aubgroup.com.au

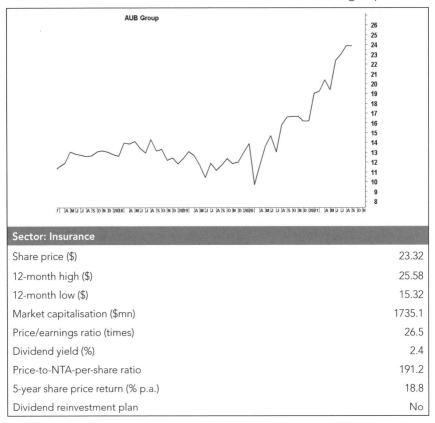

Sector: Insurance	
Share price ($)	23.32
12-month high ($)	25.58
12-month low ($)	15.32
Market capitalisation ($mn)	1735.1
Price/earnings ratio (times)	26.5
Dividend yield (%)	2.4
Price-to-NTA-per-share ratio	191.2
5-year share price return (% p.a.)	18.8
Dividend reinvestment plan	No

Sydney-based AUB Group, formerly known as Austbrokers Holdings, was established in 1985. It manages a network of insurance businesses throughout Australia and New Zealand. Its principal business is insurance broking, and it typically holds an equity stake of at least 50 per cent in each business, usually in partnership with the original owners. It also manages an underwriting agency business, which operates agencies in many specialised areas of the insurance business.

Latest business results (June 2021, full year)

AUB enjoyed another good year, with a solid rise in revenues and profits. The core Australian broking operation contributes more than half the company's turnover. It reported another double-digit rise in profits, thanks to increasing commercial premiums and cost reductions, as well as a contribution from the August 2020 acquisition of a majority stake in Experien Insurance Services, a specialty brokerage focused on the medical and dental professions. By contrast, New Zealand broking, representing about 14 per cent of company turnover, experienced its first profit decline in five years, with premiums flat for the year. It was also affected by a software accounting policy change. A new operating structure and the acquisition of 360 Underwriting Solutions helped profits rebound from the previous year for the underwriting business.

Outlook

AUB has achieved success with its model of buying a stake in an insurance broking house but, in most cases, continuing to operate it with the original owners. This has allowed the businesses to preserve their local identity and management, while benefiting from the support of a large group. The company is able to help its members develop their businesses through growth initiatives, including the addition of new products, and sometimes through appropriate bolt-on acquisitions. Since entering the New Zealand market in 2014 it has become that country's largest broking management group. It is realising excellent returns from its 40 per cent equity stake in the BizCover online broking service, which helps AUB expand its reach among small and medium-sized companies. A new partnership with accounting firm Kelly+Partners Group from December 2020 will provide AUB with further exposure to the small business sector. It is a beneficiary of rising premiums, and expects further 5 per cent to 6 per cent growth in the June 2022 year. A new structure for the underwriting business is expected to generate further increases in profits. The company also continues to seek new acquisitions. AUB's early forecast is for underlying after-tax profit in the June 2022 year of $70 million to $73 million.

Year to 30 June	2020	2021
Revenues ($mn)	303.5	313.3
EBIT ($mn)	82.8	90.4
EBIT margin (%)	27.3	28.8
Profit before tax ($mn)	76.6	83.8
Profit after tax ($mn)	53.4	65.3
Earnings per share (c)	72.45	87.93
Cash flow per share (c)	101.74	121.77
Dividend (c)	50	55
Percentage franked	100	100
Net tangible assets per share ($)	0.61	0.12
Interest cover (times)	13.4	13.7
Return on equity (%)	12.6	14.4
Debt-to-equity ratio (%)	30.0	22.7
Current ratio	1.2	1.2

Austal Limited

ASX code: ASB　　　　　　　　　　　　　　　　www.austal.com

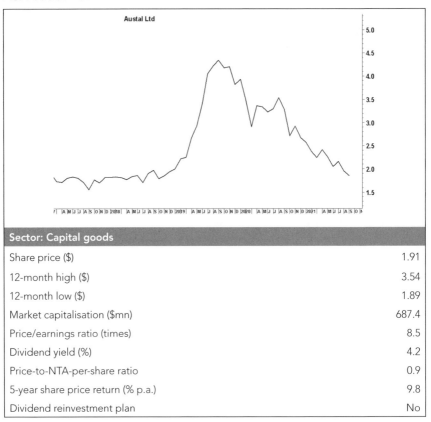

Sector: Capital goods	
Share price ($)	1.91
12-month high ($)	3.54
12-month low ($)	1.89
Market capitalisation ($mn)	687.4
Price/earnings ratio (times)	8.5
Dividend yield (%)	4.2
Price-to-NTA-per-share ratio	0.9
5-year share price return (% p.a.)	9.8
Dividend reinvestment plan	No

Perth-based shipbuilder Austal, founded in 1988, is today a leading supplier of vessels to customers around the world. These vessels include passenger and vehicle ferries, patrol boats and a range of military ships. It is also a provider of worldwide vessel maintenance and management services. It operates from shipyards in Western Australia, the US, Vietnam and the Philippines, as well as from a joint venture business in China.

Latest business results (June 2021, full year)

Austal delivered a record number of new ships, but revenues and profits fell, as the company was hit by a combination of structural and one-off issues. A key factor was a reduction in sales to the US Navy of the company's Littoral Combat Ship, as Austal transitions to the construction of new types of vessels. The company was also hurt by COVID-related costs and delays, an unfavourable currency exchange rate and reduced demand in the US for support services. US revenues fell 36 per cent, although profits actually rose, thanks to cost-cutting measures and some higher-margin contracts. Australasia — incorporating all the company's other work — reported a decline in revenues and profits, and a particularly heavy impact from the COVID-19 pandemic.

During the year the company delivered 19 ships to commercial and defence customers around the world. From its Australian shipyard the company delivered patrol boats for Australia and Trinidad and Tobago, as well as trimaran ferries for Japan and the Canary Islands. In the US the company delivered three new naval vessels. Company shipyards in Asia delivered a total of seven ferries. At June 2021 Austal had an order book worth approximately $2.5 billion.

Outlook

With some three-quarters of its business connected to its work for the US Navy, Austal now sees itself as in a period of transition, as it initiates a new steel vessel program, anticipating that much future demand from the US Navy will be for steel-hulled vessels. Until now the company has specialised in aluminium hulls. It has already received US Navy contracts for preliminary design work, and anticipates that it will be ready to begin steel vessel construction work from May 2022. It also expects increasing levels of demand in the US for support services, and it is expanding its US facilities. In Australia it sees a solid pipeline of tendering opportunities related to the government's 2020 defence strategic update, the Force Structure Plan. Austal has announced that it will sell its shareholding in its joint venture Chinese company, disappointed at levels of business there.

Year to 30 June	2020	2021
Revenues ($mn)	2086.0	1572.2
USA (%)	77	74
Australasia (%)	23	26
EBIT ($mn)	130.4	114.6
EBIT margin (%)	6.3	7.3
Gross margin (%)	11.5	14.2
Profit before tax ($mn)	123.5	107.2
Profit after tax ($mn)	89.0	81.1
Earnings per share (c)	24.98	22.55
Cash flow per share (c)	37.82	35.27
Dividend (c)	8	8
Percentage franked	0	0
Net tangible assets per share ($)	2.04	2.05
Interest cover (times)	18.9	15.5
Return on equity (%)	12.9	10.6
Debt-to-equity ratio (%)	~	~
Current ratio	2.0	1.7

Australian Ethical Investment Limited

ASX code: AEF

www.australianethical.com.au

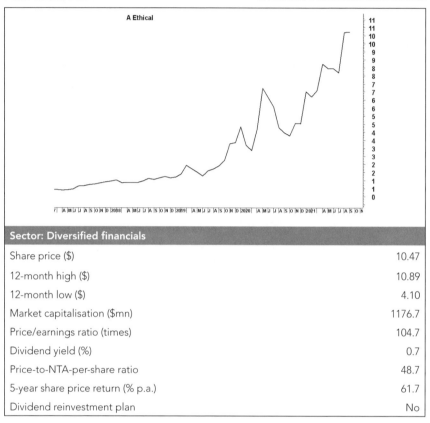

A Ethical

Sector: Diversified financials	
Share price ($)	10.47
12-month high ($)	10.89
12-month low ($)	4.10
Market capitalisation ($mn)	1176.7
Price/earnings ratio (times)	104.7
Dividend yield (%)	0.7
Price-to-NTA-per-share ratio	48.7
5-year share price return (% p.a.)	61.7
Dividend reinvestment plan	No

Australian Ethical, based in Sydney, was founded in 1986. It is a wealth management company that specialises in investments in corporations that meet a set of ethical criteria. It operates a range of wholesale and retail funds, incorporating Australian and international shares, emerging companies and fixed interest. It also manages the Australian Ethical Advocacy Fund, which seeks to engage directly with companies to pursue improved corporate behaviour. The company donates up to 10 per cent of its profits to charities and activist groups through its Australian Ethical Foundation.

Latest business results (June 2021, full year)

Further growth in new customer numbers and in net money inflows generated another strong result. Net inflows of $1.03 billion were up 56 per cent from the June 2020 year. In that year inflows had doubled from June 2019. There was particularly good growth in fund inflow from institutional investors and superannuation funds. The company received a performance fee of $2.9 million — down from $3.6 million in the previous year — relating to its Emerging Companies Fund. During the year it reduced the fees for many of its products. Funds under management of $6.1 billion at June 2021 were up 50 per cent from a year earlier.

Outlook

Australian Ethical is a small company but is a leader in a fast-growing trend towards ethical investment. One reason it has attracted attention for its funds is because of its perceived independence. Some rival ethical or green funds are actually managed by large institutional investors. The company's pledge is that it seeks out positive investments that support its three pillars of people, planet and animals. Its Ethical Charter gives details of the criteria it uses for its investments, and it provides a public list of the companies in which it is prepared to invest. In 2020 the financial information service Morningstar named Australian Ethical as one of the six leading asset managers in the field of ethical investing, selected from 40 managers around the world. It has adopted an aggressive growth strategy that in the short term will boost expenses and limit profit growth. It believes it will be possible to expand to three to five times its current size over the coming four or five years, leading eventually to higher levels of profitability. Nevertheless, despite its strong position, Australian Ethical remains heavily exposed to financial markets, and its businesses could be hurt in any sustained downturn. At June 2021 it had no debt and more than $27 million in cash holdings.

Year to 30 June	2020	2021
Revenues ($mn)	49.9	58.7
EBIT ($mn)	13.0	15.5
EBIT margin (%)	26.0	26.4
Profit before tax ($mn)	13.1	15.5
Profit after tax ($mn)	9.3	11.1
Earnings per share (c)	8.46	10.00
Cash flow per share (c)	9.27	11.06
Dividend (c)	5	7
Percentage franked	100	100
Net tangible assets per share ($)	0.19	0.22
Interest cover (times)	~	15497.0
Return on equity (%)	49.1	49.1
Debt-to-equity ratio (%)	~	~
Current ratio	2.5	2.4

Baby Bunting Group Limited

ASX code: BBN   www.babybunting.com.au

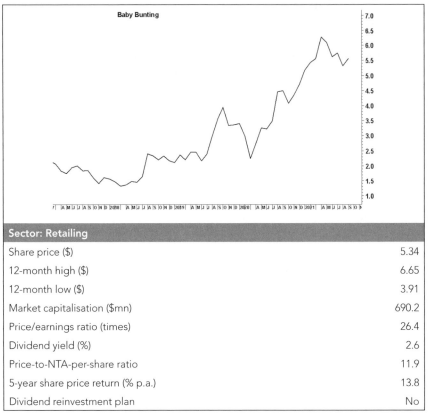

Sector: Retailing

Share price ($)	5.34
12-month high ($)	6.65
12-month low ($)	3.91
Market capitalisation ($mn)	690.2
Price/earnings ratio (times)	26.4
Dividend yield (%)	2.6
Price-to-NTA-per-share ratio	11.9
5-year share price return (% p.a.)	13.8
Dividend reinvestment plan	No

Melbourne retailer Baby Bunting started in 1979 with the opening of a store in the suburb of Balwyn. It has since grown into a nationwide chain of stores specialising in some 6000 lines of baby and nursery products, including prams, car seats, carriers, furniture, nursery items, safety goods, babywear, manchester, toys, feeding products and maternity wear.

Latest business results (June 2021, full year)

In an excellent result, sales and profits rose by double-digit amounts. Despite the pandemic, the company was able to keep all stores open during the year. On a same-store basis, sales rose 11.3 per cent, and the company also opened four new stores. There was another significant jump in sales of private label and exclusive products, up 31.1 per cent from the previous year. Online sales grew by 54.2 per cent to comprise 19.4 per cent of total turnover.

Outlook

Baby Bunting occupies a strong position in the $2.5 billion Australian baby goods retail market. With the demise of some competitors, it is now the only specialist baby goods retailer with a national presence, and its major rivals are stores such as Kmart, Target and Big W. It has numerous strategies for growth. It plans to open some four to eight new stores each year, with an eventual target of more than 100 throughout Australia, up from 60 at June 2021. Private label and exclusive products — generally providing higher profit margins than other goods — now comprise 41 per cent of sales, and the company's long-term goal is to raise this to 50 per cent. It also continues to invest in developing its digital operations. In addition, it is expanding into the services sphere, with initial offerings that include car seat and breast pump rentals, along with car seat installations and repairs. A new loyalty program has attracted 1.1 million members, with members spending 36 per cent more per transaction than non-members. The program will be expanded during the June 2022 year with additional benefits and personalised offers. In July 2020 Baby Bunting began online sales to New Zealand customers, and it has announced plans to launch a New Zealand network of at least 10 stores. It commissioned its new national distribution centre in March 2021, followed by its new store support centre in May 2021. Both are in Victoria and will reduce the company's reliance on third-party logistics, as well as providing cost efficiencies. A second distribution centre is planned for either New South Wales or Queensland.

Year to 27 June*	2020	2021
Revenues ($mn)	405.2	468.4
EBIT ($mn)	33.2	42.3
EBIT margin (%)	8.2	9.0
Gross margin (%)	36.2	37.1
Profit before tax ($mn)	27.5	36.6
Profit after tax ($mn)	19.3	26.0
Earnings per share (c)	15.16	20.20
Cash flow per share (c)	35.04	42.66
Dividend (c)	10.5	14.1
Percentage franked	100	100
Net tangible assets per share ($)	0.35	0.45
Interest cover (times)	5.8	7.5
Return on equity (%)	20.8	25.9
Debt-to-equity ratio (%)	~	~
Current ratio	1.0	1.2

* 28 June 2020

Bapcor Limited

ASX code: BAP

www.bapcor.com.au

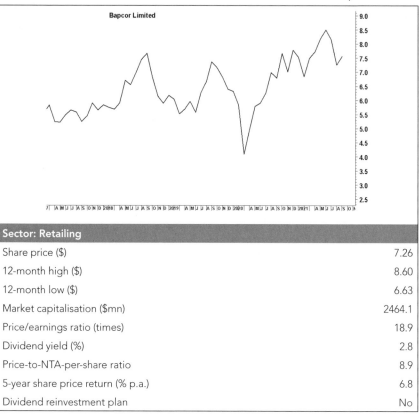

Sector: Retailing	
Share price ($)	7.26
12-month high ($)	8.60
12-month low ($)	6.63
Market capitalisation ($mn)	2464.1
Price/earnings ratio (times)	18.9
Dividend yield (%)	2.8
Price-to-NTA-per-share ratio	8.9
5-year share price return (% p.a.)	6.8
Dividend reinvestment plan	No

Melbourne company Bapcor started in 1971 as Burson Auto Parts, supplying a range of automotive products to workshops and service stations. It grew steadily, organically and by acquisition, opening stores throughout Australia, and taking its present name in 2016. It now services the automotive aftermarket under numerous brands, including Autobarn, Midas, Autopro and ABS. It has extensive operations in Australia and New Zealand, and in 2018 it opened its first stores in Thailand, in partnership with a local auto specialist company. In 2021 it acquired an equity stake in Singapore automotive parts distributor Tye Soon. Bapcor operates from more than 1000 locations in Australia, New Zealand and Thailand.

Latest business results (June 2021, full year)

Sales and profits grew strongly as the company continued to expand its network of businesses and as lockdowns eased. All four divisions recorded double-digit profit growth. An excellent result came from the Specialist Wholesale division, which comprises a range of small outlets that focus on sourcing replacement parts for the automotive aftermarket. It recorded sales growth of 27 per cent, with EBITDA surging 42 per cent, helped by a full-year contribution from the December 2019

Truckline and Diesel Drive acquisitions. The Trade division, comprising the Burson Auto Parts and the Precision Automotive Equipment business units, benefited from same-store sales growth of 14 per cent and the addition of 14 new stores. The Retail division also benefited from a big jump in same-store sales. New Zealand businesses enjoyed a recovery in sales and profits, after suffering from lockdowns in the previous year.

Outlook

Bapcor is a leader in the supply of a huge range of auto parts to more than 30 000 auto workshop customers, and this business is expected to continue to grow as the population increases. In addition, the COVID-19 pandemic has led to an increased reliance on cars for travel and commuting. The company has an ambitious five-year strategy that will lead to a steady increase in the number of outlets across all its divisions. It sees significant growth potential in Thailand, although the impact of COVID means it has so far opened just six stores there. It has taken a 25 per cent equity stake in Singapore automotive parts distributor Tye Soon, which has operations in Singapore, Malaysia, Thailand and South Korea. Bapcor views this investment as an opportunity to develop a network of Asian businesses. It expects significant cost benefits as it merges 13 distribution centres into one new state-of-the-art centre that it has opened in Victoria.

Year to 30 June	2020	2021
Revenues ($mn)	1462.7	1761.7
Specialist wholesale (%)	34	36
Trade (%)	37	35
Retail (%)	19	20
Bapcor New Zealand (%)	10	9
EBIT ($mn)	144.9	200.9
EBIT margin (%)	9.9	11.4
Gross margin (%)	46.5	46.1
Profit before tax ($mn)	125.3	186.0
Profit after tax ($mn)	89.1	130.1
Earnings per share (c)	30.35	38.33
Cash flow per share (c)	57.61	63.49
Dividend (c)	17.5	20
Percentage franked	100	100
Net tangible assets per share ($)	0.66	0.82
Interest cover (times)	7.4	13.4
Return on equity (%)	10.5	12.9
Debt-to-equity ratio (%)	10.5	15.8
Current ratio	2.0	1.9

Beach Energy Limited

ASX code: BPT   www.beachenergy.com.au

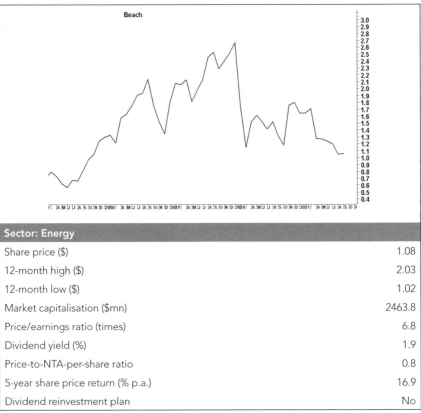

Sector: Energy	
Share price ($)	1.08
12-month high ($)	2.03
12-month low ($)	1.02
Market capitalisation ($mn)	2463.8
Price/earnings ratio (times)	6.8
Dividend yield (%)	1.9
Price-to-NTA-per-share ratio	0.8
5-year share price return (% p.a.)	16.9
Dividend reinvestment plan	No

Adelaide-based Beach Energy, with a history dating back to 1961, is a major oil and gas producer, and a key supplier of gas to eastern states. Its operations are concentrated on five production hubs — the Cooper/Eromanga Basin region of South Australia and Queensland, the Bass Basin in the Bass Strait, the Otway Basin of Victoria and South Australia, the Perth Basin and the Taranaki Basin in New Zealand. It also maintains an active exploration and development program in other areas of Australia and New Zealand.

Latest business results (June 2021, full year)

Lower oil prices and reduced sales sent revenues and profits down for another year. Total production of 25.6 million barrels of oil equivalent (boe) fell from 26.7 million barrels in the previous year, reflecting especially a declining performance from the Western Flank field in the Cooper Basin. The average realised oil price of $78.10 per barrel was down from $80.90 in the previous year. However, the average realised gas/ethane price rose 1 per cent. During the year the company achieved exploration success at its Enterprise 1 and Artisan 1 wells in the Otway Basin.

Outlook

Beach Energy shares took a hit during 2021 after the company revised down the amount of oil reserves at its Western Flank field. It sparked the possibility of a shareholder class action against the company. Beach subsequently also cut the value of its Otway Basin reserves, and for the June 2022 year it has forecast production of just 21 million to 23 million boe. It expects a substantial increase in capital spending in the June 2022 year to as much as $1.1 billion, up from $671 million in June 2021, and with a particular emphasis on projects in the Perth Basin and the Victorian Otway Basin. Thanks to its work in the Perth Basin the company expects to enter the global liquefied natural gas (LNG) market in 2023, as LNG exports begin from the Waitsia Gas Project, which is operated by Mitsui E&P Australia. Beach also plans further exploration activity in the Western Flank field with the goal of unlocking new reserves. It is ramping up drilling activity in the Otway Basin with the aim of supporting the tightening East Coast gas market and providing a stable long-term revenue stream. In New Zealand the Kupe Compression project is due to come online, extending the production life of the Kupe gas plant, and Beach is investigating further drilling opportunities in the region.

Year to 30 June	2020	2021
Revenues ($mn)	1728.2	1562.0
EBIT ($mn)	653.0	523.5
EBIT margin (%)	37.8	33.5
Gross margin (%)	38.9	38.1
Profit before tax ($mn)	639.0	518.0
Profit after tax ($mn)	461.0	363.0
Earnings per share (c)	20.22	15.92
Cash flow per share (c)	39.73	34.27
Dividend (c)	2	2
Percentage franked	100	100
Net tangible assets per share ($)	1.21	1.32
Interest cover (times)	46.6	95.2
Return on equity (%)	17.8	12.3
Debt-to-equity ratio (%)	~	1.5
Current ratio	1.1	1.7

Beacon Lighting Group Limited

ASX code: BLX   www.beaconlighting.com.au

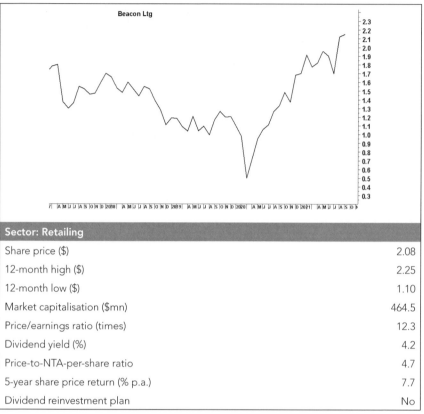

Sector: Retailing	
Share price ($)	2.08
12-month high ($)	2.25
12-month low ($)	1.10
Market capitalisation ($mn)	464.5
Price/earnings ratio (times)	12.3
Dividend yield (%)	4.2
Price-to-NTA-per-share ratio	4.7
5-year share price return (% p.a.)	7.7
Dividend reinvestment plan	No

Melbourne-based lighting specialist Beacon dates back to the launch of the first Beacon Lighting store in 1967. It steadily expanded throughout Australia, and today has 115 stores — two of them franchised — supplying a wide range of lighting fixtures and light globes, as well as ceiling fans. Its Beacon Lighting Commercial division supplies many commercial projects, including volume residential developments, apartment complexes, aged care facilities, hotels and retail fit-outs. It also operates an international wholesale business, based in Hong Kong and with a showroom in China.

Latest business results (June 2021, full year)

Sales and profits rose strongly as customers, unable to travel much, instead spent more time engaged in home renovation projects. Rising demand enabled the company to reduce the levels of discounting it had been using to drive sales, boosting margins. On a same-store basis, sales were up 13.3 per cent for the year, with particularly strong demand in Western Australia. Online sales continued to surge, up 60.3 per cent to $26 million. International business grew by 45.3 per cent to $12.3 million. Commercial sales were up 27.1 per cent. During the year the company opened three new stores.

Outlook

Beacon's business is closely linked to trends in the housing market, which recently has been strong, and it has also benefited from restrictions in travel and the resulting buoyant home renovations market, as well as moves towards home offices. It plans to continue opening new stores and has developed a variety of further strategies for long-term growth. It is placing a particular emphasis on developing its commercial business, with the opening of stores at 7:30 am, a dedicated trade marketing program and the development of trade-specific products. Sales to members of Beacon's Trade Loyalty Club rose by 50 per cent in the June 2021 year. Another growth strategy is the promotion of online business, and it has upgraded its websites in anticipation of continuing strong demand. It is working to boost exports, with sales offices in Hong Kong, Germany and the United States, and it is planning its first sales website aimed at customers in the US. Its Connected Light Solutions business supplies outdoor lighting for a variety of urban applications. Light Source Solutions distributes General Electric lighting products in Australia and New Zealand. Masson For Light works with architects to supply designer lights for prestige construction projects. With much of its product range imported, Beacon is vulnerable to currency fluctuations. At June 2021 it had net cash holdings of more than $15 million.

Year to 27 June*	2020	2021
Revenues ($mn)	251.2	289.3
EBIT ($mn)	35.4	59.5
EBIT margin (%)	14.1	20.6
Gross margin (%)	65.3	68.4
Profit before tax ($mn)	29.2	53.8
Profit after tax ($mn)	20.4	37.6
Earnings per share (c)	9.26	16.93
Cash flow per share (c)	20.39	28.83
Dividend (c)	5	8.8
Percentage franked	100	100
Net tangible assets per share ($)	0.33	0.44
Interest cover (times)	5.8	10.4
Return on equity (%)	23.9	37.8
Debt-to-equity ratio (%)	~	~
Current ratio	1.6	1.4

*28 June 2020

BHP Group Limited

ASX code: BHP   www.bhp.com

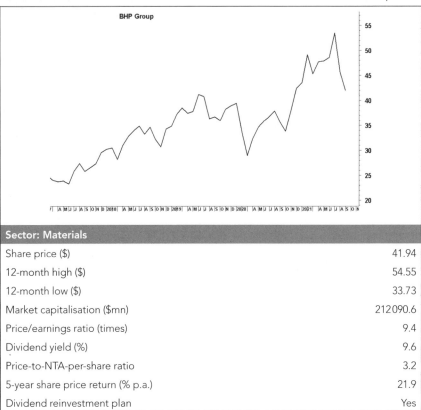

Sector: Materials	
Share price ($)	41.94
12-month high ($)	54.55
12-month low ($)	33.73
Market capitalisation ($mn)	212090.6
Price/earnings ratio (times)	9.4
Dividend yield (%)	9.6
Price-to-NTA-per-share ratio	3.2
5-year share price return (% p.a.)	21.9
Dividend reinvestment plan	Yes

BHP Group was formed in 2001 from the merger of BHP, which was founded as Broken Hill Proprietary in 1885, and Billiton, which dates back to 1851. With its headquarters in Melbourne, though with a dual listing on both the Australian and London stock exchanges, it is today one of the world's largest diversified resources companies, with a powerful portfolio of assets incorporating iron ore, copper, coal, nickel, potash, and oil and gas. It has operations in many countries. It has announced plans to sell its oil and gas operations to Woodside Petroleum.

Latest business results (June 2021, full year)

A booming iron ore market generated significant growth in sales and profits in an excellent year for the company. Iron ore revenues of US$34.5 billion were up 66 per cent from the previous year, thanks to slightly higher volumes and a 69 per cent jump in the average price, partially offset by rising costs. Iron ore represented 57 per cent of total company sales for the year but 80 per cent of underlying EBIT. Copper was also strong, with revenues up 47 per cent to US$15.7 billion and profits surging. Petroleum saw business largely flat for the year. The coal business recorded falling revenues and profits, hurt by higher costs and weaker prices. BHP also reported some major one-off expenses not included in the figures in this book, including more than US$1 billion related to the 2015 dam collapse at the Samarco iron ore mine in Brazil and US$2.8 billion in impairment costs for energy coal and potash assets. Note that BHP reports its results in US dollars. The Australian dollar figures in this book — converted at prevailing exchange rates — are for guidance only.

Outlook

BHP plans a restructuring of its operations in order to gain greater exposure to what it believes are mega-trends of decarbonisation and electrification. It will sell its oil and gas business to Woodside Petroleum, with payment in Woodside shares, which will be distributed to BHP shareholders. It also plans a US$5.7 billion investment in the Jansen Stage 1 potash project in Canada, with the construction of an underground mine and surface infrastructure. The goal is the production of around 4.35 million tonnes of potash annually from 2027, in order to meet global fertiliser demand that the company believes could double from present levels by the late 2040s. BHP also plans to end its current stock market dual-listing arrangement, leading to a more simplified and efficient corporate structure.

Year to 30 June	2020	2021
Revenues ($mn)	62 218.8	80 022.4
Iron ore (%)	48	57
Copper (%)	25	26
Coal (%)	15	8
Petroleum (%)	9	6
EBIT ($mn)	23 140.6	39 968.4
EBIT margin (%)	37.2	49.9
Profit before tax ($mn)	21 820.3	38 251.3
Profit after tax ($mn)	13 130.4	22 469.7
Earnings per share (c)	259.65	444.33
Cash flow per share (c)	434.81	621.88
Dividend (c)	174.86	402.66
Percentage franked	100	100
Net tangible assets per share ($)	13.56	13.14
Interest cover (times)	17.5	23.3
Return on equity (%)	19.2	32.6
Debt-to-equity ratio (%)	26.1	10.3
Current ratio	1.4	1.6

BlueScope Steel Limited

ASX code: BSL   www.bluescope.com

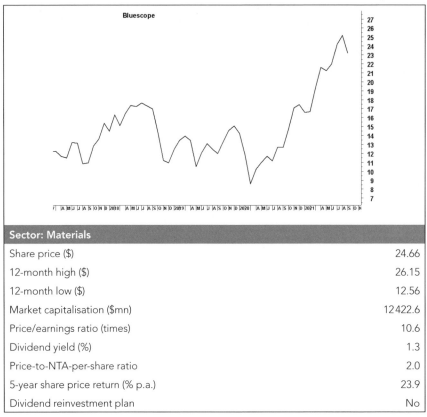

Sector: Materials	
Share price ($)	24.66
12-month high ($)	26.15
12-month low ($)	12.56
Market capitalisation ($mn)	12 422.6
Price/earnings ratio (times)	10.6
Dividend yield (%)	1.3
Price-to-NTA-per-share ratio	2.0
5-year share price return (% p.a.)	23.9
Dividend reinvestment plan	No

Melbourne-based BlueScope Steel, originally a division of BHP, was established as an independent company in 2002. It is a major international producer of steel products for a wide variety of industrial applications. It is one of the world's largest manufacturers of painted and coated steel products, including Colorbond roofing materials. The company is structured into five businesses. Australian Steel Products operates the country's largest steelworks at Port Kembla, with a focus on the building and construction industry. Building Products Asia and North America comprises metal coating, painting and roll-forming businesses. North Star BlueScope Steel is a leading American producer of hot rolled coil. Buildings North America services low-rise non-residential customers. The New Zealand and Pacific Islands division operates production facilities in New Zealand, Fiji, New Caledonia and Vanuatu.

Latest business results (June 2021, full year)

Strong demand across all its businesses generated an excellent result for BlueScope. The core Australian Steel Products division benefited from a combination of lower raw material costs, increased sales and higher global steel prices. A particularly strong home renovation market drove higher sales of metal coated and painted products.

A recovering American economy along with rising steel prices generated significantly higher profits for North American businesses. The New Zealand and Pacific Islands division moved from loss to profit on strong demand for higher-margin coated and painted products and the elimination of some loss-making products. Economic recovery in Asian markets, along with higher steel prices, contributed to strong profit growth for the company's businesses in that region.

Outlook

BlueScope occupies a solid position within the Australian economy, and to a lesser extent within the economies of the US and Asia. Its fortunes will be greatly affected by economic trends in these regions. It is also influenced by global steel prices, currency rate trends and raw material prices. At June 2021 it held net cash of more than $1.3 billion, and it is planning some major expansions to its operations. It is especially optimistic about the growth potential of its North Star steel mill in the US. This division represents 18 per cent of company turnover but more than 39 per cent of June 2021 EBIT. BlueScope already has underway a $1 billion project to boost the 2.1 million tonnes annual capacity of this plant by some 40 per cent, and is now considering an even greater expansion. It is also in the process of exploring the possibility of a $700 million to $800 million upgrade for Port Kembla.

Year to 30 June	2020	2021
Revenues ($mn)	11 284.5	12 872.9
Australian steel products (%)	45	43
Building products Asia & North America (%)	24	24
North Star BlueScope Steel (%)	15	18
Buildings North America (%)	10	8
New Zealand & Pacific Islands (%)	6	7
EBIT ($mn)	564.0	1 723.8
EBIT margin (%)	5.0	13.4
Profit before tax ($mn)	507.5	1 662.1
Profit after tax ($mn)	353.0	1 166.3
Earnings per share (c)	69.58	231.60
Cash flow per share (c)	174.75	328.24
Dividend (c)	14	31
Percentage franked	0	0
Net tangible assets per share ($)	9.59	12.08
Interest cover (times)	10.0	27.9
Return on equity (%)	5.3	16.5
Debt-to-equity ratio (%)	~	~
Current ratio	1.8	1.9

Brambles Limited

ASX code: BXB   www.brambles.com

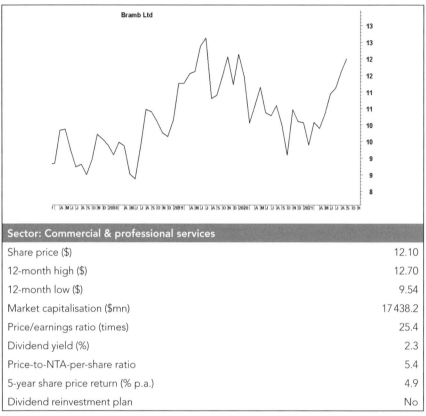

Sector: Commercial & professional services	
Share price ($)	12.10
12-month high ($)	12.70
12-month low ($)	9.54
Market capitalisation ($mn)	17 438.2
Price/earnings ratio (times)	25.4
Dividend yield (%)	2.3
Price-to-NTA-per-share ratio	5.4
5-year share price return (% p.a.)	4.9
Dividend reinvestment plan	No

Sydney-based Brambles has a history that dates back to 1875, when Walter Bramble opened a butcher's business, later expanding into transportation and logistics. Today, following a long series of acquisitions, it is the global leader in pallets, crates and container pooling services under the brand name CHEP (Commonwealth Handling Equipment Pool, a term used by the Australian government to designate pallets and other assets left in Australia by the United States Army after World War II). It owns approximately 345 million pallets, crates and containers through a network of more than 750 service centres in 60 countries.

Latest business results (June 2021, full year)

In a highly volatile business environment, Brambles enjoyed single-digit gains in revenues and profits on a constant currency basis, as demand grew steadily for its services. However, the company reports its results in US dollars, so the revenues figure edged down when converted to Australian dollars. The company benefited from price increases and from supply-chain efficiencies, more than offsetting gradually rising costs. The company saw growth in all regions, with the best result from CHEP Asia-Pacific, thanks especially to continuing expansion of the timber pallets business

in China and a large new reusable plastic container contract in Australi
Americas benefited from strong growth in the consumer staples sector. CHEP
covering Europe, the Middle East and Africa, enjoyed a pleasing recovery
automotive supplies business, which had been hurt badly in the previous year b
pandemic. As noted, Brambles reports its results in US dollars. The Australian do
figures in this book — converted at prevailing exchange rates — are for guidance onl

Outlook

Brambles is heavily influenced by trends in global trade and, more generally, by the
global economy. However, it has a level of protection from any economic downturn
in the fact that more than 80 per cent of its business is related to consumer goods,
particularly grocery items. Half its revenues come from the Americas, and it is
especially affected by the state of the US economy. In addition, it is hurt by the high
expenses of its American operations, with profit margins substantially below those
prevailing elsewhere, and it is working to drive down costs. Nevertheless, it is
concerned that a range of inflationary pressures and supply constraints it experienced
in the June 2021 second half — especially for lumber, which represents 80 per cent of
new pallet costs — could hurt its operations. Consequently, the company is
experimenting with the use of plastic pallets.

Year to 30 June	2020	2021
Revenues ($mn)	6860.3	6855.0
CHEP Americas (%)	52	50
CHEP EMEA (%)	39	40
CHEP Asia-Pacific (%)	9	10
EBIT ($mn)	1111.6	1157.0
EBIT margin (%)	16.2	16.9
Profit before tax ($mn)	994.5	1044.3
Profit after tax ($mn)	691.6	703.9
Earnings per share (c)	44.66	47.72
Cash flow per share (c)	101.95	107.04
Dividend (c)	29	27.32
Percentage franked	30	30
Net tangible assets per share ($)	2.40	2.23
Interest cover (times)	9.5	10.3
Return on equity (%)	14.7	18.6
Debt-to-equity ratio (%)	39.0	49.9
Current ratio	1.1	0.7

Solutions Limited

www.bravurasolutions.com

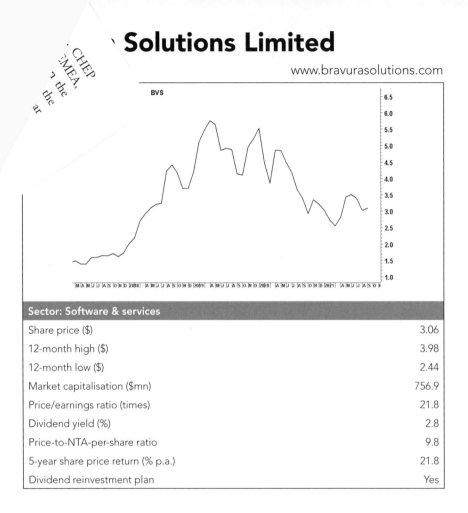

Sector: Software & services	
Share price ($)	3.06
12-month high ($)	3.98
12-month low ($)	2.44
Market capitalisation ($mn)	756.9
Price/earnings ratio (times)	21.8
Dividend yield (%)	2.8
Price-to-NTA-per-share ratio	9.8
5-year share price return (% p.a.)	21.8
Dividend reinvestment plan	Yes

Sydney-based financial software specialist Bravura was formed in 2004 from a management buyout of the wealth management business unit of CSC Australia. It has grown substantially by acquisition, and is now a leader in the provision of financial software for the wealth management and funds administration sectors. Its key product, the Sonata financial management software, is used by many blue-chip clients around the world. It operates from 17 offices in Australia, New Zealand, the United Kingdom, Poland, India and South Africa.

Latest business results (June 2021, full year)

With more than half of its revenues deriving from the UK, Bravura was hurt by a significant pandemic-related slowdown in business activity among British financial institutions, and revenues and profits were down by double-digit amounts. Both of the company's main business segments suffered. The core Wealth Management segment saw revenues down 11 per cent, with EDITDA dropping 5 per cent, due mainly to the decline in UK project work. The Funds Administration segment was hurt by a decline in UK professional services work and by lower licence fees, and recorded a 12 per cent decline in revenues, with EBITDA down 18 per cent.

The result would have been worse but for some cost-saving initiatives, including $11.5 million in savings from staffing reductions. There was also a positive impact from recent acquisitions.

Outlook

Bravura has a solid reputation for its products, many long-term contracts and a strong pipeline of potential customers. It estimates that its annual addressable market in Australia is about $1 billion, and in the UK about £1.2 billion. Currently the company has just a single-digit share of these markets, representing significant upside potential. The $42 million acquisition of Britain's Delta Financial Systems in 2020 greatly extended Bravura's core Sonata product in the field of pension administration. It sees strong potential in Australia for its new fully automated superannuation software product Sonata Alta, and in October 2020 it announced a major contract with Aware Super. It is steadily migrating clients to cloud-based delivery of its products. This helps boost recurring income, which has risen to 84 per cent of total income. It invests heavily in research and development, with $50.4 million spent in the June 2021 year. With demand improving for its products and a resumption in the UK and South Africa of projects that had been postponed due to COVID-19, the company forecasts after-tax profit growth in the mid-teens for the June 2022 year. At June 2021 Bravura had no debt and more than $73 million in cash holdings.

Year to 30 June	2020	2021
Revenues ($mn)	272.4	242.3
Wealth management (%)	66	66
Funds administration (%)	34	34
EBIT ($mn)	46.9	40.6
EBIT margin (%)	17.2	16.8
Profit before tax ($mn)	47.1	39.1
Profit after tax ($mn)	40.1	34.6
Earnings per share (c)	16.46	14.01
Cash flow per share (c)	24.44	22.63
Dividend (c)	11	8.6
Percentage franked	0	0
Net tangible assets per share ($)	0.47	0.31
Interest cover (times)	~	26.1
Return on equity (%)	13.3	10.8
Debt-to-equity ratio (%)	~	~
Current ratio	2.2	1.8

Breville Group Limited

ASX code: BRG   www.brevillegroup.com

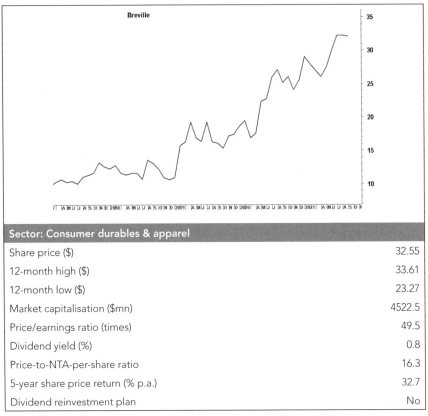

Sector: Consumer durables & apparel	
Share price ($)	32.55
12-month high ($)	33.61
12-month low ($)	23.27
Market capitalisation ($mn)	4522.5
Price/earnings ratio (times)	49.5
Dividend yield (%)	0.8
Price-to-NTA-per-share ratio	16.3
5-year share price return (% p.a.)	32.7
Dividend reinvestment plan	No

Sydney-based Breville Group traces its origins to the production of the first Breville radio in 1932. It later moved into the home appliance business and was subsequently acquired by Housewares International. In 2008 Housewares changed its name to Breville Group, and today the company is a leading designer and distributor of kitchen home appliances under the Breville and Kambrook brands. Its subsidiary in the UK distributes Breville products under the Sage brand. Breville sells its products in some 80 countries, and international business is responsible for around 80 per cent of company turnover.

Latest business results (June 2021, full year)

Breville reported an excellent result as customers around the world, limited in their ability to travel, and often working from home, spent heavily on homeware products. Business was also boosted by the company's steady moves into new markets. All regions of activity were strong, despite some supply-chain disruptions, with particularly impressive growth in demand for a third consecutive year from European consumers. Breville segments its operations into two broad divisions, Global Product and Distribution. The former, responsible for the sale of products designed and developed by Breville, again generated more than 80 per cent of company turnover, with revenues up 29 per cent — 37 per cent on a constant currency basis — and EBIT rising by 28 per cent. The company's recent entry into France, Portugal and Italy helped European sales grow 58 per cent in constant currency. The Distribution division sells products designed and developed by third parties. It achieved sales growth of 8 per cent, with EBIT up 11 per cent, and especially strong demand for air purifiers.

Outlook

Breville has been achieving great success with its strategy of developing its own lines of premium home appliances for the North American, European and Australia/New Zealand markets. North America alone now represents half of company revenues and in 2021 Europe passed Australia/New Zealand as the second-largest region. The company is boosting its product development budget considerably and is realising particular success with new coffee machines, sous vide cookers and air fryer products. Nevertheless, it is wary about the near-term outlook. It believes that while consumers still have considerable amounts of pent-up savings, there are limits to how much they can spend on more home appliances. It is also concerned about logistics delays and rising costs, and it is looking to raise prices where possible. At June 2021 Breville had no debt and cash holdings of nearly $130 million.

Year to 30 June	2020	2021
Revenues ($mn)	952.2	1187.7
EBIT ($mn)	113.1	136.4
EBIT margin (%)	11.9	11.5
Gross margin (%)	33.7	34.8
Profit before tax ($mn)	104.9	127.4
Profit after tax ($mn)	75.0	91.0
Earnings per share (c)	57.21	65.76
Cash flow per share (c)	76.73	85.18
Dividend (c)	41	26.5
Percentage franked	60	100
Net tangible assets per share ($)	1.95	1.99
Interest cover (times)	13.8	15.1
Return on equity (%)	20.4	19.7
Debt-to-equity ratio (%)	~	~
Current ratio	2.4	2.2

Carsales.com Limited

ASX code: CAR   shareholder.carsales.com.au

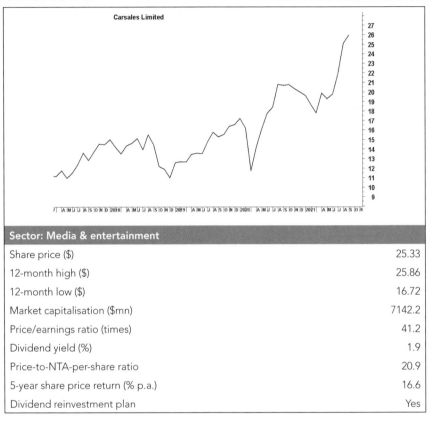

Sector: Media & entertainment	
Share price ($)	25.33
12-month high ($)	25.86
12-month low ($)	16.72
Market capitalisation ($mn)	7142.2
Price/earnings ratio (times)	41.2
Dividend yield (%)	1.9
Price-to-NTA-per-share ratio	20.9
5-year share price return (% p.a.)	16.6
Dividend reinvestment plan	Yes

Carsales.com was founded in Melbourne in 1997 and has grown to become the market leader in online automotive advertising. It also operates specialist websites for the sale of a variety of other goods, including boats, motorcycles, trucks, construction equipment, farm machinery, caravans and tyres. It has expanded abroad, with interests in automotive businesses in Asia and Latin America, and overseas business now represents more than 20 per cent of total turnover. A smaller division provides a diverse range of data services for customers, including software as a service, research and reporting, valuations, appraisals, website development and photography services. It has sold its Stratton Finance subsidiary. In August 2021 it acquired a 49 per cent stake in the US company Trader Interactive.

Latest business results (June 2021, full year)

In a difficult year, revenues and profits grew, thanks especially to the company's growing international exposure. With the COVID-19 pandemic affecting the vehicle sales market, the core Australian online advertising business managed only a modest 2 per cent rise in revenues, though effective cost control helped deliver a 9 per cent rise in profits at the EBITDA level. Asian business, represented by the company's

Korean subsidiary Encar.com, enjoyed an excellent year, with revenues up 21 per cent in local currency, though a stronger dollar and heavy marketing expenses meant that adjusted profits rose by just 6 per cent. Latin American businesses contribute less than 2 per cent of total turnover, and revenues rose in local currencies, with a substantially smaller loss than in the previous year.

Outlook

Carsales.com operates domestically in a mature market in which it has a dominant market share. It is affected by lockdowns and retail closures, which have an impact on vehicle sales advertising volumes. Nevertheless, it believes underlying market conditions remain solid, and it continues to tweak its products in order to achieve growth. It expects continuing strong progress in its Korean operations following a big investment in its Dealer Direct product. Its largest investment in Latin America is in Brazil, and the company believes the growth potential there remains strong, although business in the country has been badly hit by the COVID-19 pandemic. Carsales.com sees its $800 million acquisition of a 49 per cent holding in Trader Interactive in the US as a transformational investment. Trader Interactive is an American leader in the provision of digital markets for commercial and recreational vehicles and industrial equipment, and Carsales.com believes it can use its own technology to build on these businesses.

Year to 30 June	2020	2021
Revenues ($mn)	421.6	437.8
Online advertising services (%)	69	69
Asia (%)	19	20
Data, research & services (%)	10	9
EBIT ($mn)	203.5	227.1
EBIT margin (%)	48.3	51.9
Profit before tax ($mn)	189.2	208.4
Profit after tax ($mn)	138.2	152.8
Earnings per share (c)	56.40	61.53
Cash flow per share (c)	67.91	74.37
Dividend (c)	47	47.5
Percentage franked	100	100
Net tangible assets per share ($)	~	1.21
Interest cover (times)	14.2	12.2
Return on equity (%)	46.1	24.9
Debt-to-equity ratio (%)	125.0	~
Current ratio	3.2	4.2

CIMIC Group Limited

ASX code: CIM

www.cimic.com.au

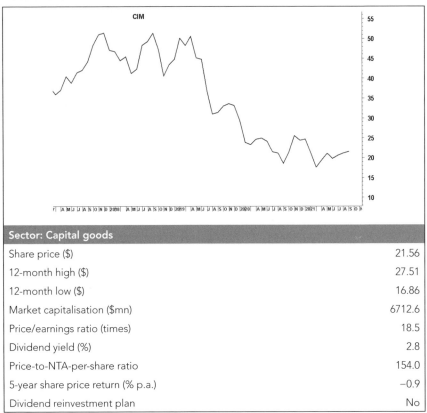

Sector: Capital goods	
Share price ($)	21.56
12-month high ($)	27.51
12-month low ($)	16.86
Market capitalisation ($mn)	6712.6
Price/earnings ratio (times)	18.5
Dividend yield (%)	2.8
Price-to-NTA-per-share ratio	154.0
5-year share price return (% p.a.)	−0.9
Dividend reinvestment plan	No

CIMIC, based in Sydney was founded in 1949, and until 2015 it was named Leighton Holdings. Its current name derives from its main businesses, Construction, Infrastructure, Mining and Concessions. It is one of Australia's largest contractors, with particular strengths in construction, engineering and a wide range of services in Australia, New Zealand and Asia. More than 78 per cent of the company's shares are owned by German construction company Hochtief, which itself is majority-owned by Spanish construction giant ACS Group.

Latest business results (June 2021, half year)

Revenues and profits edged up, after adjusting for the company's sale of half its holding in mining services provider Thiess. Construction work contributes more than 70 per cent of company income, with revenues up 4 per cent, thanks to the resumption of some work that had been postponed due to the pandemic, along with new contracts and the ramp-up of major tunnelling projects. Services revenues rose 7 per cent, again due especially to the resumption of deferred work. Both the Construction and the Services divisions recorded small increases in profits. During the June 2021 half the company received $10.4 billion worth of new work, exceeding the $6.8 billion received for the full year 2020. At June 2021 the company held work in hand of $33.3 billion, slightly higher than the figure of June 2020. The $2.2 billion sale in December 2020 of a 50 per cent stake in its subsidiary Thiess led to a sharp reduction in debt.

Outlook

CIMIC is a leading participant in the Australian infrastructure construction market, and stands to be a significant beneficiary as the federal and state governments boost spending as a means of stimulating economic recovery. It also sees potential for its services activities, pointing to high levels of underinvestment in asset maintenance by the owners of many assets, along with a growing trend to outsource maintenance services to specialist providers. Having retained a 50 per cent holding in Thiess, it will continue to benefit from that company's strong exposure to the resources sector. CIMIC is a member of the consortium that has been named as preferred bidder to do the tunnelling for Melbourne's planned $15.8 billion North East Link toll road. In New South Wales it is involved in the $1.95 billion Sydney M6 Motorway Stage 1 project and the $1.5 billion project to provide operations and maintenance for the rail infrastructure of the state's regional network. CIMIC forecasts a December 2021 after-tax profit of $400 million to $430 million.

Year to 31 December	2019	2020
Revenues ($mn)	10 806.1	9 004.2
EBIT ($mn)	788.3	598.9
EBIT margin (%)	7.3	6.7
Profit before tax ($mn)	699.6	438.9
Profit after tax ($mn)	595.6	371.5
Earnings per share (c)	183.77	116.84
Cash flow per share (c)	264.99	208.71
Dividend (c)	71	60
Percentage franked	100	20
Interest cover (times)	8.9	3.7
Return on equity (%)	40.6	49.3
Half year to 30 June	2020	2021
Revenues ($mn)	4 401.1	4 612.5
Profit before tax ($mn)	237.6	247.1
Profit after tax ($mn)	205.3	207.8
Earnings per share (c)	63.90	66.80
Dividend (c)	0	42
Percentage franked	~	20
Net tangible assets per share ($)	~	0.14
Debt-to-equity ratio (%)	170.6	28.7
Current ratio	1.3	1.1

Clover Corporation Limited

ASX code: CLV www.clovercorp.com.au

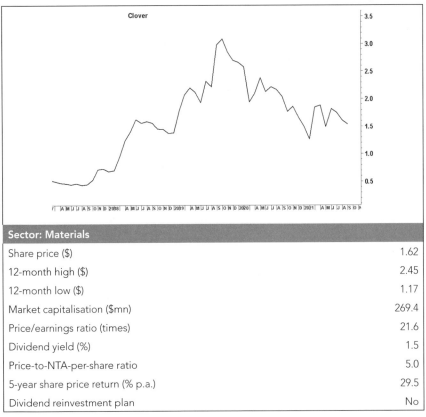

Sector: Materials	
Share price ($)	1.62
12-month high ($)	2.45
12-month low ($)	1.17
Market capitalisation ($mn)	269.4
Price/earnings ratio (times)	21.6
Dividend yield (%)	1.5
Price-to-NTA-per-share ratio	5.0
5-year share price return (% p.a.)	29.5
Dividend reinvestment plan	No

Melbourne-based Clover, founded in 1988 as a family-owned company, develops value-added nutrients for use in foods or as nutritional supplements. Its key product is docosahexaenoic acid (DHA), a form of omega 3. It sells this under the Nu-Mega and Ocean Gold range of tuna oils. It also markets nutritional oil powders, based on technology developed by the Commonwealth Scientific and Industrial Research Organisation (CSIRO). In addition, the company has developed technology that allows nutritional oils to be added to infant formula, foods and beverages. Overseas customers account for more than half of company sales.

Latest business results (January 2021, half year)

Sales and profits fell sharply. The company attributed this mainly to the COVID-19 pandemic, though with more than half of its sales invoiced in US dollars it was also hurt by the strengthening Australian dollar. Sales to customers in Australia and New Zealand slumped from $21.2 million in the January 2020 half to $11.4 million in January 2021. Much of this business represents demand from Chinese buyers — including students and tourists — who purchase infant formula in Australia for resale to customers in China. However, the pandemic has led to a precipitous decline in both tourist and international student numbers, while at the same time the Chinese market has become more competitive. By contrast, revenues from sales directly to Asia, Europe and the Americas all rose, thanks to product initiatives and new customers. Clover has initiated legal proceedings against a company and an individual it claims are infringing its intellectual property rights. It also took a $0.6 million hit from the delayed opening of a new spray drying facility. It said that without these additional expenses its after-tax profit would have been $3.3 million.

Outlook

Clover expects a slow recovery in sales as the pandemic eases. With so much of its output sold abroad it is wary of shipping constraints, and it is also affected by currency movements. It is placing a particular emphasis on European markets, thanks to new European Union legislation requiring a minimum DHA content in infant formula, and has established a warehouse in the Netherlands. It also expects continuing growth in American and Asian markets. It has developed a promising new, highly concentrated omega 3 powder, which is undergoing trials with potential customers, and it has several other new products awaiting release during 2021, targeted at the health food market. It expects July 2021 revenues to be between $60 million and $70 million.

Year to 31 July	2019	2020
Revenues ($mn)	76.7	88.3
EBIT ($mn)	14.3	18.2
EBIT margin (%)	18.6	20.7
Profit before tax ($mn)	14.0	17.7
Profit after tax ($mn)	10.1	12.5
Earnings per share (c)	6.12	7.51
Cash flow per share (c)	6.36	7.92
Dividend (c)	2.375	2.5
Percentage franked	100	100
Interest cover (times)	44.9	31.1
Return on equity (%)	24.3	24.3
Half year to 31 January	2020	2021
Revenues ($mn)	37.6	29.4
Profit before tax ($mn)	6.4	3.3
Profit after tax ($mn)	4.6	2.5
Earnings per share (c)	2.79	1.51
Dividend (c)	0	0.5
Percentage franked	~	100
Net tangible assets per share ($)	0.30	0.32
Debt-to-equity ratio (%)	32.0	7.1
Current ratio	4.9	8.0

Cochlear Limited

ASX code: COH   www.cochlear.com

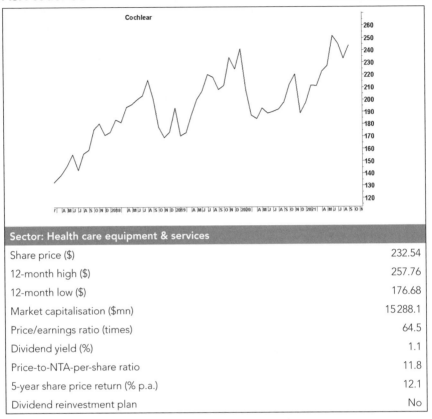

Sector: Health care equipment & services	
Share price ($)	232.54
12-month high ($)	257.76
12-month low ($)	176.68
Market capitalisation ($mn)	15 288.1
Price/earnings ratio (times)	64.5
Dividend yield (%)	1.1
Price-to-NTA-per-share ratio	11.8
5-year share price return (% p.a.)	12.1
Dividend reinvestment plan	No

Sydney-based Cochlear, founded in 1981, has around 60 per cent of the world market for cochlear bionic-ear implants, which are intended to assist the communication ability of people suffering from severe hearing impediments. It also sells the Baha bone-anchored hearing implant, as well as a range of acoustic products. With manufacturing facilities and technology centres in Australia, Sweden, Belgium and the US, it has sales in over 100 countries, and overseas business accounts for more than 90 per cent of revenues and profits.

Latest business results (June 2021, full year)

Sales were higher and profits rebounded strongly, having crashed in the previous year when the COVID-19 pandemic halted elective surgery in many countries. The result would have been stronger but for the strength of the dollar during the year. Cochlear implant sales rose 15 per cent to 36 456 units, with revenues up 10 per cent, thanks to market growth and the rescheduling of surgeries from the previous year. Services revenues rose 11 per cent, with the October 2020 launch in Europe and the US of the Nucleus Kanso 2 sound processor driving demand for upgrades. Acoustics revenues were up by 12 per cent, though still below pre-COVID levels.

Outlook

Cochlear continues to launch new products at an impressive rate, with a high level of research and development, and this is helping it maintain its market leadership. It sees a significant unmet and addressable clinical need globally for cochlear and acoustic implants, and it is stepping up its marketing activities. A particular recent focus has been adults and seniors in developed markets, which it regards as its biggest opportunity, given the large and growing market size and a current penetration rate of only about 3 per cent. The company points to research suggesting that good hearing is an important contributor to healthy ageing. Another key target is children in emerging markets. The current penetration rate is only about 10 per cent, but the company expects this to rise as awareness builds of cochlear implants and wealth grows in many emerging economies. It sees great potential for its new-generation Osia 2 acoustic system, which delivers a significant improvement in performance and quality of life for bone conduction patients. It has received regulatory approval in the US, and is experiencing high levels of demand there. The company forecasts a June 2022 after-tax profit of $265 million to $285 million. However, it remains vulnerable to currency fluctuations and further disruptions to elective surgery due to the COVID pandemic.

Year to 30 June	2020	2021
Revenues ($mn)	1352.3	1497.6
Cochlear implants (%)	61	60
Services (%)	29	29
Acoustics (%)	10	11
EBIT ($mn)	206.9	330.2
EBIT margin (%)	15.3	22.0
Gross margin (%)	74.5	72.6
Profit before tax ($mn)	198.0	321.8
Profit after tax ($mn)	153.8	236.7
Earnings per share (c)	266.48	360.34
Cash flow per share (c)	400.76	481.37
Dividend (c)	160	255
Percentage franked	100	0
Net tangible assets per share ($)	15.09	19.76
Interest cover (times)	23.2	39.3
Return on equity (%)	14.5	15.3
Debt-to-equity ratio (%)	~	~
Current ratio	1.8	3.1

Codan Limited

ASX code: CDA www.codan.com.au

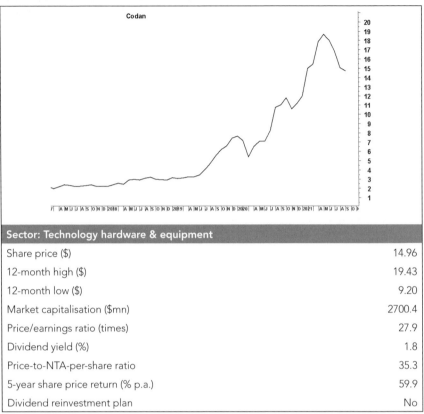

Sector: Technology hardware & equipment	
Share price ($)	14.96
12-month high ($)	19.43
12-month low ($)	9.20
Market capitalisation ($mn)	2700.4
Price/earnings ratio (times)	27.9
Dividend yield (%)	1.8
Price-to-NTA-per-share ratio	35.3
5-year share price return (% p.a.)	59.9
Dividend reinvestment plan	No

Adelaide electronics company Codan was founded in 1959. It is a leading world manufacturer of metal-detecting products, including Minelab metal detectors for hobbyists, gold detectors for small-scale miners and landmine detectors for humanitarian applications. A second division produces high-frequency communication radios for military and humanitarian use. Codan sells to more than 150 countries, and overseas sales represent more than 85 per cent of company revenues. In July 2021 it sold its Minetec subsidiary to Caterpillar Holdings Australia. Also in 2021 it acquired two American communication technology companies, Domo Tactical Communications and Zetron.

Latest business results (June 2021, full year)

Codan enjoyed another excellent year, with strong growth in sales and profits, thanks once again to high demand worldwide for its metal-detecting equipment. The core Metal Detection division saw sales up by 38 per cent, with profits surging 46 per cent. In the previous year the figures had been 30 per cent and 45 per cent respectively. In part, this growth reflected the company's strategy of expanding its range to include lower-priced detectors for hobbyists, which has helped it gain market share. The new

GPX6000 unit helped it maintain market leadership in artisanal gold detectors. The Communications division, which had enjoyed strong growth in the previous year, this time saw sales and profits fall, as the COVID-19 pandemic led to deferred spending by customers, and travel limitations hindered the company's marketing efforts. The small Tracking Solutions division, incorporating the now-sold Minetec business, experienced a big jump in sales, and it moved from loss to profit.

Outlook

Codan is a significant force in two niche high-tech product areas. Its high-margin metal detectors dominate the African artisanal gold mining market, and the new GPX6000 unit, released in 2021, is expected to make a significant contribution in the June 2022 year. In the recreational market it has achieved success with the Vanquish detector, now in its second year. The new MF5 mine detector is expected to expand Codan's sales in the landmine sector. The Communications division has been transformed by its two 2021 acquisitions. Domo Tactical Communications, acquired for $114 million, develops products that provide wireless transmission of video and other data services for military and tactical applications. Zetron, acquired for $59 million, develops emergency response technologies for public safety, transportation, utilities, healthcare and natural resources customers. Both companies provide technology that is complementary to Codan's own, offering the potential for a range of new products and markets as well as synergy benefits.

Year to 30 June	2020	2021
Revenues ($mn)	348.0	437.0
Metal detection (%)	68	75
Communications (%)	30	22
EBIT ($mn)	88.9	131.2
EBIT margin (%)	25.5	30.0
Gross margin (%)	56.5	55.6
Profit before tax ($mn)	89.0	130.8
Profit after tax ($mn)	63.8	97.3
Earnings per share (c)	35.47	53.68
Cash flow per share (c)	46.95	64.17
Dividend (c)	18.5	27
Percentage franked	100	100
Net tangible assets per share ($)	0.89	0.42
Interest cover (times)	~	368.5
Return on equity (%)	27.8	35.3
Debt-to-equity ratio (%)	~	0.5
Current ratio	2.2	1.1

Collins Foods Limited

ASX code: CKF

www.collinsfoods.com

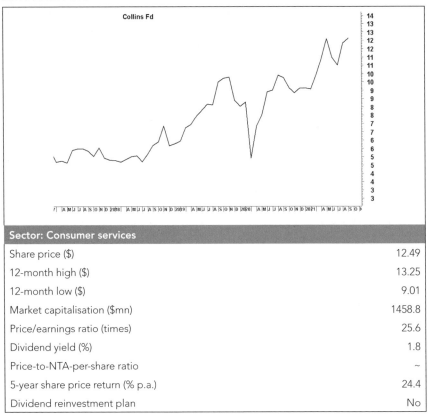

Sector: Consumer services	
Share price ($)	12.49
12-month high ($)	13.25
12-month low ($)	9.01
Market capitalisation ($mn)	1458.8
Price/earnings ratio (times)	25.6
Dividend yield (%)	1.8
Price-to-NTA-per-share ratio	~
5-year share price return (% p.a.)	24.4
Dividend reinvestment plan	No

Collins Foods, based in Brisbane, dates back to 1968 when it obtained the KFC fried chicken franchise for Queensland. Today it owns and operates KFC outlets across Australia, and is the country's largest KFC franchisee. It also owns KFC stores in Germany and the Netherlands. It has closed its Sizzler restaurant business in Australia, though it continues to operate as a franchisor of Sizzler restaurants in Thailand and Japan. It has launched the Taco Bell Mexican restaurant brand in Australia.

Latest business results (May 2021, full year)

Collins achieved another year of rising sales and profits, thanks to flourishing business for its domestic KFC outlets. The company recorded same-store revenue growth of a high 12.9 per cent in Australia. It also benefited from the opening of 11 new outlets domestically during the year, and profits rose strongly. However, KFC Europe was hurt by COVID-related restrictions. Its European restaurants depend more on dine-in business than do the Australian restaurants, and an effective lockdown was in place there for much of the second half of the financial year. Consequently, same-store sales in Europe fell by 0.6 per cent and profits were sharply lower. The company opened three new restaurants in the Netherlands. The new Taco Bell business recorded strong growth, with the opening of four new restaurants, though it remained in the red. The Asian Sizzler business made a small profit. At the end of the period the company operated 251 franchised KFC restaurants in Australia, with a further 29 in the Netherlands and 17 in Germany. It also ran 16 franchised Taco Bell restaurants in Australia. It operated as franchisor for 64 Sizzler restaurants in Asia.

Outlook

Collins has experienced significant disruptions from the COVID-19 pandemic, though its Australian stores have benefited greatly from growing demand for takeaway food by people confined to their homes. As restrictions ease in Europe it is experiencing a strong recovery in sales, and it plans to open three new outlets in the Netherlands, with a longer-term goal of two to four new outlets annually in that country. In Australia the company plans to open at least 66 new KFC restaurants by May 2028, with nine to 12 planned for the May 2022 year. It also expects to accelerate its rollout of new Taco Bell outlets, thanks to a pleasing customer response to this business, with nine to 12 restaurants in the pipeline for May 2022, including an initial move into Western Australia.

Year to 2 May*	2020	2021
Revenues ($mn)	952.8	1065.9
KFC restaurants Australia (%)	83	84
KFC restaurants Europe (%)	14	13
Taco Bell restaurants (%)	2	3
EBIT ($mn)	86.9	90.6
EBIT margin (%)	9.1	8.5
Gross margin (%)	52.8	52.5
Profit before tax ($mn)	54.9	61.2
Profit after tax ($mn)	48.1	56.9
Earnings per share (c)	41.26	48.81
Cash flow per share (c)	80.66	89.70
Dividend (c)	20	23
Percentage franked	100	100
Net tangible assets per share ($)	~	~
Interest cover (times)	2.7	3.1
Return on equity (%)	13.6	15.8
Debt-to-equity ratio (%)	56.2	48.4
Current ratio	1.0	0.8

*3 May 2020

Commonwealth Bank of Australia

ASX code: CBA   www.commbank.com.au

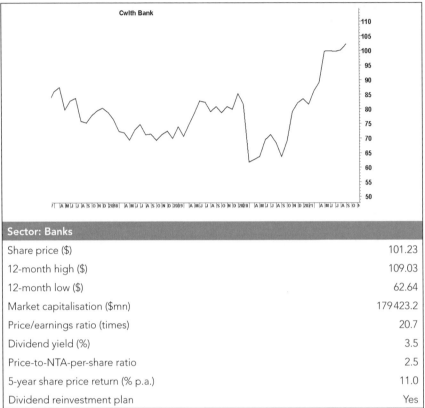

Cwlth Bank

Sector: Banks	
Share price ($)	101.23
12-month high ($)	109.03
12-month low ($)	62.64
Market capitalisation ($mn)	179 423.2
Price/earnings ratio (times)	20.7
Dividend yield (%)	3.5
Price-to-NTA-per-share ratio	2.5
5-year share price return (% p.a.)	11.0
Dividend reinvestment plan	Yes

The Commonwealth Bank, based in Sydney, was founded in 1911. It is today one of Australia's largest banks, and one of the country's top providers of home loans, personal loans and credit cards, as well as the largest holder of deposits. Commonwealth Securities is Australia's largest online stockbroker. It has significant interests in New Zealand through ASB Bank. It owns Bankwest in Western Australia.

Latest business results (June 2021, full year)

The cash profit rose in a good result in a volatile environment, reversing three straight years of decline. The core Retail Banking Services division — which includes the home loans and retail deposit businesses — enjoyed a 16 per cent rise in profits, thanks in particular to a 33 per cent increase in new home lending. The Business Banking division achieved an 11 per cent rise in profits as the bank continued to gain market share in business lending. The smaller Institutional Banking and Markets division saw a particularly impressive 46 per cent jump in profits, thanks to higher income from commodities financing and institutional lending. New Zealand was also very strong, with profits up 43 per cent, thanks to growth in lending and deposit volumes. The bank's operating expenses were up by 2 per cent, including a 4 per cent rise in the wage bill as it hired extra staff in a bid to boost its digital expertise. Pressure from falling interest rates and price competition sent the net interest margin down four basis points to 2.02 per cent. Loan impairments of $554 million were down from $2.5 billion in the previous year.

Outlook

Commonwealth Bank occupies a powerful position in the domestic economy as well as in the local banking industry. Thanks to a large branch network, offering many cross-selling opportunities, it has pricing power that has generally enabled it to maintain a cost advantage over some of its rivals. It expects the Australian economy to rebound late in 2021, with contributions from significant accumulated household savings, a strong housing market and relatively low levels of unemployment. However, it is wary of competitive pressures and the impact on its businesses of continuing low interest rates. It is rolling out a range of new products that are designed to compete with smaller fintech companies. It plans the launch late in 2021 of a new digital mortgage brand, Unloan, that will take advantage of cloud computing. It also plans to introduce two new advanced payments terminals, along with related apps.

Year to 30 June	2020	2021
Operating income ($mn)	23 761.0	24 156.0
Net interest income ($mn)	18 610.0	18 839.0
Operating expenses ($mn)	10 895.0	11 359.0
Profit before tax ($mn)	10 348.0	12 243.0
Profit after tax ($mn)	7 296.0	8 653.0
Earnings per share (c)	412.50	488.59
Dividend (c)	298	350
Percentage franked	100	100
Non-interest income to total income (%)	21.7	22.0
Net tangible assets per share ($)	36.80	40.49
Cost-to-income ratio (%)	45.9	47.0
Return on equity (%)	10.3	11.5
Return on assets (%)	0.7	0.8

Costa Group Holdings Limited

ASX code: CGC   investors.costagroup.com.au

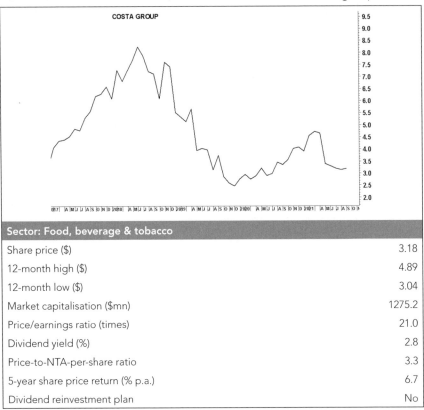

Sector: Food, beverage & tobacco	
Share price ($)	3.18
12-month high ($)	4.89
12-month low ($)	3.04
Market capitalisation ($mn)	1275.2
Price/earnings ratio (times)	21.0
Dividend yield (%)	2.8
Price-to-NTA-per-share ratio	3.3
5-year share price return (% p.a.)	6.7
Dividend reinvestment plan	No

Melbourne-based horticultural company Costa Group has roots that go back to the establishment of a fruit store in Geelong, Victoria, in the nineteenth century. It has grown steadily, organically and through acquisition, and is today one of Australia's leading producers, distributors and exporters of fresh fruit and vegetables. It segments its output into five core categories — berries, mushrooms, glasshouse-grown tomatoes, citrus and avocados. It receives royalty income from the licensing of its blueberry varietals in Australia and abroad. It also manages berry-growing operations in Morocco and China. In July 2021 it acquired Queensland citrus grower 2PH Farms.

Latest business results (June 2021, half year)

Revenues were flat from the June 2020 half but profits fell. The company's core business is the domestic sale of its produce, and revenues fell 7 per cent, with profits dropping by nearly 25 per cent. During the period the company suffered substantial damage from a hailstorm in northern Victoria, and it was also affected by lower avocado prices. International business saw revenues rise 25 per cent with profits up 28 per cent, thanks to growth in the company's operations in both Morocco and China. Though international activities contribute only about a quarter of total revenues, they were responsible for two-thirds of June 2021 profit. Costa also operates a trading and services business, Costa Farms and Logistics, which carries out logistics, wholesaling and marketing operations within Australia. It represents about 11 per cent of company income, and revenues and profits were down.

Outlook

Costa plays an important role in the Australian economy as a leading grower and distributor of foodstuffs, and its business is relatively resistant to economic fluctuations. However, it operates in a competitive industry, and with activities that are very dependent on weather conditions. In addition, it has been affected by pandemic-related labour shortages. It expects further solid growth in its successful international operations, and is expanding its Chinese and Moroccan blueberry farms with additional plantings and, in China, a new packing facility. Domestically, it aims to expand its fresh food logistics and distribution business, and in July 2021 it acquired Select Fresh Group, a prominent Western Australian wholesale foodstuffs distributor. The $219 million acquisition of 2PH Farms, the largest citrus grower in northern Australia, will complement Costa's existing citrus-growing operations and provide access to new markets, notably in Asia and the US. The company also expects it to add around 10 per cent to its EPS figure, and deliver substantial cost-saving synergies.

Year to 27 December*	2019	2020
Revenues ($mn)	1030.8	1164.9
EBIT ($mn)	46.1	88.0
EBIT margin (%)	4.5	7.6
Profit before tax ($mn)	37.3	81.2
Profit after tax ($mn)	26.6	60.8
Earnings per share (c)	8.08	15.16
Cash flow per share (c)	34.91	39.27
Dividend (c)	5.5	9
Percentage franked	100	100
Interest cover (times)	5.2	13.1
Return on equity (%)	5.3	10.6
Half year to 27 June**	2020	2021
Revenues ($mn)	612.4	612.4
Profit before tax ($mn)	57.3	54.2
Profit after tax ($mn)	43.4	37.4
Earnings per share (c)	10.82	9.33
Dividend (c)	4	4
Percentage franked	100	100
Net tangible assets per share ($)	0.94	0.98
Debt-to-equity ratio (%)	29.5	32.0
Current ratio	1.5	1.5

*29 December 2019
**28 June 2020

Credit Corp Group Limited

ASX code: CCP   www.creditcorpgroup.com.au

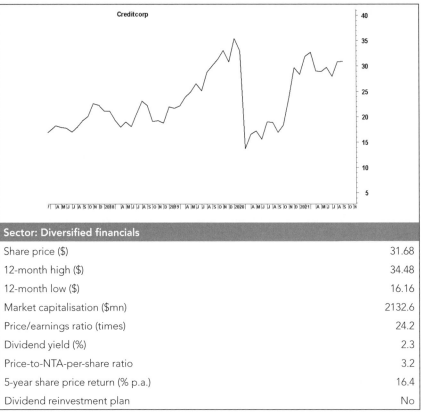

Sector: Diversified financials	
Share price ($)	31.68
12-month high ($)	34.48
12-month low ($)	16.16
Market capitalisation ($mn)	2132.6
Price/earnings ratio (times)	24.2
Dividend yield (%)	2.3
Price-to-NTA-per-share ratio	3.2
5-year share price return (% p.a.)	16.4
Dividend reinvestment plan	No

Sydney-based Credit Corp was formed in 1992, although it has its origins in companies that started in the early 1970s. It provides debt collection services to companies in numerous industries, including the finance, insurance, legal and government sectors, though with a specialty in consumer credit card debt. It has operations in the United States and in New Zealand. It also runs a consumer lending business in Australia and New Zealand.

Latest business results (June 2021, full year)

A further sharp rise in Credit Corp's US debt collection business, along with growth in this activity in Australia, offset weakness in consumer lending to generate a rise in revenues and profits. The company's core business — representing around 58 per cent of turnover — is its Australia/New Zealand debt collection operations, and revenues and profits rose, helped by the acquisition during the financial year of a large amount of debt from struggling rival Collection House. A reduction in employee expenses, due to some salary cuts, also aided the result. US revenues and profits doubled as this operation continued to grow in scale and boost market share. The US now represents some 20 per cent of company revenues, though profit margins remain below those in

Australia. The consumer lending business saw profitability down as borrowers took advantage of a range of stimulus measures — including early superannuation withdrawal — to make an unprecedented level of loan prepayments. However, the June 2021 loan book of $184 million was up a touch from $181 million a year earlier.

Outlook

Credit Corp's main business effectively involves buying consumer debt at a discount to its face value, then seeking to recover an amount in excess of the purchase price. Often this recovery takes the form of phased payments over an extended period, and Credit Corp thus has substantial recurring income. Setting an appropriate price for the acquisition of parcels of debt is one of the keys to success, and Credit Corp has acquired considerable expertise in this. During the first phase of the COVID-19 pandemic in 2020 it suffered from a reduction in the amount of consumer debt available for purchase, as banks and other institutions initiated forbearance programs, allowing their customers extended periods in which to pay amounts that they owed. But this began to change during 2021, with increasing volumes of consumer debt available. The company is optimistic that US operations will continue to grow. Its early forecast is for a June 2022 after-tax profit of $85 million to $95 million.

Year to 30 June	2020	2021
Revenues ($mn)	313.4	374.8
EBIT ($mn)	124.6	131.7
EBIT margin (%)	39.8	35.2
Profit before tax ($mn)	113.9	125.9
Profit after tax ($mn)	79.6	88.1
Earnings per share (c)	131.21	130.92
Cash flow per share (c)	149.18	147.02
Dividend (c)	36	72
Percentage franked	100	100
Net tangible assets per share ($)	8.82	9.90
Interest cover (times)	11.6	22.7
Return on equity (%)	15.0	14.0
Debt-to-equity ratio (%)	~	~
Current ratio	5.0	5.6

CSL Limited

ASX code: CSL

www.csl.com

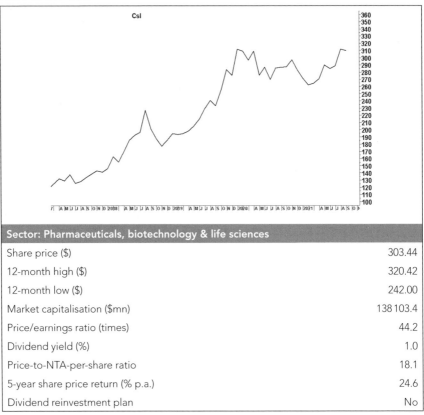

Sector: Pharmaceuticals, biotechnology & life sciences	
Share price ($)	303.44
12-month high ($)	320.42
12-month low ($)	242.00
Market capitalisation ($mn)	138 103.4
Price/earnings ratio (times)	44.2
Dividend yield (%)	1.0
Price-to-NTA-per-share ratio	18.1
5-year share price return (% p.a.)	24.6
Dividend reinvestment plan	No

Melbourne-based CSL, formerly the state-owned Commonwealth Serum Laboratories, was founded in 1916. It has grown organically and through acquisition to become a major global biotechnology company, with operations in numerous countries — with particular strength in the US, Australia, Germany, the UK, China and Switzerland — and more than 90 per cent of revenues derive from outside Australia. Its principal business now, through its CSL Behring division, is the provision of plasma-derived coagulation therapies for the treatment of a range of medical conditions. CSL Plasma, a subdivision of CSL Behring, is a major global collector of human blood plasma. The Seqirus division is one of the world's largest influenza vaccine companies and a producer of other prescription medicines and pharmaceutical products. CSL enjoys high margins and high market shares for many of its products.

Latest business results (June 2021, full year)

CSL recorded a double-digit rise in revenues and profits, though it reports its results in US dollars, and the increase was a little more subdued when converted to Australian dollars. There was continuing steady demand for the company's core immunoglobulin products, including a 15 per cent rise in sales of the subcutaneous product Hizentra.

Albumin sales jumped 61 per cent, although this partly reflected a pandemic-related fall in the previous year. Altogether the CSL Behring division saw sales up 9 per cent and EBIT rising by 8 per cent. The Seqirus division — representing the remaining 16 per cent of company turnover — enjoyed particularly strong demand for influenza vaccines. Revenues for this division rose 34 per cent and EBIT jumped ahead by 82 per cent. As noted, CSL reports its results in US dollars. The figures in this book have been converted to Australian dollars based on prevailing exchange rates.

Outlook

CSL remains a powerhouse biotechnology company, with an impressive research and development capability and a solid pipeline of potential new products. However, management have described the June 2022 year as a period of transition, and the initial forecast is for a decline in profits. In particular, the company is concerned that the COVID-19 pandemic has sparked a sharp decline in blood donations, leading to increased plasma collection costs, despite continuing strong underlying demand for the company's therapies. It expects continuing good growth in its vaccines business, with new products under development and strong demand for influenza vaccines as a result of the COVID-19 pandemic. CSL manufactures the AstraZeneca COVID-19 vaccine in Australia, and has been engaged in research on other COVID vaccines.

Year to 30 June	2020	2021
Revenues ($mn)	12 748.7	13 130.9
EBIT ($mn)	3 937.0	4 118.4
EBIT margin (%)	30.9	31.4
Gross margin (%)	55.4	55.2
Profit before tax ($mn)	3 728.6	3 898.8
Profit after tax ($mn)	3 047.1	3 125.0
Earnings per share (c)	6 71.45	686.84
Cash flow per share (c)	805.52	830.08
Dividend (c)	292.75	293.93
Percentage franked	0	5
Net tangible assets per share ($)	14.00	16.73
Interest cover (times)	18.9	18.8
Return on equity (%)	35.7	30.3
Debt-to-equity ratio (%)	73.5	47.7
Current ratio	3.0	2.4

CSR Limited

ASX code: CSR

www.csr.com.au

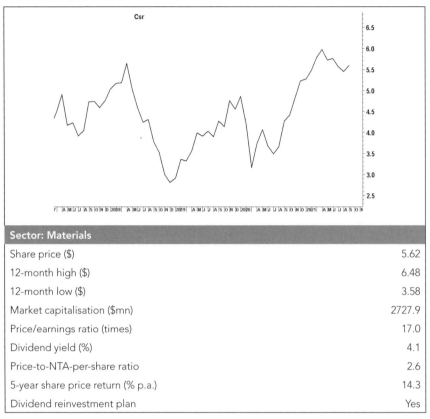

Sector: Materials	
Share price ($)	5.62
12-month high ($)	6.48
12-month low ($)	3.58
Market capitalisation ($mn)	2727.9
Price/earnings ratio (times)	17.0
Dividend yield (%)	4.1
Price-to-NTA-per-share ratio	2.6
5-year share price return (% p.a.)	14.3
Dividend reinvestment plan	Yes

Sydney-based CSR, founded in 1855 as a sugar refiner, is now a leading manufacturer of building products for residential and commercial construction, with distribution throughout Australia and New Zealand. Its brands include Gyprock plasterboard, Bradford insulation, Monier roof tiles, Hebel concrete products and PGH Bricks and Pavers. It is also a joint venture partner in Australia's second-largest aluminium smelter at Tomago. In addition, it operates a residential and industrial property development business based on former industrial sites.

Latest business results (March 2021, full year)

Profits recovered after two years of decline, and despite a dip in revenues, thanks to operational efficiencies and solid demand from the home-building and renovations markets. Property sales also made a big contribution. The company's largest business, Gyprock plasterboard, enjoyed an excellent year, and PGH Bricks benefited from productivity gains. By contrast, Hebel concrete products and AFS concrete wall systems both experienced lower profits, due to their exposure to high-density housing, which suffered declining demand. In addition, the company's aluminium business took a hit, having surged in the previous year, with profits down 60 per cent following a sharp decline in aluminium prices. A major settlement of the company's Horsley Park industrial development in Sydney contributed $54 million to EBIT.

Outlook

Low interest rates and government incentives are fuelling an upswing in home building, and CSR is a prominent beneficiary, with detached housing responsible for 54 per cent of building product sales. It expects the trend to continue well into 2022, and is forecasting strong demand for bricks, roofing and insulation products. With a network of over 170 manufacturing and distribution sites, it believes it has the flexibility to boost production to meet growing demand. It also believes that travel restrictions, forcing people to stay at home, could stimulate home renovation activity. This could be partially offset by weaker demand in the commercial building sector, although this represents only 20 per cent of CSR's building products business. But it has also warned that labour shortages in the construction industry could have an impact on business. It expects a recovery in its aluminium division, having locked in sales prices with a new hedging program that took advantage of a rally in aluminium pricing. Property will also continue to make a solid contribution, with $146 million in Horsley Park sales expected over three years, including an EBIT contribution of $18 million in the March 2022 year. Further development projects are expected to generate substantial earnings over the coming 10 years.

Year to 31 March	2020	2021
Revenues ($mn)	2212.5	2122.4
Building products (%)	72	72
Aluminium (%)	28	28
EBIT ($mn)	209.8	223.0
EBIT margin (%)	9.5	10.5
Gross margin (%)	30.3	28.5
Profit before tax ($mn)	192.8	211.3
Profit after tax ($mn)	134.8	160.4
Earnings per share (c)	27.32	33.07
Cash flow per share (c)	47.52	52.90
Dividend (c)	10	23
Percentage franked	50	100
Net tangible assets per share ($)	2.04	2.16
Interest cover (times)	12.3	19.1
Return on equity (%)	12.0	14.7
Debt-to-equity ratio (%)	~	~
Current ratio	2.3	1.7

Data#3 Limited

ASX code: DTL   www.data3.com

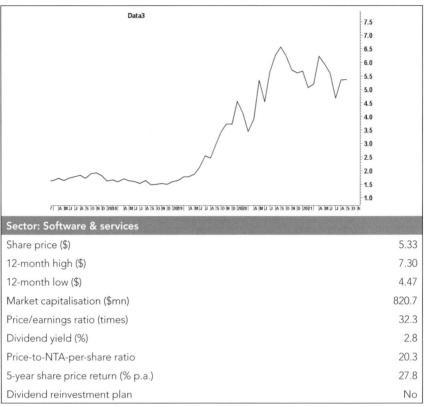

Sector: Software & services	
Share price ($)	5.33
12-month high ($)	7.30
12-month low ($)	4.47
Market capitalisation ($mn)	820.7
Price/earnings ratio (times)	32.3
Dividend yield (%)	2.8
Price-to-NTA-per-share ratio	20.3
5-year share price return (% p.a.)	27.8
Dividend reinvestment plan	No

Brisbane-based IT consultant Data#3 was formed in 1984 from the merger of computer software consultancy Powell, Clark and Associates with IBM typewriter dealer Albrand Typewriters and Office Machines. Today it operates from offices around Australia and in Fiji, providing information and communication technology services to a wide range of businesses that include banking and finance, mining, tourism and leisure, legal, health care, manufacturing, distribution, government and utilities.

Latest business results (June 2021, full year)

In a volatile period, Data#3 achieved a third consecutive year of higher sales and profits. The company's major market of Queensland performed poorly, but most other regions were strong. Data#3 divides its activities broadly into three segments. The first of these, software solutions, involves managing clients' software investments. This business performed well, with continuing strong growth in public cloud income, up 36 per cent for the year to $792 million. A second segment, infrastructure solutions, helps clients maximise returns from infrastructure investments in servers, storage, networks and devices, and this business also achieved solid growth, including gains in market share, though with some margin pressure. A third, much smaller business segment is services, which benefited from new contract wins. The company reported a significant backlog of orders at the end of the financial year due to supply constraints. It said pre-tax profit would have been about $3 million higher but for these constraints.

Outlook

Data#3 has adopted a strategic plan with three key long-term objectives — to deliver sustained profit growth, to boost its services revenues, with enhanced margins, and to expand its cloud services revenues. The COVID-19 pandemic has led to a slowing in demand from some clients, but the company now expects the Australian IT market to grow at a record rate in the June 2022 year. Recurring revenue from government bodies and large corporate customers represents more than 60 per cent of total company turnover. It has noted that cyber-security has become its customers' major priority, and this is an important focus for the company. However, it is concerned that hardware supply constraints, based on a global shortage of semiconductors, will continue for a further 12 months to 18 months, affecting business. In the longer term it believes companies are set for a digital transformation based on such technologies as artificial intelligence, the internet of things, blockchain and 3D printing, presenting many opportunities for new business. At June 2021 Data#3 had no debt and cash holdings of more than $200 million, and it continues to seek out expansion opportunities.

Year to 30 June	2020	2021
Revenues ($mn)	1623.8	1955.2
EBIT ($mn)	34.1	37.7
EBIT margin (%)	2.1	1.9
Profit before tax ($mn)	34.1	36.9
Profit after tax ($mn)	23.6	25.4
Earnings per share (c)	15.35	16.51
Cash flow per share (c)	19.10	20.43
Dividend (c)	13.9	15
Percentage franked	100	100
Net tangible assets per share ($)	0.24	0.26
Interest cover (times)	2621.5	52.2
Return on equity (%)	47.6	46.8
Debt-to-equity ratio (%)	~	~
Current ratio	1.1	1.1

Dicker Data Limited

ASX code: DDR   www.dickerdata.com.au

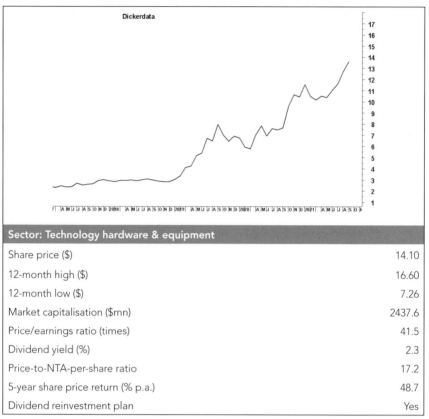

Sector: Technology hardware & equipment	
Share price ($)	14.10
12-month high ($)	16.60
12-month low ($)	7.26
Market capitalisation ($mn)	2437.6
Price/earnings ratio (times)	41.5
Dividend yield (%)	2.3
Price-to-NTA-per-share ratio	17.2
5-year share price return (% p.a.)	48.7
Dividend reinvestment plan	Yes

Sydney-based technology distributor Dicker Data dates back to its establishment by David Dicker in 1978. Today it is a leader in Australia and New Zealand in the wholesale distribution of computer hardware, software and related products to some 7000 customers, with a particular focus on small and medium-sized companies. It is the leading Australian distributor for some of the world's leading technology brands. Chief executive officer David Dicker and co-founder and director Fiona Brown between them own more than 65 per cent of the company's equity. In July 2021 Dicker Data acquired Exeed Group, New Zealand's second-largest distributor of IT products.

Latest business results (June 2021, half year)

Revenues and profits continued to rise. Hardware sales represent about three-quarters of company turnover, and these rose by 8 per cent from the June 2020 half, despite some supply constraints. There was particularly strong growth for networking products. By contrast, software sales rose by just 2 per cent. These had experienced substantial growth in the previous year as increasing numbers of people began to work from home. Five new vendors contributed sales of $14.5 million. New Zealand sales — about 7.5 per cent of the total — rose 18.5 per cent, though with just a small contribution to company profits.

Outlook

Dicker Data has a strong position in Australia's IT distribution sector, with an approximate 27 per cent market share in the corporate and commercial segment. Though this is a low-margin business, it has grown to such a scale that it has become very profitable. The company is unusual in that CEO David Dicker takes no salary. In addition, its policy is to pay out its entire profits in dividends, and these are generally distributed quarterly. It has become a major beneficiary of the digital transformation of businesses in Australia, and believes the remote-working trend will continue, with people's homes becoming sub-branches of their offices. It expects the roll-out of 5G digital connectivity to have a revolutionary impact in accelerating the development of artificial intelligence and machine learning technologies, leading to increased demand for both hardware and software. The $68 million acquisition of Exeed Group will double the company's New Zealand sales. In addition, Exeed works in the multi-billion-dollar retail sector, which Dicker Data regards as a significant untapped revenue opportunity. The company is concerned about the global semiconductor chip shortage, which has led to supply disruptions and order backlogs since late 2020. With strong demand continuing from customers, Dicker Data sees shortages enduring into the foreseeable future.

Year to 31 December	2019	2020
Revenues ($mn)	1758.5	1998.8
EBIT ($mn)	81.4	85.0
EBIT margin (%)	4.6	4.3
Profit before tax ($mn)	75.9	81.9
Profit after tax ($mn)	54.3	57.2
Earnings per share (c)	33.69	34.02
Cash flow per share (c)	36.53	37.81
Dividend (c)	28	33
Percentage franked	100	100
Interest cover (times)	14.7	27.0
Return on equity (%)	62.1	44.6
Half year to 30 June	2020	2021
Revenues ($mn)	1005.8	1066.5
Profit before tax ($mn)	42.0	45.9
Profit after tax ($mn)	29.4	32.1
Earnings per share (c)	17.08	18.58
Dividend (c)	15	19.5
Percentage franked	100	100
Net tangible assets per share ($)	0.75	0.82
Debt-to-equity ratio (%)	45.8	51.0
Current ratio	1.2	1.1

Elders Limited

ASX code: ELD

www.elders.com.au

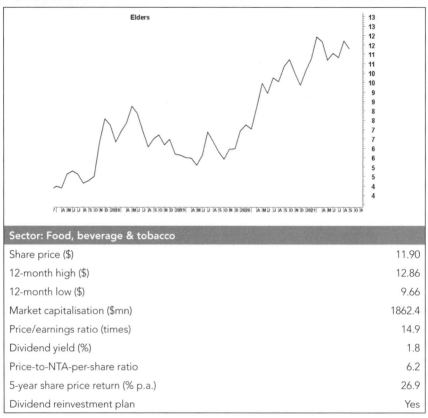

Sector: Food, beverage & tobacco

Share price ($)	11.90
12-month high ($)	12.86
12-month low ($)	9.66
Market capitalisation ($mn)	1862.4
Price/earnings ratio (times)	14.9
Dividend yield (%)	1.8
Price-to-NTA-per-share ratio	6.2
5-year share price return (% p.a.)	26.9
Dividend reinvestment plan	Yes

Adelaide-based agribusiness giant Elders dates back to 1839, when Scotsman Alexander Elder established a store in South Australia. It has grown and undergone many transformations, until today it is a leader in a range of businesses serving rural Australia. It is a prominent supplier of agricultural products, including seeds, fertilisers, chemicals and animal health products. It is a leading agent for the sale of wool, grain and livestock. It is also a major provider of financial and real estate services to the rural sector. An operation in China imports, processes and distributes Australian meat.

Latest business results (March 2021, half year)

In a favourable period for rural Australia, Elders achieved an excellent result, with strength in all regions and across all product lines. Elders groups its business into three broad divisions. The main one of these, Branch Network, representing three-quarters of total turnover, incorporates agricultural retail products, agency services, and real estate and financial services. It saw a strong rise in sales and profits, along with margin improvement, and with particularly pleasing growth in demand for Elders' own brand of crop protection and animal health products. The Wholesale Products division, which supplies rural merchandise to retailers throughout Australia, represents 15 per cent of turnover, and it too achieved excellent growth. A third smaller division, Feed and Processing Services, includes two feedlots and the company's Chinese activities. Profits were down for this division, due mainly to pricing pressure on feeder cattle at the Killara feedlot.

Outlook

Elders is heavily geared to the rural economy, and the near-term outlook is for further buoyancy, with continuing strong demand for fertilisers, crop protection products and animal feed. As one of Australia's agribusiness leaders, Elders expects to continue to benefit, and it has developed an ambitious eight-point plan aimed at winning market shares across all its products and services, along with higher profits and moves into new product lines. Its 2019 acquisition of Australian Independent Rural Retailers has significantly boosted its wholesaling operation. Low interest rates and the favourable seasonal conditions should help boost the real estate business. The company is benefiting from growing demand from city dwellers seeking to move to cheaper homes in the country. The company is also optimistic about the outlook for its high-margin agency services. Elders is seeking to grow through acquisition, in order to expand its client base and boost its product offerings, and it has said that it has a strong pipeline of potential bolt-on acquisitions.

Year to 30 September	2019	2020
Revenues ($mn)	1626.0	2092.6
EBIT ($mn)	64.4	107.7
EBIT margin (%)	4.0	5.1
Gross margin (%)	21.3	20.6
Profit before tax ($mn)	60.4	104.1
Profit after tax ($mn)	68.9	122.9
Earnings per share (c)	56.97	79.79
Cash flow per share (c)	61.21	106.91
Dividend (c)	18	22
Percentage franked	100	100
Interest cover (times)	16.0	30.0
Return on equity (%)	17.3	21.1
Half year to 31 March	2020	2021
Revenues ($mn)	900.2	1100.5
Profit before tax ($mn)	45.2	69.3
Profit after tax ($mn)	52.0	68.2
Earnings per share (c)	34.10	43.70
Dividend (c)	9	20
Percentage franked	100	20
Net tangible assets per share ($)	1.46	1.92
Debt-to-equity ratio (%)	19.8	23.5
Current ratio	1.2	1.2

Evolution Mining Limited

ASX code: EVN   www.evolutionmining.com.au

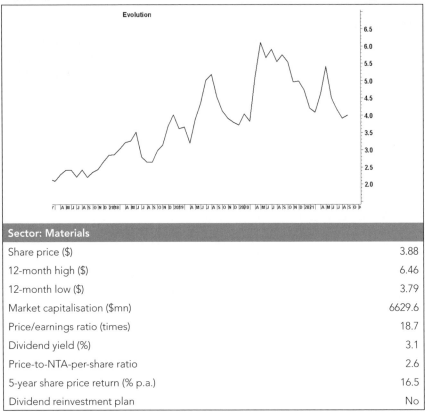

Sector: Materials	
Share price ($)	3.88
12-month high ($)	6.46
12-month low ($)	3.79
Market capitalisation ($mn)	6629.6
Price/earnings ratio (times)	18.7
Dividend yield (%)	3.1
Price-to-NTA-per-share ratio	2.6
5-year share price return (% p.a.)	16.5
Dividend reinvestment plan	No

Gold mining company Evolution Mining, based in Sydney, was formed in 2011 from the merger of Catalpa Resources and Conquest Mining and the acquisition of two mines from Newcrest Mining. It now operates five fully owned mines — Cowal in New South Wales, Mt Carlton and Mt Rawdon in Queensland, Mungari in Western Australia and Red Lake in Ontario, Canada. It also holds an interest in the Ernest Henry copper-gold project in Queensland. In August 2021 it acquired a portfolio of Kalgoorlie mining assets from Northern Star Resources.

Latest business results (June 2021, full year)

A 9 per cent fall in gold output for the year, along with higher production costs, sent revenues and profits down. Total gold production for the year of 680 788 ounces was down from 746 463 ounces in the June 2020 year, with all Australian mines recording declines. Production costs for the year averaged $1215 per ounce, up from $1043, in part a reflection of the high costs prevailing at Red Lake in Canada. The average gold price received by the company edged up to $2369 per ounce, from $2274 in the previous year. The result also included copper and silver revenues of $259 million, up from $204 million in the previous year.

Outlook

Evolution's strategy is to build its gold reserves through developing or acquiring new assets, while also improving the quality of its portfolio and driving down expenses in order to remain a low-cost producer. In particular, it has aimed at delivering operational stability and predictability through the ownership of a number of similar-sized mines, rather than holding just a single mine or a dominant mine. Its target is to own six to eight mines, and it has said it is continually looking for additional long-life, low-cost assets to add to its portfolio. It is investing heavily in Red Lake, acquired in 2020, with the aim of boosting production and driving down operating costs. In May 2021 it acquired Canada's Battle North Corporation for $354 million. Battle North's assets include a processing mill adjacent to Red Lake. Evolution's $400 million acquisition of Kalgoorlie mining operations from Northern Star Resources delivers it a portfolio of assets near its Mungari mine, with the potential for significant cost savings. Evolution has set a gold production target of 700 000 ounces to 760 000 ounces for the June 2022 year, with an average cost of $1220 to $1280 per ounce. However, the company has expressed concern that labour and skill shortages, exacerbated by state border closures, could force costs higher.

Year to 30 June	2020	2021
Revenues ($mn)	1941.9	1864.1
Cowal (%)	32	27
Ernest Henry (%)	20	24
Red Lake (%)	4	16
Mungari (%)	15	15
Mt Rawdon (%)	10	10
EBIT ($mn)	584.5	511.7
EBIT margin (%)	30.1	27.5
Gross margin (%)	33.8	31.1
Profit before tax ($mn)	576.5	496.2
Profit after tax ($mn)	405.4	354.3
Earnings per share (c)	23.81	20.74
Cash flow per share (c)	49.22	43.01
Dividend (c)	16	12
Percentage franked	100	100
Net tangible assets per share ($)	1.45	1.48
Interest cover (times)	72.8	33.0
Return on equity (%)	16.6	14.2
Debt-to-equity ratio (%)	7.7	17.8
Current ratio	2.0	1.3

Fiducian Group Limited

ASX code: FID www.fiducian.com.au

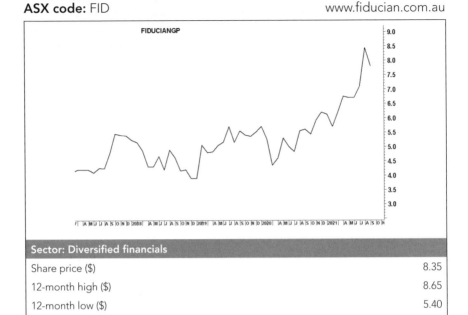

Sector: Diversified financials	
Share price ($)	8.35
12-month high ($)	8.65
12-month low ($)	5.40
Market capitalisation ($mn)	262.5
Price/earnings ratio (times)	21.6
Dividend yield (%)	3.2
Price-to-NTA-per-share ratio	11.2
5-year share price return (% p.a.)	24.3
Dividend reinvestment plan	No

Sydney financial services company Fiducian Group was founded in 1996 by executive chairman Indy Singh, who owns more than a third of the company equity. Initially it specialised in the provision of masterfund, client administration and financial planning services to financial advisory groups. It has since expanded and is now a holding company with five divisions — Fiducian Portfolio Services is in charge of trustee and superannuation services; Fiducian Investment Management Services operates the company's managed funds; Fiducian Services is the administration service provider for all the company's products; Fiducian Financial Services manages the company's financial planning businesses; and Fiducian Business Services provides accounting and business services. In 2019 the company acquired the financial planning business of Tasmanian financial services group MyState.

Latest business results (June 2020, full year)

Revenues and underlying profits rose once more in a solid result. For reporting purposes the company divides its operations into three broad segments. The largest of these now is funds management, which enjoyed a solid increase in revenues and profits, thanks to the company's success in selecting strongly performing funds to offer to its clients. The financial planning business experienced a small dip in revenues, and it made a small loss, with the company continuing to invest in seeking out new businesses to add to its network of advisers. Funds under advice rose from $3 billion in June 2020 to $3.7 billion. The corporate and platform administration segment incorporates all the company's other businesses, and revenues and profits were higher. At June 2021 the total funds under management, advice and administration of $10.4 billion was up by 30 per cent from a year earlier.

Outlook

Fiducian managed 46 financial planning offices across Australia at June 2021, both company-owned and franchised, with a total of 72 authorised representatives. It is continually seeking new offices to join the group, and it has also been achieving solid organic growth. At the same time, Fiducian itself has been named as a possible takeover target for a larger financial institution. The funds management business offers a suite of 14 funds, and the company believes that its method of choosing fund managers with differing investment styles offers the ability to deliver above-average returns with greater diversification and reduced risks. Fiducian management have stated that their long-term goal is to deliver consistent double-digit earnings growth. However, the company is vulnerable to any major downturn in financial markets. At June 2021 it had no debt and cash holdings of more than $19 million.

Year to 30 June	2020	2021
Revenues ($mn)	54.7	58.6
Funds management (%)	36	39
Financial planning (%)	37	33
Platform administration (%)	27	28
EBIT ($mn)	14.6	16.7
EBIT margin (%)	26.8	28.5
Profit before tax ($mn)	14.9	16.9
Profit after tax ($mn)	10.5	12.2
Earnings per share (c)	33.28	38.73
Cash flow per share (c)	44.11	50.27
Dividend (c)	23	26.9
Percentage franked	100	100
Net tangible assets per share ($)	0.54	0.75
Interest cover (times)	~	~
Return on equity (%)	28.7	30.1
Debt-to-equity ratio (%)	~	~
Current ratio	2.4	2.9

Fortescue Metals Group Limited

ASX code: FMG   www.fmgl.com.au

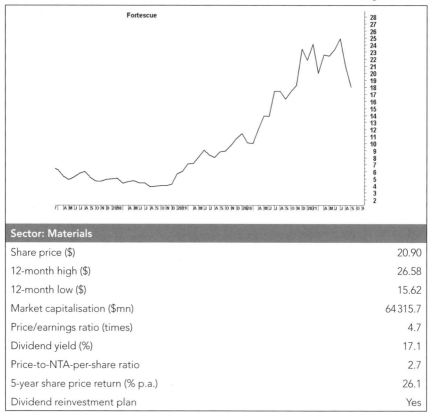

Sector: Materials	
Share price ($)	20.90
12-month high ($)	26.58
12-month low ($)	15.62
Market capitalisation ($mn)	64 315.7
Price/earnings ratio (times)	4.7
Dividend yield (%)	17.1
Price-to-NTA-per-share ratio	2.7
5-year share price return (% p.a.)	26.1
Dividend reinvestment plan	Yes

Perth-based Fortescue was founded in 2003. It has been responsible for discovering and developing some of the largest iron ore mines in the world and is today one of the world's largest iron ore producers, with operations that are centred on several mine sites in the Pilbara region. It also operates its own heavy-haul railway between its mines and its Herb Elliott Port at Port Hedland. Around 90 per cent of its sales are to China.

Latest business results (June 2021, full year)

A surging iron ore price generated a powerhouse result for Fortescue, with revenues up strongly and profits more than doubling. Sales of 182.2 million tonnes were up 2 per cent from the previous year, and the average price of US$135 per tonne was 72 per cent higher. Average production costs of US$13.93 per tonne were up 8 per cent, due to a stronger dollar, increasing energy costs, a tight labour market and expenses associated with the ramping up of the new Eliwana project. During the year the company moved from a net debt position to net cash, and at June 2021 it had net cash holdings of US$2.68 billion. Note that Fortescue reports its results in US dollars. The Australian dollar figures in this book — converted at prevailing exchange rates — are for guidance only.

Outlook

Its heavy debt burden brought Fortescue near to collapse in 2012, and since then it has been devoting enormous efforts into making itself more financially stable. In 2012 its basic production costs were as high as US$50 a tonne, but they have since fallen substantially, and are now among the lowest in the world. It maintains an active exploration and development program at its Pilbara properties as well as an exploration portfolio that encompasses copper-gold projects in Western Australia and ventures throughout South America. With the start of Eliwana operations in December 2020 the company has a further source of low-cost ore to support future sales. Its other major development is the US$3.3 billion to US$3.5 billion Iron Bridge Magnetite project, which is expected to begin production by December 2022. The company has launched Fortescue Future Industries, a global green energy business, with a particular focus on green hydrogen, which the company predicts could become a US$12 trillion market by 2050. Nevertheless, Fortescue's near-term fortunes are tied intimately to the price of iron ore, which can be volatile. It forecasts iron ore shipments during the June 2022 year of 180 million tonnes to 185 million tonnes.

Year to 30 June	2020	2021
Revenues ($mn)	18 579.7	29 321.1
EBIT ($mn)	10 017.4	19 665.8
EBIT margin (%)	53.9	67.1
Gross margin (%)	55.2	69.5
Profit before tax ($mn)	9 695.7	19 371.1
Profit after tax ($mn)	6 862.3	13 546.1
Earnings per share (c)	223.00	440.22
Cash flow per share (c)	288.13	498.64
Dividend (c)	176	358
Percentage franked	100	100
Net tangible assets per share ($)	6.23	7.68
Interest cover (times)	31.1	66.7
Return on equity (%)	40.0	63.3
Debt-to-equity ratio (%)	1.9	~
Current ratio	2.3	2.3

Grange Resources Limited

ASX code: GRR   www.grangeresources.com.au

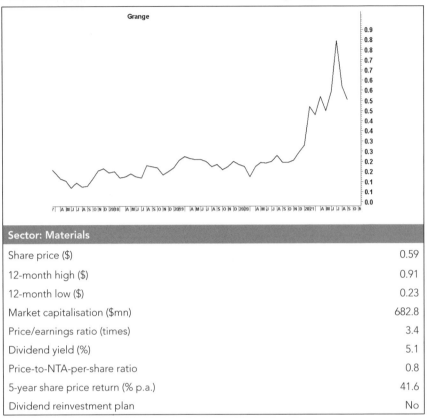

Sector: Materials	
Share price ($)	0.59
12-month high ($)	0.91
12-month low ($)	0.23
Market capitalisation ($mn)	682.8
Price/earnings ratio (times)	3.4
Dividend yield (%)	5.1
Price-to-NTA-per-share ratio	0.8
5-year share price return (% p.a.)	41.6
Dividend reinvestment plan	No

Based in Burnie, Tasmania, Grange Resources is an iron ore producer. It dates back to the 1980s when it was a Western Australian gold-copper miner with the name Sabminco. It is today involved in three major projects — the Savage River magnetite iron ore mine and the Port Latta pellet plant and port facility, both in Tasmania, and a 70-per-cent share in the Southdown Magnetite Project in Western Australia's Great Southern region. It has abandoned its moves into the luxury housing development business.

Latest business results (June 2021, half year)

A booming iron ore market sent revenues and profits soaring for Grange. The company recorded sales of 1.27 million tonnes of iron ore products, mainly iron ore pellets, about 1 per cent more than in the June 2020 period. It received an average price of $339.21 per tonne, 92 per cent higher than in June 2020. Production costs of $100.23 per tonne were up 2 per cent. About three-quarters of the iron ore was shipped to China, with nearly 20 per cent for Korea. The company also received about $1 million in property development revenues, down from nearly $11 million in the June 2020 period.

Outlook

Grange's fortunes are quite dependent on movements in the iron ore market, which in turn have become fairly reliant on Chinese political and economic trends. The company's business involves mining magnetite from its Savage River mine and then refining it at the Port Latta plant into an iron ore concentrate that can be used for steel production. It estimates that Savage River has a mine life that will extend into the 2030s, and it is involved in pre-feasibility study work to determine how best to maximise efficient and effective future mining operations. Port Latta can produce more than 2 million tonnes of iron ore pellets annually and Grange plans to boost this. The company holds long-term supply contracts for 1 million tonnes of its annual production, and the remainder is sold via a spot sales tendering and contracting process. It is carrying out a pre-feasibility study at its Southdown Magnetite Project in Western Australia, with a view to initiating mining operations. It expects the study to be completed by the end of 2021 and is seeking strategic investors to join it in the development of the mine. After losing money, it has ended its three-year-old joint venture to develop luxury apartments in Melbourne. At June 2021 Grange had net cash holdings of more than $380 million.

Year to 31 December	2019	2020
Revenues ($mn)	368.6	526.3
EBIT ($mn)	75.5	224.6
EBIT margin (%)	20.5	42.7
Gross margin (%)	22.4	43.9
Profit before tax ($mn)	81.6	208.9
Profit after tax ($mn)	77.3	203.2
Earnings per share (c)	6.68	17.56
Cash flow per share (c)	8.58	19.38
Dividend (c)	2	3
Percentage franked	100	100
Interest cover (times)	~	14.3
Return on equity (%)	15.3	32.7
Half year to 30 June	**2020**	**2021**
Revenues ($mn)	242.0	450.6
Profit before tax ($mn)	83.7	294.0
Profit after tax ($mn)	65.6	205.3
Earnings per share (c)	5.79	17.79
Dividend (c)	1	2
Percentage franked	100	100
Net tangible assets per share ($)	0.51	0.77
Debt-to-equity ratio (%)	~	~
Current ratio	4.7	4.9

GUD Holdings Limited

ASX code: GUD

www.gud.com.au

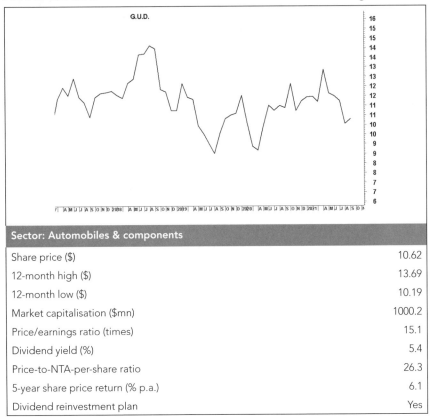

Sector: Automobiles & components	
Share price ($)	10.62
12-month high ($)	13.69
12-month low ($)	10.19
Market capitalisation ($mn)	1000.2
Price/earnings ratio (times)	15.1
Dividend yield (%)	5.4
Price-to-NTA-per-share ratio	26.3
5-year share price return (% p.a.)	6.1
Dividend reinvestment plan	Yes

GUD, based in Melbourne and founded in 1940, is a manufacturer and distributor of a diversified range of auto and industrial products. Its main automotive brands include Ryco, Wesfil, Goss, Brown and Watson International (BWI) — incorporating the Narva and Projecta brands — Griffiths Equipment, Innovative Mechatronic Group (IMG), AA Gaskets and Disc Brakes Australia. The company also manufactures and distributes Davey water pumps and water treatment products.

Latest business results (June 2021, full year)

A booming car parts business powered GUD to a strong rise in revenues and profits, seeing it rebound from the decline of the previous year and overcome weakness in water products. Sales for the core Automotive division surged 34 per cent, with roughly half this from acquisitions and the remainder from organic growth. All main product areas achieved double-digit sales growth, led by excellent performances from BWI and IMG, and the company also benefited from its decision to maintain high inventory levels, even during a period when demand was weakening. The Davey water products operation saw modest sales growth but profits fell sharply as the pandemic forced the idling of production lines, boosted costs, generated significant order backlogs and hurt much of the company's export business. Though 20 per cent of sales, Davey contributed only about 5 per cent of total company profit.

Outlook

Having divested itself of a series of businesses, GUD is now focused on the steadily growing Australian automotive after-market sector. It continues to broaden the product ranges for its various brands and it is also seeking to expand exports. It hopes to secure further acquisitions and has developed a set of acquisition criteria that it believes will boost profitability. It is looking especially for acquisitions related to the four-wheel-drive/sports utility vehicle and the electric vehicle markets. Already about 60 per cent of its automotive sales are unrelated to the combustion engine. Much of the demand for GUD's products is from vehicles more than five years old, and the company estimates that this segment will grow from 14.4 million vehicles in 2020 to 16.2 million by 2025. The company also expects more use of cars as Australians avoid public transport and as they opt for domestic tourism rather than overseas travel. GUD is working to boost profits for its low-margin Davey division, and has been spending heavily on restructuring this business and on developing new products. However, with supply chain disruptions continuing, it believes that a return to normal operations will take some time.

Year to 30 June	2020	2021
Revenues ($mn)	438.0	557.0
Automotive (%)	76	80
Davey (%)	24	20
EBIT ($mn)	81.7	101.2
EBIT margin (%)	18.7	18.2
Gross margin (%)	46.1	44.1
Profit before tax ($mn)	71.1	90.8
Profit after tax ($mn)	50.9	64.0
Earnings per share (c)	58.72	70.35
Cash flow per share (c)	76.02	90.77
Dividend (c)	37	57
Percentage franked	100	100
Net tangible assets per share ($)	~	0.40
Interest cover (times)	7.7	9.7
Return on equity (%)	18.4	19.3
Debt-to-equity ratio (%)	51.7	37.7
Current ratio	2.7	2.7

GWA Group Limited

ASX code: GWA

www.gwagroup.com.au

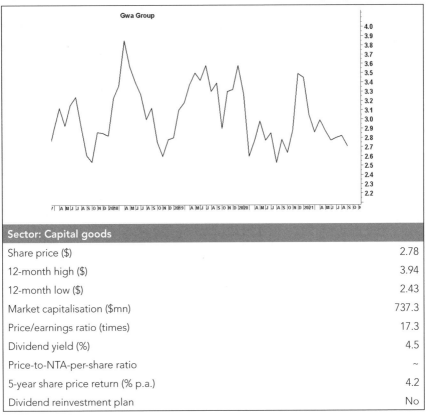

Sector: Capital goods	
Share price ($)	2.78
12-month high ($)	3.94
12-month low ($)	2.43
Market capitalisation ($mn)	737.3
Price/earnings ratio (times)	17.3
Dividend yield (%)	4.5
Price-to-NTA-per-share ratio	~
5-year share price return (% p.a.)	4.2
Dividend reinvestment plan	No

Brisbane-based GWA is a prominent designer, importer and distributor of residential and commercial bathroom and kitchen products, marketed under brands that include Caroma, Dorf, Fowler, Stylus and Clark. About 13 per cent of its sales are in New Zealand, with 8 per cent to other countries, primarily the United Kingdom. In 2019 it acquired the New Zealand company Methven, which designs and manufactures showers, taps and valves.

Latest business results (June 2021, full year)

For the second straight year revenues rose but profits fell, with first-half weakness followed by a solid recovery in the second half. Revenues in Australia actually fell by 1 per cent for the year, including a 6.2 per cent decline in the first half. Sales rose to both the retail market and the builders segment. However, the commercial and multi-residential segments remained weak, hurting profits, as commercial sales generally generate higher margins than do sales to other market segments. New Zealand revenues were up by 14.5 per cent, with other international sales rising by 12.4 per cent. Price rises of around 5 per cent, implemented in August 2020, helped mitigate the impact of rising costs. The continuing integration into the company of the Methven acquisition delivered cost synergies of $3 million.

Outlook

After a long series of restructurings GWA is now almost completely exposed to a bathroom and kitchen fixtures market that in Australia is worth up to $1.4 billion annually. It claims market shares as high as 50 per cent for some of its products, with an overall share of about 23 per cent. It has targeted three sectors — renovations and replacements, commercial construction and detached housing — and is developing new, high-margin products specifically for these markets. It is experiencing growing demand in the detached residential market, but just subdued growth in commercial demand. It expects further weakness in the multi-residential segment, due to COVID-related border closures and travel restrictions. It sees great potential for its Caroma Smart Command intelligent bathroom system, which enables the monitoring and management of water usage in commercial buildings. This product has now been installed in 127 sites, up from 49 installations as of June 2020. In response to the COVID-19 pandemic, it has introduced its Caroma GermGard anti-bacterial glazing product for sanitaryware. It continues to work on reducing its cost base, and expects $3 million in supply-chain savings in the June 2022 year. It will also benefit from price increases of up to 3 per cent that were implemented in July 2021.

Year to 30 June	2020	2021
Revenues ($mn)	398.7	405.7
EBIT ($mn)	71.8	68.5
EBIT margin (%)	18.0	16.9
Gross margin (%)	40.4	40.4
Profit before tax ($mn)	63.2	60.4
Profit after tax ($mn)	44.9	42.3
Earnings per share (c)	17.02	16.03
Cash flow per share (c)	24.74	23.76
Dividend (c)	11.5	12.5
Percentage franked	100	100
Net tangible assets per share ($)	~	~
Interest cover (times)	8.3	8.5
Return on equity (%)	15.9	14.7
Debt-to-equity ratio (%)	51.1	34.9
Current ratio	1.7	1.7

Hansen Technologies Limited

ASX code: HSN   www.hansencx.com

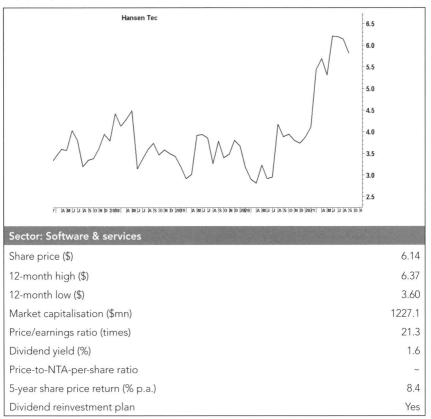

Sector: Software & services	
Share price ($)	6.14
12-month high ($)	6.37
12-month low ($)	3.60
Market capitalisation ($mn)	1227.1
Price/earnings ratio (times)	21.3
Dividend yield (%)	1.6
Price-to-NTA-per-share ratio	~
5-year share price return (% p.a.)	8.4
Dividend reinvestment plan	Yes

Melbourne company Hansen Technologies dates back to an IT business launched in 1971. It later moved into the development of billing software systems and is today a significant global provider of these services, specialising in the electricity, gas, water, pay television and telecommunications sectors. Hansen has offices around the world, and services some 600 customers across 16 product lines in over 80 countries. In September 2021 the private equity firm BGH Capital withdrew its $1.3 billion takeover bid for Hansen.

Latest business results (June 2021, full year)

Revenues rose and profits soared in an excellent result, which would have been even stronger but for currency volatility. New contract wins and expanded contracts with existing customers lay behind the increase in revenues. Notable new customers included Telefonica and DISH in 5G telecommunications, Western Power in smart energy and Nautilus Solar in renewable energy. Altogether, about 51 per cent of business came from the gas, electricity and water industries, with the remainder from communications businesses. During the year the company achieved great success in

cutting costs, and this lay behind a big improvement in profit margins. I'
employee expenses were down 11 per cent and the repayment of a la'
company debt led to a sharp reduction in interest payments. Pander
restrictions meant that the travel budget plunged.

Outlook

Though a small company, Hansen has developed a high reputation for its servic
Once it does business with a customer it stands to benefit further from a long-term
stream of recurring revenue. Hansen's particular strategy is growth by acquisition, and
with the billing services industry still fragmented and largely regionalised, it expects
further attractive acquisition opportunities to present themselves. In particular, it is
aiming at assets that own intellectual property and with recurring revenue streams
that will help Hansen move into new regions or market segments. It has a dedicated
mergers and acquisitions team that has developed a proactive relationship with many
brokers and bankers around the world, and has the ability to move quickly if it finds
the right opportunities. To help reduce costs it has been making a significant
investment in development centres in Vietnam and India. It sees the rapid pace of
regulatory change in many countries as a particular tailwind that creates growing
demand for its services. The company's target is $500 million in revenues in the June
2025 year with EBITDA of $160 million to $175 million, compared to $120 million
in June 2021.

Year to 30 June	2020	2021
Revenues ($mn)	301.4	307.7
EBIT ($mn)	38.3	74.8
EBIT margin (%)	12.7	24.3
Profit before tax ($mn)	30.3	70.1
Profit after tax ($mn)	26.2	57.3
Earnings per share (c)	13.23	28.81
Cash flow per share (c)	34.62	49.36
Dividend (c)	8	10
Percentage franked	23	38
Net tangible assets per share ($)	~	~
Interest cover (times)	4.8	16.2
Return on equity (%)	10.5	21.2
Debt-to-equity ratio (%)	45.1	22.7
Current ratio	1.6	0.7

Iarvey Norman Holdings Limited

ASX code: HVN   www.harveynormanholdings.com.au

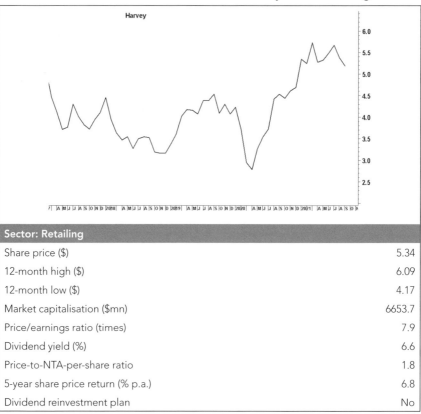

Harvey

Sector: Retailing	
Share price ($)	5.34
12-month high ($)	6.09
12-month low ($)	4.17
Market capitalisation ($mn)	6653.7
Price/earnings ratio (times)	7.9
Dividend yield (%)	6.6
Price-to-NTA-per-share ratio	1.8
5-year share price return (% p.a.)	6.8
Dividend reinvestment plan	No

Sydney-based Harvey Norman, established in 1982, operates a chain of 297 retail stores specialising in electrical and electronic goods, home appliances, furniture, flooring, carpets and manchester items, throughout Australia, New Zealand, Ireland, Northern Ireland, Singapore, Malaysia, Slovenia and Croatia, under the Harvey Norman, Domayne and Joyce Mayne banners. The 192 Australian stores are independently held as part of a franchise operation, from which Harvey Norman receives income for advisory and advertising services. It also receives a considerable amount of income from its own stores, from its $3.4 billion property portfolio and from the provision of finance to franchisees and customers.

Latest business results (June 2021, full year)

Harvey Norman enjoyed another excellent year, as travel-restricted consumers spent heavily on their homes. Strong sales allowed the company to reduce discounting and raise some prices, and profit margins were higher. Total store sales — franchise and company-owned — rose 15 per cent to $9.72 billion. Sales of $2.28 billion by the company's own stores were up 20 per cent, with pre-tax profit surging 70 per cent. The 15 Irish stores were especially strong, with sales up 47 per cent and the pre-tax profit rising threefold. Franchise income received by Harvey Norman rose 30 per cent to $1.24 billion. The property business reported a 68 per cent rise in pre-tax profit, although this was largely the result of property revaluations. The company said that excluding the impact of property revaluations its total after-tax profit was $743.1 million. During the year the company opened 12 new stores, in Singapore, Malaysia, New Zealand, Ireland and Croatia.

Outlook

Harvey Norman reported that sales fell at most of its stores in the early months of the June 2022 financial year, although much of this was due to government-mandated lockdowns. Nevertheless, it remains uncertain how much money consumers can continue to spend on their homes, though with Christmas on the horizon the company was optimistic about a quick recovery in spending when lockdowns lifted. Anticipating supply chain delays, it has increased inventories. It has high fixed costs, so even modest increases in sales can translate to much larger increases in earnings. Nevertheless, its business is also highly exposed to economic conditions and consumer spending trends, and it could be affected by rising unemployment or growing economic weakness. It continues to expand, with plans to open three new stores abroad in the June 2022 year and three franchised complexes in Australia. In 2023 it plans an initial move into Hungary, with two stores.

Year to 30 June	2020	2021
Revenues ($mn)	3545.8	4438.6
Retail (%)	65	63
Franchising operations (%)	26	27
Property (%)	8	9
EBIT ($mn)	714.7	1227.7
EBIT margin (%)	20.2	27.7
Gross margin (%)	32.2	33.6
Profit before tax ($mn)	661.3	1182.5
Profit after tax ($mn)	480.5	841.4
Earnings per share (c)	39.19	67.53
Cash flow per share (c)	46.33	74.54
Dividend (c)	18	35
Percentage franked	100	100
Net tangible assets per share ($)	2.72	3.05
Interest cover (times)	13.4	27.2
Return on equity (%)	14.5	23.0
Debt-to-equity ratio (%)	~	7.6
Current ratio	1.7	1.5

IDP Education Limited

ASX code: IEL   www.idp.com

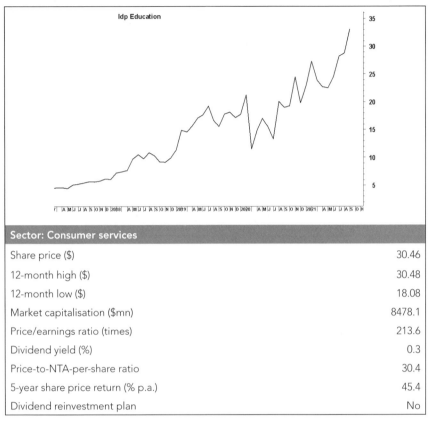

Sector: Consumer services	
Share price ($)	30.46
12-month high ($)	30.48
12-month low ($)	18.08
Market capitalisation ($mn)	8478.1
Price/earnings ratio (times)	213.6
Dividend yield (%)	0.3
Price-to-NTA-per-share ratio	30.4
5-year share price return (% p.a.)	45.4
Dividend reinvestment plan	No

Melbourne-based IDP Education dates back to 1969 and the launch of the Australian Asian Universities Cooperation Scheme, aimed at helping Asian students study in Australia. In 1981 it changed its name to the International Development Program (IDP), and opened a series of offices throughout Asia. It has since expanded through acquisition and organic growth, and today helps students from around the world find placements in higher education programs in English-speaking countries. It also works with University of Cambridge ESOL Examinations and the British Council to administer worldwide testing for the International English Language Testing System. About 25 per cent of IDP's equity is held by 38 Australian universities.

Latest business results (June 2021, full year)

Revenues fell and profits crashed as lockdowns and travel restrictions severely hurt business. A modest second-half recovery was insufficient to overcome a sharp decline in business in the first half. More than half the company's turnover derives from its English language testing services, and revenues were largely flat, with only a small decline in profits. Altogether 1.15 million tests were administered, 5 per cent more than in the previous year, despite periods of lockdown in many of the company's countries of operation. Profits would actually have risen but for unfavourable currency exchange rates. The company's other main business, student placement services, saw revenues and profits down by double-digit amounts. Australian operations were particularly badly hit due to border restrictions. A smaller business involves English language teaching at nine schools in Cambodia and Vietnam. Government-mandated closures forced courses to move online, and revenues and profits fell sharply.

Outlook

IDP faces challenges while the COVID-19 pandemic restricts international travel. Around two-thirds of its revenues and three-quarters of its profits have been coming from Asia, and particularly from China and India, which the company has noted are the key engines of growth for the international education industry more broadly. Demand for international education services remains high in both countries. However, the company's largest study destination by volume is Australia, and it is unclear when international students will be able to return. Two other prominent study destinations for the company are the United Kingdom and Canada, and there are signs that campuses there are set to reopen. Testing demand also looks set to grow. In August 2021 IDP acquired for £130 million the British Council's English language testing business in India. It expects this to add 13 per cent to its EPS figure, as well as delivering cost-saving synergy benefits of up to $8 million annually.

Year to 30 June	2020	2021
Revenues ($mn)	587.1	528.7
Asia (%)	66	60
Rest of World (%)	24	31
Australasia (%)	10	9
EBIT ($mn)	107.8	64.1
EBIT margin (%)	18.4	12.1
Profit before tax ($mn)	102.6	58.9
Profit after tax ($mn)	67.9	39.7
Earnings per share (c)	26.14	14.26
Cash flow per share (c)	41.88	27.76
Dividend (c)	16.5	8
Percentage franked	17	0
Net tangible assets per share ($)	0.95	1.00
Interest cover (times)	20.8	12.1
Return on equity (%)	24.9	10.3
Debt-to-equity ratio (%)	~	~
Current ratio	2.5	2.5

Infomedia Limited

ASX code: IFM　　　　　　　　　　　www.infomedia.com.au

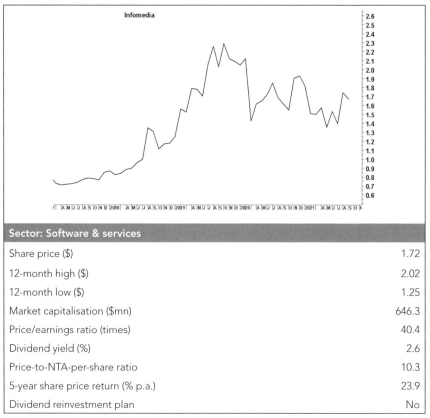

Sector: Software & services	
Share price ($)	1.72
12-month high ($)	2.02
12-month low ($)	1.25
Market capitalisation ($mn)	646.3
Price/earnings ratio (times)	40.4
Dividend yield (%)	2.6
Price-to-NTA-per-share ratio	10.3
5-year share price return (% p.a.)	23.9
Dividend reinvestment plan	No

Sydney electronic data company Infomedia was formed in 1987, and has grown into a world leader in the development of specialised electronic catalogues. Its main product is the Microcat electronic parts catalogue for the automotive industry, with versions for most leading car companies. Sold to customers in 186 countries, the catalogue enables service personnel in a motor dealership to identify the correct replacement parts for a vehicle. The company also produces the Superservice data management product, which provides automotive dealers with a range of service, repair and warranty management tools. Another product is Infodrive, which provides auto companies with data analytics. In June 2021 it acquired the American parts e-commerce platform SimplePart.

Latest business results (June 2021, full year)

Revenues rose but profits fell, as pandemic-related restrictions delayed the implementation of some contracts. The company also reported a double-digit rise in expenses as it spent heavily on its new Next Gen software. With the majority of its business abroad, it also felt an unfavourable impact from currency fluctuations. The Asia-Pacific region again enjoyed the best result, with a big increase in Superservice sales in Australia and growing strength in South-East Asia. European sales were subdued due to uncertainty sparked by Brexit and the pandemic, and American business was hurt by travel restrictions and lockdowns. Nevertheless, both Europe and America recorded modest revenue rises.

Outlook

In a fiercely competitive global automobile market, car dealerships now often make more profit from the supply of parts and service than they do from actual car sales. It is this fast-growing after-sales sector that is the target market for Infomedia. It believes that parts and servicing requirements are set to become more complex as a result of moves towards automated and electric vehicles. It also points to a rise in the number of older cars on the roads, stimulating demand for parts and servicing. It has rolled out its Next Gen parts and services software, one of the largest development projects in its history. It believes the Next Gen electronic parts catalogues will provide dealerships with innovative tools, including a major data analytics capability, that will enable them to boost sales and productivity significantly. The acquisition of SimplePart, at a price of up to US$45 million, expands the company's e-commerce offerings and broadens its customer base. Infomedia achieved $35 million in new contract wins in 2020 and 2021, and this will help power growth in coming years. It forecasts revenues of $117 million to $123 million in the June 2022 year.

Year to 30 June	2020	2021
Revenues ($mn)	94.6	97.4
EBIT ($mn)	25.5	20.0
EBIT margin (%)	27.0	20.5
Profit before tax ($mn)	25.0	20.4
Profit after tax ($mn)	18.6	16.0
Earnings per share (c)	5.69	4.26
Cash flow per share (c)	12.08	11.50
Dividend (c)	4.3	4.45
Percentage franked	70	84
Net tangible assets per share ($)	0.23	0.17
Interest cover (times)	46.1	~
Return on equity (%)	17.0	10.4
Debt-to-equity ratio (%)	~	~
Current ratio	5.8	4.3

Integral Diagnostics Limited

ASX code: IDX   www.integraldiagnostics.com.au

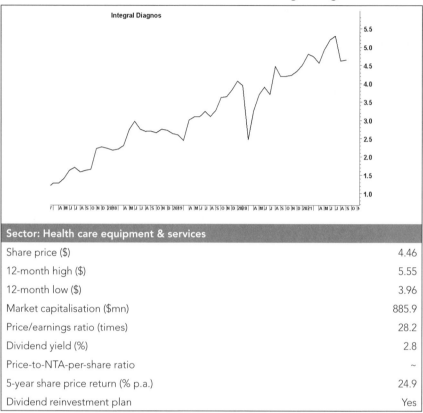

Sector: Health care equipment & services	
Share price ($)	4.46
12-month high ($)	5.55
12-month low ($)	3.96
Market capitalisation ($mn)	885.9
Price/earnings ratio (times)	28.2
Dividend yield (%)	2.8
Price-to-NTA-per-share ratio	~
5-year share price return (% p.a.)	24.9
Dividend reinvestment plan	Yes

Melbourne-based healthcare services company Integral Diagnostics got its start in 2002 with the formation of its Lake Imaging brand in Ballarat. It has since grown through acquisition and is today one of Australia's largest radiology providers, with operations at 55 sites in Victoria, Queensland and Western Australia. It is also active in New Zealand, with a further 12 sites. Its services include x-ray, ultrasound, computed tomography, magnetic resonance imaging (MRI) and nuclear medicine. In November 2019 it acquired Imaging Queensland and in September 2020 it acquired Ascot Radiology in New Zealand.

Latest business results (June 2021, full year)

The impact of recent acquisitions, along with solid organic growth, helped Integral Diagnostics overcome a pandemic-related slowdown in some of its operations, and it posted another good result. It achieved organic revenue growth of 12.2 per cent in Australia, and the average fee per examination rose 3.3 per cent, driven by moves to higher-end procedures and a rise in Medicare payments. Operating costs rose as a percentage of revenues, due to rising wages for radiologists, increased costs related to higher-end procedures and the necessity to spend more on personal protective equipment because of the COVID-19 pandemic. New Zealand revenues of $46.2 million were up from $24.8 million in the previous year, thanks to the Ascot Radiology acquisition and 12.5 per cent organic growth. Capital spending of $23.1 million was down from $26.1 million in the previous year, with the major item of expenditure the installation of an MRI spine centre at the Gold Coast.

Outlook

Integral Diagnostics operates through a variety of brands — Lake Imaging in Victoria, Imaging Queensland and South Coast Radiology in Queensland, Apex Radiology in Western Australia and Specialist Radiology Group, Trinity MRI and Ascot Radiology in New Zealand. With growing and ageing populations in both countries, it believes that long-term fundamentals are strong. In addition, the industry remains quite fragmented, presenting opportunities for further consolidation. However, in the short term the company is concerned that continuing lockdowns in both Australia and New Zealand will hurt business. It plans a large increase in capital spending in the June 2022 year to as much as $44 million, including $11 million to develop four new radiology clinics and $8 million on new technology and equipment upgrades. It has launched IDXt, a teleradiology business. Teleradiology involves the remote analysis of radiological patient images. In February 2021 Integral Diagnostics entered into a joint venture with Medica Group, the UK market leader in teleradiology services.

Year to 30 June	2020	2021
Revenues ($mn)	275.6	350.7
EBIT ($mn)	43.6	54.0
EBIT margin (%)	15.8	15.4
Profit before tax ($mn)	35.3	45.2
Profit after tax ($mn)	23.0	31.3
Earnings per share (c)	12.43	15.80
Cash flow per share (c)	26.29	33.44
Dividend (c)	9.5	12.5
Percentage franked	100	100
Net tangible assets per share ($)	~	~
Interest cover (times)	5.3	6.1
Return on equity (%)	13.0	12.9
Debt-to-equity ratio (%)	54.2	53.6
Current ratio	1.1	1.1

IPH Limited

ASX code: IPH   www.iphltd.com.au

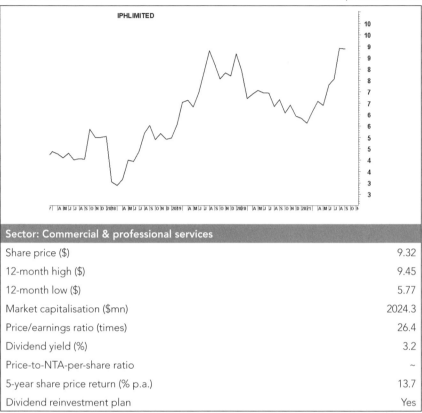

Sector: Commercial & professional services	
Share price ($)	9.32
12-month high ($)	9.45
12-month low ($)	5.77
Market capitalisation ($mn)	2024.3
Price/earnings ratio (times)	26.4
Dividend yield (%)	3.2
Price-to-NTA-per-share ratio	~
5-year share price return (% p.a.)	13.7
Dividend reinvestment plan	Yes

Sydney-based IPH, formed in 2014 but with roots that stretch back to 1887, is a holding company for a group of businesses offering a wide range of intellectual property services and products. These include the filing, prosecution, enforcement and management of patents, designs, trademarks and other intellectual property. The company also develops data analytics software through its subsidiary Practice Insight. IPH operates from offices in Australia, New Zealand, Singapore, Malaysia, China, Indonesia, Thailand and Hong Kong.

Latest business results (June 2021, full year)

Revenues and profits edged down, although this largely reflected currency movements, and on a like-for-like basis business advanced. For reporting purposes the company segments its operations into Australian and New Zealand businesses, representing about three-quarters of total turnover, and Asian businesses. Underlying revenues and profits fell slightly in Australia and New Zealand, reflecting a 5 per cent decline in patent filings. However, cost synergies from the successful integration of Xenith IP Group, acquired in 2019, sent profits higher on a like-for-like basis. Asia too saw revenues and profits down, though on a like-for-like basis they rose, with particular strength in China and Hong Kong.

Outlook

IPH has established itself as one of the leaders in the intellectual property business in Australia, New Zealand and South-East Asia. It has expanded steadily, through organic growth and acquisition. As it grows it achieves economies of scale that boost margins. It has become the largest filer of patents in Singapore, where it opened an office in 1997. It classifies the US, Western Europe, Japan and South Korea as the primary markets in its business, and its expressed aim is to establish itself in other regions. Its $192 million acquisition of Xenith has boosted its share of the domestic intellectual property market from around 20 per cent to more than 35 per cent and has delivered significant cost synergies. It is achieving success with its strategy of leveraging its network of companies, and domestic subsidiaries are now among the foremost clients of its trademark and patent operations in Beijing and Hong Kong. It continues to seek out further acquisition opportunities. In October 2020 it acquired Baldwins IP, a leading New Zealand intellectual property specialist, and in July 2021 it acquired Applied Marks, one of Australia's leading online automated trademark application platforms. It plans to use this company's technology to develop a new digital services function within the group. The acquisition will also allow IPH to address the retail online trademark market.

Year to 30 June	2020	2021
Revenues ($mn)	365.7	359.7
EBIT ($mn)	111.3	108.5
EBIT margin (%)	30.4	30.2
Profit before tax ($mn)	104.2	102.6
Profit after tax ($mn)	77.7	76.2
Earnings per share (c)	36.68	35.26
Cash flow per share (c)	52.96	52.60
Dividend (c)	28.5	29.5
Percentage franked	100	45
Net tangible assets per share ($)	~	~
Interest cover (times)	15.8	18.3
Return on equity (%)	22.0	17.9
Debt-to-equity ratio (%)	18.8	12.9
Current ratio	3.0	2.7

IRESS Limited

ASX code: IRE   www.iress.com

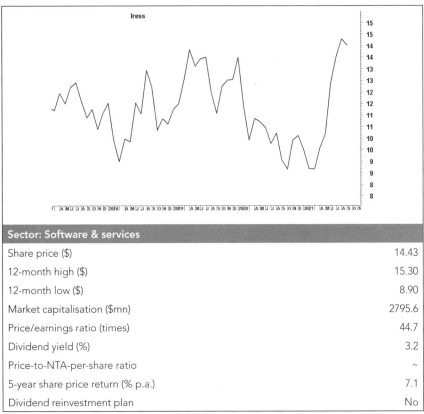

Sector: Software & services	
Share price ($)	14.43
12-month high ($)	15.30
12-month low ($)	8.90
Market capitalisation ($mn)	2795.6
Price/earnings ratio (times)	44.7
Dividend yield (%)	3.2
Price-to-NTA-per-share ratio	~
5-year share price return (% p.a.)	7.1
Dividend reinvestment plan	No

Melbourne-based IRESS was founded in 1993. It produces the IRESS (Integrated Real-time Equity System) share market information system, used widely throughout the Australian investment community. Within the IRESS system it offers a portfolio of information and trading products with numerous applications for stockbrokers, fund managers and other financial professionals. It is also active in wealth management services, with its Xplan financial planning software. A third activity is the Mortgages division, which provides mortgage processing software. The company has expanded its operations to New Zealand, Europe, North America, Singapore, Hong Kong and South Africa. In 2020 it acquired the ASX-listed financial technology company OneVue Holdings.

Latest business results (June 2021, half year)

Revenues and profits rose, reflecting the OneVue acquisition, which was completed in November 2020, along with a strong performance from the Mortgages division and from North American operations. The Asia-Pacific region represents more than half of total turnover. As well as benefiting from OneVue, this segment enjoyed continuing growth in Asian business and a 5 per cent rise in Australian revenues. The United Kingdom and Europe are the other main contributors to company income, and revenues edged up on a constant currency basis — though they fell slightly in Australian dollars — thanks to new and continuing projects with key clients. The small Mortgages division was boosted by new client wins, and North American operations benefited from a major regulatory change that required additional project work from clients. Economic uncertainty hurt South African business.

Outlook

IRESS's businesses are strongly geared to levels of financial market activity, which can lead to volatility in its operations. It is also vulnerable to structural changes in the financial sector. Nevertheless, its products are widely used in Australia, and the company reports high levels of customer loyalty, with recurring revenues responsible for some 90 per cent of total turnover. It benefits from the steady growth of superannuation assets, and it also expects considerable synergy benefits as it integrates Xplan with OneVue. The company calculates that it has an addressable market across the investment infrastructure, superannuation and UK wealth sectors worth more than $5 billion, and it has announced an ambitious growth plan, with the aim of more than doubling after-tax profit by 2025. Much of this involves upgrading and integrating its various software platforms into a single, cloud-based technology platform, and it expects to spend $30 million during 2022 and 2023 on this work. In September 2021 Swedish private equity firm EQT Fund Management withdrew its takeover bid for IRESS.

Year to 31 December	2019	2020
Revenues ($mn)	508.9	542.6
EBIT ($mn)	96.6	86.1
EBIT margin (%)	19.0	15.9
Profit before tax ($mn)	88.5	78.1
Profit after tax ($mn)	65.1	59.1
Earnings per share (c)	37.87	32.28
Cash flow per share (c)	59.53	53.78
Dividend (c)	46	46
Percentage franked	30	38
Interest cover (times)	11.8	10.8
Return on equity (%)	15.2	11.6
Half year to 30 June	2020	2021
Revenues ($mn)	270.7	290.2
Profit before tax ($mn)	35.1	50.4
Profit after tax ($mn)	26.3	40.9
Earnings per share (c)	15.00	21.40
Dividend (c)	16	16
Percentage franked	35	80
Net tangible assets per share ($)	~	~
Debt-to-equity ratio (%)	8.7	31.6
Current ratio	1.7	1.3

JB Hi-Fi Limited

ASX code: JBH

investors.jbhifi.com.au

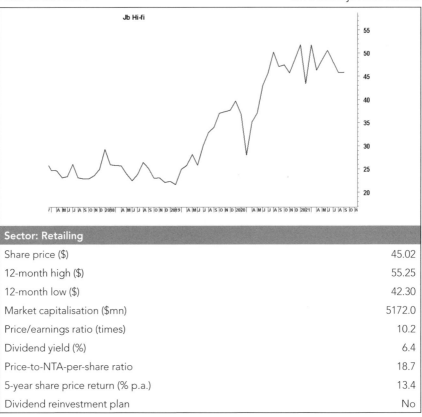

Sector: Retailing	
Share price ($)	45.02
12-month high ($)	55.25
12-month low ($)	42.30
Market capitalisation ($mn)	5172.0
Price/earnings ratio (times)	10.2
Dividend yield (%)	6.4
Price-to-NTA-per-share ratio	18.7
5-year share price return (% p.a.)	13.4
Dividend reinvestment plan	No

Melbourne-based JB Hi-Fi dates back to the opening in 1974 of a single recorded music store in the Melbourne suburb of East Keilor. It has since grown into a nationwide chain of home electronic and home appliance products outlets, and it has also expanded to New Zealand. In 2016 it acquired The Good Guys chain of home appliance stores. Its JB Hi-Fi Solutions division sells to the commercial, educational and insurance sectors. The company also maintains a growing online presence. At the end of June 2021 it operated 197 JB Hi-Fi and JB Hi-Fi Home stores in Australia, 14 JB Hi-Fi stores in New Zealand and 105 The Good Guys stores in Australia.

Latest business results (June 2021, full year)

In another excellent result, sales rose and profits raced ahead, as the COVID 19 pandemic led Australian consumers to spend heavily on items for the home. There was a particularly strong performance from The Good Guys, with sales up 13.7 per cent but EBIT surging by 90 per cent, as continuing cost control measures had a big impact. Demand was especially buoyant for the refrigeration, laundry, floorcare, portable appliance and visual segments. Profit margins at The Good Guys are now similar to those at JB Hi-Fi Australia. At JB Hi-Fi Australia sales were up 12 per cent, with strong demand for computers, communications equipment, games hardware and small appliances. JB Hi-Fi New Zealand saw sales up 17.4 per cent, and it moved from loss to profit. Online sales grew 78.1 per cent to represent nearly 12 per cent of total turnover.

Outlook

JB Hi-Fi has a strong brand image throughout Australia and great customer loyalty. It has shown an impressive ability to contain costs. It continues to open new stores, though at a slower pace than in previous years. It is boosting floor space at its stores for growth categories such as mobile phones, gaming and connected technology. It is also working to strengthen its online operations. Its business continues to be affected by the COVID-19 pandemic. While demand remains strong it is able to cut back on discounting and even raise some prices. However, a series of lockdowns in several states has forced it to close stores temporarily. It could also be hurt by rising freight costs and possible supply-chain disruptions. It expects to see continuing solid growth for its JB Hi-Fi Solutions division, which services commercial customers. At June 2021 JB Hi-Fi had no debt and cash holdings of $263 million.

Year to 30 June	2020	2021
Revenues ($mn)	7918.9	8916.1
JB Australia (%)	67	67
The Good Guys (%)	30	30
JB New Zealand (%)	3	3
EBIT ($mn)	511.3	743.1
EBIT margin (%)	6.5	8.3
Gross margin (%)	21.4	22.2
Profit before tax ($mn)	476.0	720.0
Profit after tax ($mn)	332.7	506.1
Earnings per share (c)	289.56	440.85
Cash flow per share (c)	476.15	624.56
Dividend (c)	189	287
Percentage franked	100	100
Net tangible assets per share ($)	0.65	2.41
Interest cover (times)	14.5	32.2
Return on equity (%)	31.0	41.9
Debt-to-equity ratio (%)	~	~
Current ratio	0.9	1.1

Jumbo Interactive Limited

ASX code: JIN   www.jumbointeractive.com

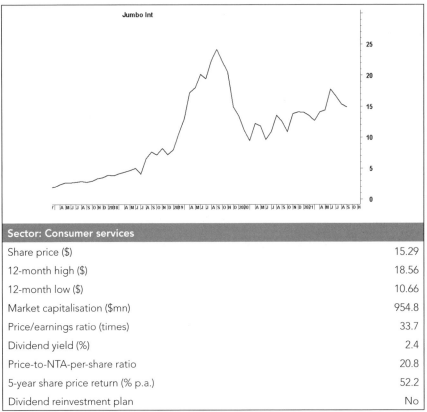

Sector: Consumer services	
Share price ($)	15.29
12-month high ($)	18.56
12-month low ($)	10.66
Market capitalisation ($mn)	954.8
Price/earnings ratio (times)	33.7
Dividend yield (%)	2.4
Price-to-NTA-per-share ratio	20.8
5-year share price return (% p.a.)	52.2
Dividend reinvestment plan	No

Jumbo Interactive was founded in Brisbane in 1995 as an internet service provider, but has since evolved into a major operator of internet services for lotteries. Its core business, Oz Lotteries, involves the sale of lottery services for Tabcorp at its ozlotteries.com website. These lotteries include OzLotto, Powerball, Lotto and Lucky Lotteries. It has introduced a Software-as-a-Service (SaaS) business, called Powered by Jumbo, that manages lotteries for charitable organisations and other institutions. It has also launched a Managed Services division to provide lottery management services on an international basis. In 2019 Jumbo entered the British market with the acquisition of lottery manager Gatherwell. In August 2021 it announced plans to acquire Canadian lottery manager Stride Management.

Latest business results (June 2021, full year)

Revenues recorded a double-digit rise, but the increase in profits was more modest as the company invested for future growth. Large Powerball and OzLotto jackpots are an important stimulus to sales, and there were 38 of these during the year, compared to 39 in the previous year. However, their average value was down substantially from $40.1 million to $31.8 million. Nevertheless, the total transaction value during the year of all Jumbo's business was $487 million, up 37 per cent from the previous year. The new Powered by Jumbo service brought in revenues of nearly $5 million and the new Managed Services division recorded $3.3 million in revenues, most of this derived from the company's new British subsidiary Gatherwell.

Outlook

Jumbo is a significant beneficiary of the Australian love of gambling. A new software platform and a vigorous marketing campaign have helped stimulate its recent growth. It is also enjoying success with new apps for mobile devices, and reports that these have succeeded in attracting a new demographic of younger customers. Consequently, 33 per cent of Australian lottery ticket sales are now online, up from 28 per cent in the June 2020 year. It sees great potential from its Stride Management acquisition, which brings in 750 000 new customers and should add more than $120 million to annual total transaction value. Stride operates in only two of Canada's provinces, and Jumbo sees considerable scope for expansion. The company also expects solid growth from its Powered by Jumbo business, which is steadily attracting new customers, in both Australia and the UK. The new Managed Services division provides services such as prize procurement, lottery game design, campaign marketing, customer relationships and draw management, and is building customer numbers in the UK and Australia.

Year to 30 June	2020	2021
Revenues ($mn)	71.2	83.3
EBIT ($mn)	37.2	39.1
EBIT margin (%)	52.3	46.9
Profit before tax ($mn)	38.0	39.1
Profit after tax ($mn)	26.5	28.3
Earnings per share (c)	42.47	45.39
Cash flow per share (c)	52.08	58.58
Dividend (c)	35.5	36.5
Percentage franked	100	100
Net tangible assets per share ($)	0.87	0.73
Interest cover (times)	~	2298.3
Return on equity (%)	33.9	34.5
Debt-to-equity ratio (%)	~	~
Current ratio	3.2	2.9

Macquarie Group Limited

ASX code: MQG   www.macquarie.com.au

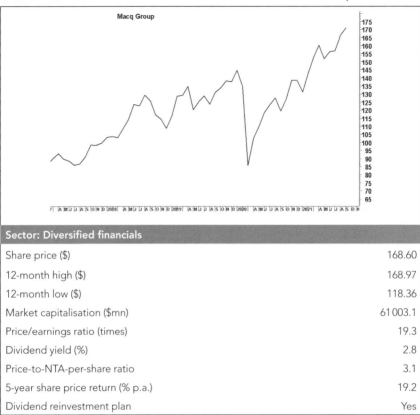

Sector: Diversified financials	
Share price ($)	168.60
12-month high ($)	168.97
12-month low ($)	118.36
Market capitalisation ($mn)	61 003.1
Price/earnings ratio (times)	19.3
Dividend yield (%)	2.8
Price-to-NTA-per-share ratio	3.1
5-year share price return (% p.a.)	19.2
Dividend reinvestment plan	Yes

Sydney-based Macquarie Group was established in 1969 as Hill Samuel Australia, a subsidiary of a British merchant bank. It is now Australia's leading locally owned investment bank, with a wide spread of activities and boasting special expertise in specific industries that include resources and commodities, energy, financial institutions, infrastructure and real estate. It has offices in 32 markets around the world, and international business accounts for more than two-thirds of total company income.

Latest business results (March 2021, full year)

Profits rebounded after the decline of the previous year, when the COVID-19 pandemic affected many of its operations. However, the good result was dependent on a 50 per cent jump in profits for the Commodities and Global Markets division, the largest of the bank's four broad operating segments. This business benefited from increased volatility in commodity prices, with a strong contribution related to North American gas, power, oil and precious metal contracts. There was also increased trading activity in foreign exchange, interest rate and credit products. The bank's other large operating segment, Macquarie Asset Management, which recorded higher profits in the previous year, this time saw its profits down by 5 per cent. This reflected an equity-accounted loss from Macquarie AirFinance, and lower profits from asset sales and decreased performance fees when compared with the previous year. Of the two smaller operating segments, Banking and Financial Services saw its profits in line with the previous year, with higher interest and trading income offset by higher staff and technology costs, in part due to the pandemic. The fourth operating segment, Macquarie Capital, recorded a 15 per cent decline in profits, largely due to fewer asset realisations compared with the previous year.

Outlook

At a time of global economic uncertainty, Macquarie is not prepared to make forecasts for the March 2022 year, although it is well able to profit from economic ambiguity and market volatility. Around 55 per cent of its profits are in the form of stable, annuity-style earnings, which reduces risk. Nevertheless, it has already said that it expects commodities income to fall significantly, following the buoyant March 2021 year. It continues to expand. In April 2021 it acquired Waddell & Reed Financial, one of the oldest wealth management companies in the US, bringing US$76 billion in assets under management. In July 2021 it announced plans to acquire AMP Capital's global equity and fixed income business, bringing a further $60 billion in assets under management. It is also placing a particular emphasis on building up a portfolio of decarbonisation assets.

Year to 31 March	2020	2021
Operating income ($mn)	12 325.0	12 774.0
Net interest income ($mn)	1 859.0	2 195.0
Operating expenses ($mn)	8 871.0	8 867.0
Profit before tax ($mn)	3 454.0	3 907.0
Profit after tax ($mn)	2 731.0	3 015.0
Earnings per share (c)	819.54	871.54
Dividend (c)	430	470
Percentage franked	40	40
Non-interest income to total income (%)	84.9	82.8
Net tangible assets per share ($)	50.21	53.91
Cost-to-income ratio (%)	72.0	69.4
Return on equity (%)	14.1	14.0
Return on assets (%)	1.2	1.2

Magellan Financial Group Limited

ASX code: MFG 　　　　　www.magellangroup.com.au

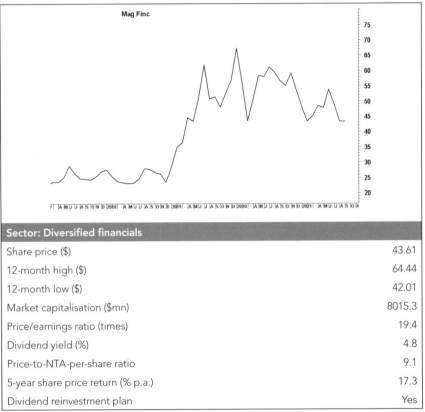

Sector: Diversified financials	
Share price ($)	43.61
12-month high ($)	64.44
12-month low ($)	42.01
Market capitalisation ($mn)	8015.3
Price/earnings ratio (times)	19.4
Dividend yield (%)	4.8
Price-to-NTA-per-share ratio	9.1
5-year share price return (% p.a.)	17.3
Dividend reinvestment plan	Yes

Sydney-based Magellan is a specialist investment management company that evolved in 2006 from the ASX-listed Pengana Hedgefunds Limited. Its main business is Magellan Asset Management, which offers managed funds to retail and institutional investors, with particular specialties in global equities, global listed infrastructure, Australian equities — through Airlie Funds Management, which it acquired in 2018 — and sustainable asset investments.

Latest business results (June 2021, full year)

Revenues and the after-tax profit fell in a mixed year for the company. Management and services fees rose again, up 7 per cent to $635 million. However, performance fees fell for the second straight year, down 63 per cent to $30 million. Once again the company achieved success in containing its basic costs, and its cost-to-income ratio fell to an impressive 16.9 per cent, down from 19.7 per cent a year earlier. At June 2021 Magellan had funds under management of $113.9 billion, up from $97.2 billion a year earlier, thanks to its investment performance and net inflows of $4.5 billion.

Outlook

Magellan continues to expand, and funds under management exceed those of two rivals, Platinum Asset Management and Perpetual. It has a record of strong, long-term performance in global equities — despite some underperformance in the June 2021 year — and has become a significant beneficiary of moves by Australian investors to diversify into overseas markets. It also benefits from the reputation and stock-picking prowess of its Chairman and Chief Investment Officer Hamish Douglass. Nevertheless, it remains heavily dependent on the state of financial markets, and it would suffer from any big sell-off in equities, or from a prolonged bear market. In addition, more than 80 per cent of funds under management are exposed to currency fluctuations. It has restructured its Magellan Global Fund in order to make it more attractive to investors, with both open-ended and closed-ended unit class options. In June 2021 it launched Magellan FuturePay, offering investors a predictable monthly income through the implementation of a high-quality, low-volatility investment strategy. The company sees high long-term growth potential for this product, which is aimed especially at retirees. Through its Magellan Capital Partners division the company has made three major strategic investments — in the financial services firm Barrenjoey Capital Partners, in technology services provider FinClear Holdings and in restaurant chain Guzman y Gomez — aimed at delivering significant long-term value. In order to tap into a trend towards ethical investing, the company has opened its Magellan Sustainable Fund to retail investors.

Year to 30 June	2020	2021
Revenues ($mn)	672.6	665.5
EBIT ($mn)	570.6	588.7
EBIT margin (%)	84.8	88.5
Profit before tax ($mn)	573.2	587.7
Profit after tax ($mn)	438.3	412.7
Earnings per share (c)	241.46	225.03
Cash flow per share (c)	245.37	228.89
Dividend (c)	214.9	211.2
Percentage franked	75	75
Net tangible assets per share ($)	5.08	4.77
Interest cover (times)	~	587.5
Return on equity (%)	49.2	40.5
Debt-to-equity ratio (%)	~	~
Current ratio	9.8	1.6

McMillan Shakespeare Limited

ASX code: MMS

www.mmsg.com.au

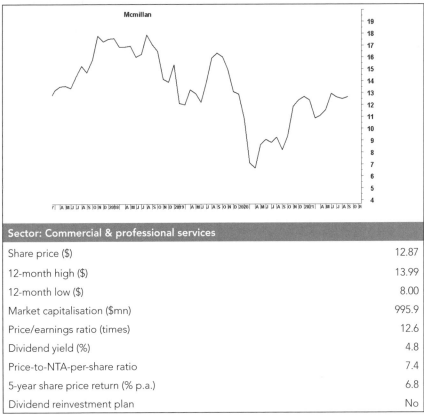

Sector: Commercial & professional services	
Share price ($)	12.87
12-month high ($)	13.99
12-month low ($)	8.00
Market capitalisation ($mn)	995.9
Price/earnings ratio (times)	12.6
Dividend yield (%)	4.8
Price-to-NTA-per-share ratio	7.4
5-year share price return (% p.a.)	6.8
Dividend reinvestment plan	No

Melbourne-based McMillan Shakespeare, founded in 1988, is a specialist provider of salary packaging and vehicle leasing and finance services. It operates under three broad categories. The Group Remuneration Services division provides administrative services for salary packaging. It also arranges motor vehicle novated leases — three-way agreements between an employer, employee and financier to lease a vehicle — as well as providing related ancillary services such as insurance. The Asset Management division arranges financing and provides related management services for motor vehicles, commercial vehicles and equipment. The third division, Retail Financial Services, manages financial services for motor vehicles. McMillan Shakespeare has operations in New Zealand and the United Kingdom.

Latest business results (June 2021, full year)

Sales and revenues rose, in a good year for the company. The Group Remuneration Services division saw just a modest rise in revenues and profits. Total salary packages under management declined, with 109 new client wins insufficient to offset a major loss relating to the New South Wales public health network. Novated leases rose by 2 per cent. This division is responsible for 42 per cent of company revenues but contributes three-quarters of company profit. The Asset Management division enjoyed a big jump in sales and profits, with a reduction in the supply of new cars generating increased demand for higher-margin used vehicles. This business recorded 30 new client wins during the year. However, the Retail Financial Services division was hit by lockdowns, vehicle supply constraints and continuing regulatory uncertainty, and profits fell.

Outlook

McMillan Shakespeare occupies a strong position in its main businesses in Australia, with high profit margins and continuing growth from a strong pipeline of prospective customers. The company's three-year Beyond 2020 transformational program is working to reduce the cost base, with a big investment in upgrading digital platforms. At the heart of McMillan Shakespeare's operations is the Group Remuneration Services division, which is suffering from constraints in the supply of new vehicles, and has been unable to meet all customer orders in a timely manner, despite some strong growth in demand. However, the division's new Plan Partners business, which assists participants in the government's National Disability Insurance Scheme, has been enjoying excellent growth, with funds under administration of $1.2 billion. The Asset Management division has achieved success in restructuring its underperforming British operations and returning them to profit. Following a strategic review of its Retail Financial Services division, in August 2021 the company agreed to sell the division's retail business to the current management team.

Year to 30 June	2020	2021
Revenues ($mn)	493.1	544.2
Asset management (%)	46	47
Group remuneration services (%)	44	42
Retail financial services (%)	10	11
EBIT ($mn)	100.6	120.8
EBIT margin (%)	20.4	22.2
Profit before tax ($mn)	92.7	112.7
Profit after tax ($mn)	69.0	79.2
Earnings per share (c)	87.44	102.37
Cash flow per share (c)	192.94	189.10
Dividend (c)	34	61.3
Percentage franked	100	100
Net tangible assets per share ($)	1.14	1.74
Interest cover (times)	12.7	14.8
Return on equity (%)	23.0	31.8
Debt-to-equity ratio (%)	75.2	6.8
Current ratio	1.7	1.7

Medibank Private Limited

ASX code: MPL www.medibank.com.au

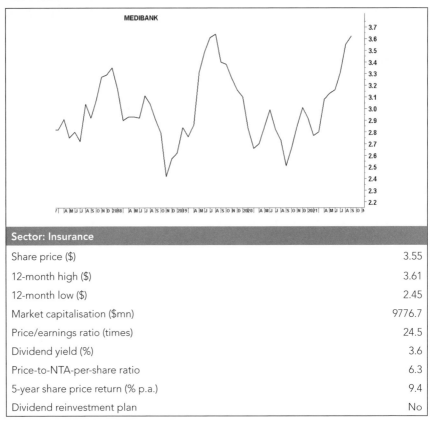

MEDIBANK

Sector: Insurance	
Share price ($)	3.55
12-month high ($)	3.61
12-month low ($)	2.45
Market capitalisation ($mn)	9776.7
Price/earnings ratio (times)	24.5
Dividend yield (%)	3.6
Price-to-NTA-per-share ratio	6.3
5-year share price return (% p.a.)	9.4
Dividend reinvestment plan	No

Melbourne-based Medibank Private was established by the Australian government in 1976 as a not-for-profit private health insurer under the Health Insurance Commission. It was privatised and listed on the ASX in 2014. Today it is Australia's largest private health insurer, with a market share of 27 per cent, operating under the Medibank and ahm brands. It has also branched into other areas, including travel insurance, pet insurance, life insurance, income protection and funeral insurance. Its Medibank Health division specialises in the provision of healthcare services over the phone, online or face-to-face.

Latest business results (June 2021, full year)

Revenues and profits rose in a solid year for Medibank. In the previous year profits had fallen sharply. Policyholder numbers grew by a net 3.5 per cent during the year to 1.89 million — exceeding total industry growth of 3.1 per cent — with most of this increase again concentrated in the budget ahm health insurance brand, which is aimed at younger customers. Premium revenues rose 2.1 per cent. Against this, net claims rose by just 1.4 per cent for the year — compared to a 3 per cent increase in the previous year — delivering a healthy profit, although this in part reflected deferred surgeries that will be taken up in subsequent years. The company also benefited with a $120 million profit from its $3 billion investment portfolio. In addition, it reported a 2.3 per cent reduction in its management expenses. The very small Medibank Health business saw its profits up 13 per cent.

Outlook

Medibank occupies a central role in the national health sector. Nevertheless, its business is heavily regulated, and it is difficult to achieve significant growth. In addition, as the population ages, customer claim volumes have been growing, often faster than premium rises. Maintaining a tight control on expenses is important for the company, and it has a target of $40 million in annual productivity savings in the three years to June 2024. It has introduced new dental and optical networks, with reduced rates for members, along with an enhanced rewards program. It has significantly boosted its telehealth services and in January 2021 it launched My Home Hospital, aimed at providing hospital-level care to patients in their own homes. It is also investing in hospitals that aim to provide members with short-stay surgical procedures. The company is aiming for a further 3 per cent policyholder growth in the June 2022 year, and forecasts that claims will rise by about 2.4 per cent.

Year to 30 June	2020	2021
Revenues ($mn)	6769.6	6910.4
EBIT ($mn)	436.6	515.1
EBIT margin (%)	6.4	7.5
Profit before tax ($mn)	461.0	528.3
Profit after tax ($mn)	367.3	398.7
Earnings per share (c)	13.34	14.48
Cash flow per share (c)	17.94	18.91
Dividend (c)	12	12.7
Percentage franked	100	100
Net tangible assets per share ($)	0.52	0.57
Interest cover (times)	~	~
Return on equity (%)	19.6	21.5
Debt-to-equity ratio (%)	~	~
Current ratio	1.8	1.8

Metcash Limited

ASX code: MTS

www.metcash.com

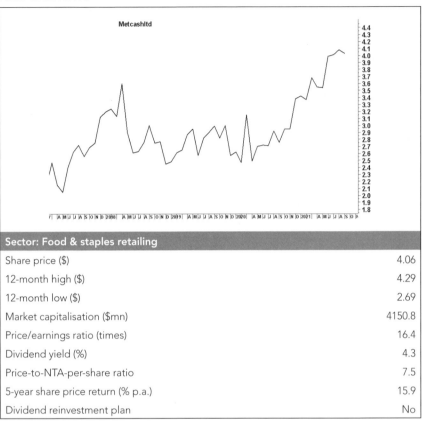

Sector: Food & staples retailing	
Share price ($)	4.06
12-month high ($)	4.29
12-month low ($)	2.69
Market capitalisation ($mn)	4150.8
Price/earnings ratio (times)	16.4
Dividend yield (%)	4.3
Price-to-NTA-per-share ratio	7.5
5-year share price return (% p.a.)	15.9
Dividend reinvestment plan	No

Sydney-based Metcash, with a history dating back to the 1920s, is a leading food and liquor wholesaler. Its Food division supports a network of more than 1600 independently owned grocery stores and supermarkets, mainly under the IGA and Foodland brands. The Liquor division is Australia's largest supplier of liquor to independently owned liquor retailers, with more than 12 000 customers. These include the Independent Brands Australia (IBA) network of Cellarbrations, The Bottle-O, Duncans, Thirsty Camel, IGA Liquor, Big Bargain and Porters. The Hardware division operates the Independent Hardware Group, which supplies more than 1500 stores, including the Mitre 10 and Home Timber & Hardware chains. In 2020 the company took a majority interest in Total Tools, Australia's largest independent tool network.

Latest business results (April 2021, full year)

Metcash reported an excellent result, with sales and profits growing strongly. The core Food division saw sales up 2 per cent and underlying EBIT rise by 5 per cent. On a same-store basis the IGA chain achieved a 10.5 per cent increase in sales as it benefited from a shift in consumer behaviour, including an increased preference for shopping at local neighbourhood stores, rather than at large shopping malls, and more cooking at home. The Liquor division achieved a 19 per cent jump in revenues, with EBIT up 22 per cent, as COVID-related restrictions boosted home consumption and sparked a sharp decline in duty-free liquor sales. The Hardware division recorded an excellent 32 per cent surge in sales, with EBIT up by nearly 62 per cent. Excluding the September 2020 acquisition of an interest in Total Tools, the gains were 18 per cent and 33 per cent. This business was another beneficiary of COVID-related restrictions, which inspired a move to more home improvement projects. Though just 11 per cent of company revenues, the Hardware division now represents more than a third of total profit.

Outlook

Metcash is reaping the rewards of its five-year MFuture restructuring process that has cut costs and enhanced the attractiveness of its offerings. It plans a further $375 million in capital spending over three years under this program. In particular, it will boost its online food and liquor business, which has been growing in popularity during the pandemic. It wishes to expand its hardware store network, including raising the number of Total Tools stores from 88 to 130 by 2025. It also plans to build its liquor business with a strong move into high-margin private label brands and an expansion of its New Zealand operations.

Year to 30 April	2020	2021
Revenues ($mn)	13 025.4	14 315.3
Food (%)	62	58
Liquor (%)	28	31
Hardware (%)	10	11
EBIT ($mn)	296.5	364.7
EBIT margin (%)	2.3	2.5
Gross margin (%)	10.1	10.3
Profit before tax ($mn)	282.9	358.8
Profit after tax ($mn)	198.8	252.7
Earnings per share (c)	21.84	24.75
Cash flow per share (c)	39.11	40.78
Dividend (c)	12.5	17.5
Percentage franked	100	100
Net tangible assets per share ($)	0.76	0.54
Interest cover (times)	21.8	61.8
Return on equity (%)	15.3	19.2
Debt-to-equity ratio (%)	~	~
Current ratio	1.3	1.2

Michael Hill International Limited

ASX code: MHJ   investor.michaelhill.com

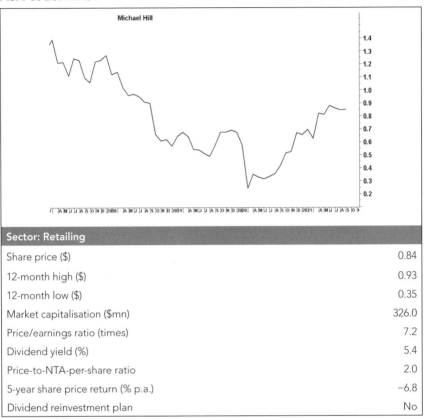

Michael Hill

Sector: Retailing	
Share price ($)	0.84
12-month high ($)	0.93
12-month low ($)	0.35
Market capitalisation ($mn)	326.0
Price/earnings ratio (times)	7.2
Dividend yield (%)	5.4
Price-to-NTA-per-share ratio	2.0
5-year share price return (% p.a.)	−6.8
Dividend reinvestment plan	No

Jewellery retailer Michael Hill dates back to the opening of its first store in Whangarei, New Zealand, in 1979. It grew steadily, expanding to Australia and Canada, and it moved its headquarters to Brisbane. Today it incorporates 285 stores, with 150 in Australia, 86 in Canada and 49 in New Zealand.

Latest business results (June 2021, full year)

Sales rose strongly and profits surged back, with strength in all regions. In the previous year the company's businesses had been severely hurt by pandemic-related lockdowns. Australian sales were up 17.1 per cent, or 13 per cent on a same-store basis, despite some further store shutdowns during the year. New Zealand sales rose 19.1 per cent in local currency, and 7.1 per cent on a same-store basis. New Zealand profit margins soared to their highest level in five years. Canadian operations were hit by some further lockdowns, and sales there rose 6.9 per cent in local currency. Total company online sales jumped 53.4 per cent to $35 million, with notably high profit margins. The result was helped by financial support from suppliers, landlords and local governments. During the year the company opened one new store and closed six.

Outlook

Michael Hill has a combination of strategies that it believes can deliver sustainable long-term growth, though it remains concerned that further lockdowns could hurt business in the near term. A key tactic is the elevation of the Michael Hill brand, driving its transition from a name associated with discount-led promotions into a brand for unique high-margin, high-quality jewellery. In the June 2021 year branded collections represented 42.1 per cent of total sales, up from 37.3 per cent a year earlier. The company is also investing heavily to strengthen its online presence, including an integrated marketplace roll-out in the June 2022 year that incorporates a presence on third-party digital channels. It is experimenting with various means of integrating online and physical business, including a new 'click and collect' option that will be introduced by Christmas 2021. Nevertheless, it views its physical stores as fundamental to its success, with a new retail incentive scheme intended to drive sales, reduce costs and boost margins. It is also working to speed up the process for introducing new products to its customers. The new Brilliance by Michael Hill loyalty program has grown from 200 000 members in June 2020 to 800 000 in June 2021, and the company is already finding that members shop more frequently and spend more than other customers.

Year to 27 June*	2020	2021
Revenues ($mn)	492.1	556.5
Australia (%)	54	56
Canada (%)	25	22
New Zealand (%)	21	21
EBIT ($mn)	14.1	72.4
EBIT margin (%)	2.9	13.0
Gross margin (%)	60.6	62.7
Profit before tax ($mn)	4.5	64.8
Profit after tax ($mn)	3.1	45.3
Earnings per share (c)	0.79	11.68
Cash flow per share (c)	15.13	24.91
Dividend (c)	1.5	4.5
Percentage franked	0	0
Net tangible assets per share ($)	0.33	0.41
Interest cover (times)	1.5	9.5
Return on equity (%)	1.9	26.1
Debt-to-equity ratio (%)	~	~
Current ratio	1.4	1.8

*28 June 2020

Mineral Resources Limited

ASX code: MIN   www.mineralresources.com.au

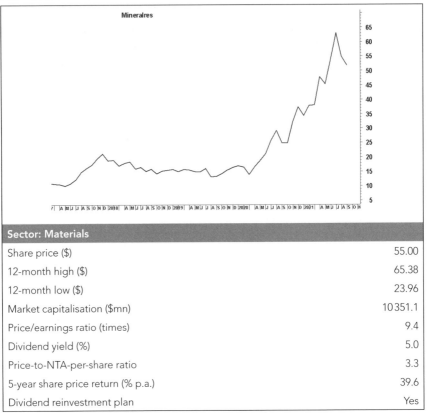

Sector: Materials	
Share price ($)	55.00
12-month high ($)	65.38
12-month low ($)	23.96
Market capitalisation ($mn)	10351.1
Price/earnings ratio (times)	9.4
Dividend yield (%)	5.0
Price-to-NTA-per-share ratio	3.3
5-year share price return (% p.a.)	39.6
Dividend reinvestment plan	Yes

Mineral Resources, based in Perth, was founded in 1993, and is a mining and mining services company. Its mining services side incorporates several subsidiaries. These include CSI Mining Services, which provides contract crushing, screening and processing services to the resources sector, Process Minerals International, a minerals processor and exporter with a specialty in bringing new mines into production, and Mining Wear Parts, a newly acquired business that provides specialist parts to the mining, quarrying and recycling industries. The company's mining side comprises iron ore production assets and holdings in the Wodgina lithium mine and the Mount Marion lithium project.

Latest business results (June 2021, full year)

Mineral Resources enjoyed another excellent year, as booming iron ore demand and soaring prices generated strong gains in revenues and profits. Total iron ore sales of 17.27 million tonnes were up 23 per cent from the previous year, and the average price received by the company of $177 per tonne was 60 per cent higher than in the June 2020 year. Partially offsetting these gains were increased haulage and shipping costs and a tighter labour market. Lithium operations continued to be weak, reflecting a decline in sales prices. Mining services operations again performed very well, with double-digit increases in revenues and profits, thanks to a high level of demand from the company's own mining activities as well as from external mine operators.

Outlook

Mineral Resources is actively seeking to expand its iron ore exposure, with the aim of developing a long-term, sustainable export business for this commodity. In the June 2022 year it expects sales to rise to at least 20 million tonnes from its two core production hubs of Utah Point and Yilgarn. It is actively working to build a major new iron ore province around the Ashburton area of the West Pilbara. In May 2021 the company acquired a small stake in the Australian Premium Iron venture, and in July 2021 it announced the $400 million acquisition of a 40 per cent holding in the Red Hill iron ore project. The company believes it could eventually be shipping 30 million tonnes of iron ore annually from Ashburton. It is also optimistic about the long-term outlook for its lithium exposure, thanks to expected high demand from manufacturers of electric vehicles and batteries. Its mining service operations continue to grow, including the development of significant new transport and port facilities. Nevertheless, Mineral Resources is vulnerable to iron ore price fluctuations and to rising costs in some of its businesses.

Year to 30 June	2020	2021
Revenues ($mn)	2124.7	3733.6
EBIT ($mn)	571.5	1642.8
EBIT margin (%)	26.9	44.0
Profit before tax ($mn)	481.0	1557.0
Profit after tax ($mn)	334.0	1103.0
Earnings per share (c)	177.35	584.80
Cash flow per share (c)	280.15	721.58
Dividend (c)	100	275
Percentage franked	100	100
Net tangible assets per share ($)	11.81	16.83
Interest cover (times)	6.3	19.1
Return on equity (%)	18.4	40.3
Debt-to-equity ratio (%)	~	~
Current ratio	2.0	2.1

Monadelphous Group Limited

ASX code: MND   www.monadelphous.com.au

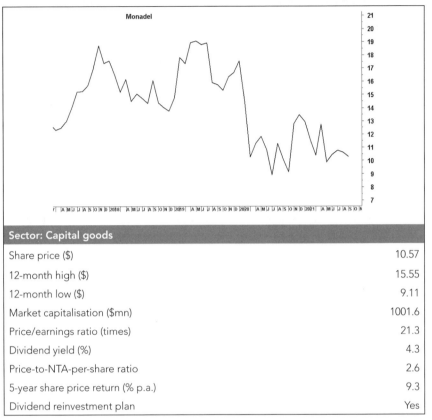

Sector: Capital goods	
Share price ($)	10.57
12-month high ($)	15.55
12-month low ($)	9.11
Market capitalisation ($mn)	1001.6
Price/earnings ratio (times)	21.3
Dividend yield (%)	4.3
Price-to-NTA-per-share ratio	2.6
5-year share price return (% p.a.)	9.3
Dividend reinvestment plan	Yes

Perth-based Monadelphous, established in 1972, is an engineering company that provides a wide range of construction, maintenance, project management and support services to the minerals, energy and infrastructure industries. It operates from branches throughout Australia, with a client base that includes most of the country's resource majors. It has also established a presence in overseas markets that include New Zealand, China, Mongolia, Papua New Guinea, Chile and the Philippines.

Latest business results (June 2021, full year)

Revenues and profits bounced back from the slump of the previous year, as the resources industry recovered from disruptions caused by the COVID-19 pandemic and customers also sought to capitalise on strong commodity prices, especially for iron ore. Monadelphous saw its iron ore projects nearly double in value during the year, to represent more than half of company income. The Engineering Construction division saw revenues jump 59 per cent from the previous year, with significant work from both BHP and Rio Tinto. By contrast the Maintenance and Industrial Services division was weak, with lower levels of demand from the oil and gas sector driving down revenues by 7 per cent. Overseas business — 46 per cent of it in Chile and 11 per cent in Mongolia — was responsible for 7 per cent of total revenues. During the year the company secured $950 million in new contracts and contract extensions.

Outlook

Monadelphous plays an important role in the Australian minerals, energy and infrastructure industries, and it stands to benefit from expected buoyant conditions over coming years. However, it believes its June 2022 revenues will fall, before recovering again in the following financial year, due to the timing of some major projects. It sees strong commodity prices as providing support for projects related to lithium, gold, copper and nickel. In addition, it is experiencing a steady recovery in work for the oil and gas sector, and expects this to continue to grow with the development of new LNG projects. It is also optimistic about the outlook for clean energy, with opportunities for its Zenviron renewable energy joint venture in the wind energy sector, and with hydrogen developments also showing potential. But the company is concerned about skills shortages, which are driving labour costs higher and leading to delays in completing projects. In addition, up to 50 per cent of its workforce flies in from other states, and COVID-related travel restrictions are a further burden. At June 2021 Monadelphous had net cash holdings of more than $170 million.

Year to 30 June	2020	2021
Revenues ($mn)	1488.7	1754.2
Services (%)	71	56
Construction (%)	29	44
EBIT ($mn)	57.6	73.0
EBIT margin (%)	3.9	4.2
Gross margin (%)	6.9	6.4
Profit before tax ($mn)	55.1	70.4
Profit after tax ($mn)	36.5	47.1
Earnings per share (c)	38.65	49.70
Cash flow per share (c)	71.73	84.46
Dividend (c)	35	45
Percentage franked	100	100
Net tangible assets per share ($)	4.02	4.13
Interest cover (times)	22.8	27.5
Return on equity (%)	9.4	12.1
Debt-to-equity ratio (%)	~	~
Current ratio	2.0	1.9

Money3 Corporation Limited

ASX code: MNY

www.money3.com.au

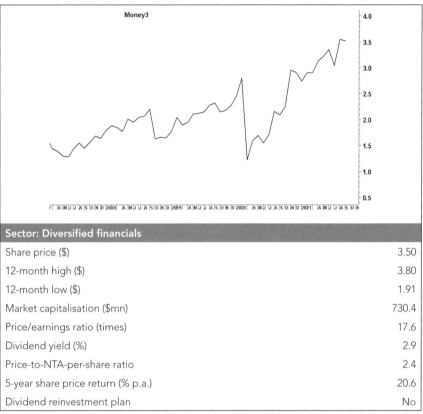

Sector: Diversified financials	
Share price ($)	3.50
12-month high ($)	3.80
12-month low ($)	1.91
Market capitalisation ($mn)	730.4
Price/earnings ratio (times)	17.6
Dividend yield (%)	2.9
Price-to-NTA-per-share ratio	2.4
5-year share price return (% p.a.)	20.6
Dividend reinvestment plan	No

Melbourne-based moneylender Money3 was formally established in 2005 through the consolidation of nine separate loans businesses operating in Melbourne and Geelong. In 2019 it sold its online and branch-based small-loans business, and it now specialises in vehicle loans and small personal loans. It entered the New Zealand car loans business with the acquisition in 2019 of Go Car Finance. In 2021 it acquired the vehicle loans specialist Automotive Financial Services and the General Motors Financial Company subsidiary GMF Australia.

Latest business results (June 2021, full year)

The two acquisitions early in 2021 helped power Money3 to a jump in revenues and profits, overcoming a weak first half when pandemic-related lockdowns hit business. Australian revenues rose 10 per cent to $113 million, with EBITDA surging 44 per cent. There was a notable increase in new loan origination from Automotive Financial Services in its initial months with the company. New Zealand enjoyed an excellent year, with revenues up by nearly 50 per cent — thanks to 90 per cent loan growth — and profits racing ahead by 174 per cent. At June 2021 the total company loan book of $601 million was up from $433 million a year earlier.

Outlook

With its origins as a provider of short-term unsecured loans, also known as payday lending, Money3 had come under some government and social pressures, with questions raised about the ethics of its activities. Consequently, it had been working to transform itself into a diversified financial services company. It is now mainly a specialist provider of vehicle finance. It has taken a significant step forward with its two new acquisitions. Automotive Financial Services, acquired for $10.8 million, specialises in vehicle loans of up to $100 000 with a particular forte in commercial vehicles. GMF Australia, acquired for $17 million, had some 700 customers who purchased a new vehicle through a Holden dealership in 2018 and 2019. Thanks to its acquisitions, Money3 now operates within a target market in Australia and New Zealand that it estimates is worth more than $40 billion annually, and it sees substantial scope for growth. It is investing in new digital systems that lower operating costs and make customer interactions increasingly smooth. With international travel still restricted in both Australia and New Zealand, it has reported continuing strong demand for car and caravan finance, and it expects lending growth of at least 20 per cent in the June 2022 year. Its target is for a loan book of $1 billion by June 2024.

Year to 30 June	2020	2021
Revenues ($mn)	124.0	145.1
EBIT ($mn)	58.3	75.0
EBIT margin (%)	47.0	51.7
Profit before tax ($mn)	43.7	56.4
Profit after tax ($mn)	30.3	39.2
Earnings per share (c)	16.50	19.85
Cash flow per share (c)	17.52	21.01
Dividend (c)	8	10
Percentage franked	100	100
Net tangible assets per share ($)	1.23	1.46
Interest cover (times)	4.0	4.0
Return on equity (%)	12.4	13.4
Debt-to-equity ratio (%)	50.1	61.1
Current ratio	10.8	3.8

Newcrest Mining Limited

ASX code: NCM www.newcrest.com

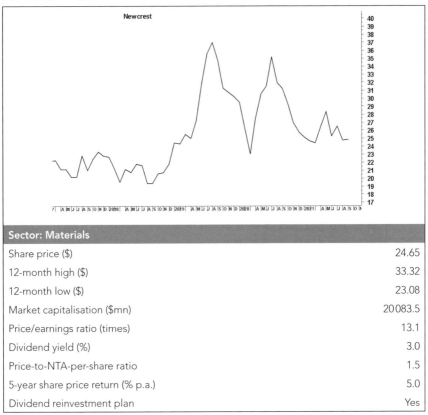

Sector: Materials	
Share price ($)	24.65
12-month high ($)	33.32
12-month low ($)	23.08
Market capitalisation ($mn)	20083.5
Price/earnings ratio (times)	13.1
Dividend yield (%)	3.0
Price-to-NTA-per-share ratio	1.5
5-year share price return (% p.a.)	5.0
Dividend reinvestment plan	Yes

Melbourne-based Newcrest, Australia's leading gold producer and one of the largest in the world, was established in 1966 as a subsidiary of the American company Newmont Mining. It also produces copper. It has four major mining projects — Telfer in Western Australia, Cadia in New South Wales, Lihir in Papua New Guinea and a 70 per cent holding in Red Chris in Canada. It has two further projects that are under development — a 50 per cent holding in Wafi-Golpu in Papua New Guinea and the joint venture Havieron operation in Western Australia. It holds a 32 per cent interest in Lundin Gold, which operates the Fruta del Norte gold-silver mine in Ecuador.

Latest business results (June 2021, full year)

A higher gold price helped generate a big increase in profits for Newcrest. Total gold production of 2 093 322 ounces was 4 per cent down on the previous year, in part reflecting the divestment of the Indonesian Gosowong mine in March 2020. But the average price received of US$1796 per ounce of gold was 17 per cent higher than in the previous year. Production costs of US$911 per ounce were 6 per cent higher than in the preceding year. Newcrest also produced 142 724 tonnes of copper, up 4 per cent from the preceding year, and received an average price of US$3.66 per pound, which was a jump of 42 per cent. Copper now represents around a quarter of total company income. Note that Newcrest reports its results in US dollars. The Australian dollar figures in this book — converted at prevailing exchange rates — are for guidance only.

Outlook

Newcrest expects a further decline in gold production in the June 2022 year, to between 1.8 million and 2 million ounces. Copper production is also likely to fall, to between 125 000 and 130 000 tonnes. In particular, it seems possible that production at its cornerstone Cadia mine has peaked and is now in steady decline. In response, the company has embarked on a variety of projects, including significant expansion work at Cadia in a bid to prolong its life. At Red Chris in British Columbia, in which Newcrest acquired a 70 per cent stake in 2019, an extensive drilling program is aimed at discovering new reserves of high-grade gold and copper. At its Havieron project, Newcrest hopes to find gold deposits that will enable it to extend the life of the nearby Telfer mine. At June 2021 Newcrest had net cash holdings of US$238 million.

Year to 30 June	2020	2021
Revenues ($mn)	5684.1	6021.1
Cadia (%)	46	48
Lihir (%)	30	31
Telfer (%)	15	16
Red Chris (%)	5	5
EBIT ($mn)	1826.1	2328.9
EBIT margin (%)	32.1	38.7
Gross margin (%)	34.5	38.7
Profit before tax ($mn)	1578.3	2194.7
Profit after tax ($mn)	1087.0	1531.6
Earnings per share (c)	140.06	187.53
Cash flow per share (c)	260.33	295.95
Dividend (c)	36.23	74.50
Percentage franked	100	100
Net tangible assets per share ($)	15.27	16.48
Interest cover (times)	7.4	17.4
Return on equity (%)	9.3	11.8
Debt-to-equity ratio (%)	6.6	~
Current ratio	2.9	3.0

NIB Holdings Limited

ASX code: NHF

www.nib.com.au

Sector: Insurance	
Share price ($)	6.59
12-month high ($)	8.05
12-month low ($)	4.06
Market capitalisation ($mn)	3016.5
Price/earnings ratio (times)	18.7
Dividend yield (%)	3.6
Price-to-NTA-per-share ratio	8.3
5-year share price return (% p.a.)	11.4
Dividend reinvestment plan	Yes

Newcastle private health insurer NIB Holdings was established as the Newcastle Industrial Benefits Hospital Fund in 1952 by workers at the BHP steelworks. It subsequently demutualised and became the first private health insurer to list on the ASX. It is also active in New Zealand. Other businesses are travel insurance and the provision of specialist insurance services to international students and workers in Australia.

Latest business results (June 2021, full year)

Revenues rose again and profits rebounded strongly, having crashed a year before when the company was hit by rising claims from its members and by losses in its travel insurance business. The company's flagship Australian Residents Health Insurance, representing 85 per cent of company income, saw premium revenues increase by 4.9 per cent to $2.2 billion. Policyholder numbers grew by a net 4.2 per cent, compared to industry growth of 3.1 per cent. The total claims expense rose by just 0.9 per cent, compared to a 5.3 per cent rise in the previous year, and profits were up strongly. New Zealand health insurance represents a further 10 per cent of company turnover. It enjoyed a solid year, with single-digit increases in revenues and profits. But other businesses were weak. The company's formerly high-margin health insurance program for international students and workers in Australia was hit by border closures and a large increase in claims. Revenues were down and this business fell into the red. The travel insurance business also saw revenues fall sharply, and it too generated a loss.

Outlook

NIB continues to see its policyholder base grow faster than the industry average. It benefits from its exposure in New Zealand, where it is the country's second-largest health insurer. It has expressed the belief that the COVID-19 pandemic has heightened community awareness of the risk of disease and the need for insurance protection, sparking increases in new policyholder numbers. However, the company has also noted that the pandemic has led some older Australians to defer treatment, which could mean a higher level of claims in future. In addition, as the population ages, it faces growing numbers of claims from members, at a time when healthcare costs are rising. It is working to branch into new areas of business. It has launched a new joint venture company, Honeysuckle Health, aimed at using data analytics to deliver healthcare programs. It has also formed a partnership with Chinese pharmaceutical company Tasly to enter the Chinese health insurance market, and made its first sales in July 2021.

Year to 30 June	2020	2021
Premium revenues ($mn)	2473.1	2580.8
EBIT ($mn)	129.1	237.8
EBIT margin (%)	5.2	9.2
Profit before tax ($mn)	125.0	231.0
Profit after tax ($mn)	90.1	161.1
Earnings per share (c)	19.75	35.24
Cash flow per share (c)	27.30	42.24
Dividend (c)	14	24
Percentage franked	100	100
Net tangible assets per share ($)	0.55	0.80
Interest cover (times)	31.5	35.0
Return on equity (%)	15.0	25.2
Debt-to-equity ratio (%)	5.8	2.6
Current ratio	1.7	1.9

Nick Scali Limited

ASX code: NCK www.nickscali.com.au

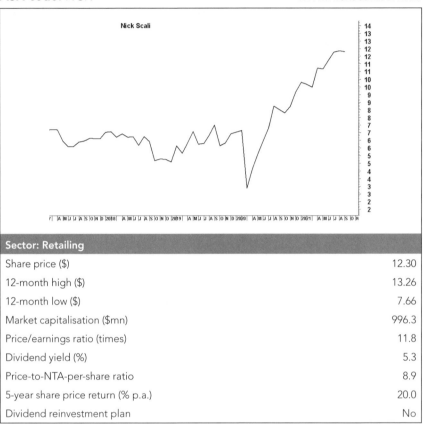

Sector: Retailing	
Share price ($)	12.30
12-month high ($)	13.26
12-month low ($)	7.66
Market capitalisation ($mn)	996.3
Price/earnings ratio (times)	11.8
Dividend yield (%)	5.3
Price-to-NTA-per-share ratio	8.9
5-year share price return (% p.a.)	20.0
Dividend reinvestment plan	No

Sydney-based Nick Scali is one of Australia's largest furniture importers and retailers, with a history dating back more than 50 years. It specialises in leather and fabric lounge suites along with dining room and bedroom furniture. It has six distribution centres and at June 2021 operated 61 Nick Scali Furniture stores, including four in New Zealand.

Latest business results (June 2021, full year)

Nick Scali achieved a superb result, with sales increasing and profits doubling as Australians cocooned at home and redirected spending from travel and restaurants to furniture and homewares. The company also achieved great success in controlling costs, which boosted margins. The good result came despite rising freight and supply chain expenses. Same-store sales revenues rose 34 per cent, with additional growth from three new stores opened during the year. Total sales orders were $401.6 million, and at June 2021 the company had an order backlog that was 35 per cent higher than a year earlier. There was particularly strong growth in New Zealand, with orders up 95 per cent from the previous year, or 40 per cent on a same-store basis. The Nick

Scali online store, launched only in April 2020, achieved sales orders of $18.3 million, up from $3 million in the previous year, with the EBIT contribution rising from $0.6 million to $8.8 million.

Outlook

Nick Scali is directly affected by trends in consumer spending, interest rates, currency movements, housing sales, renovation activity and the general economy. It is severely affected by the continuing lockdowns in several Australian states, which force it temporarily to close stores. In addition, the company has expressed concern about lockdowns in Asian countries where it sources its stock, as well as ongoing supply chain disruptions and fast-rising global shipping costs. It continues to seek out opportunities to open new stores, and expects to open three or more new ones during the June 2022 year, with an eventual target of a total of 73 stores throughout Australia and a further 13 in New Zealand. A new property in Adelaide is being developed to become the flagship store for that city. It is also working to expand its online presence, and believes this business offers great potential for continuing growth. In addition, it is seeking to grow by acquisition, and in July 2021 confirmed that it was in discussions about a possible purchase of the Plush Sofas business, which operates 46 stores. At June 2021 Nick Scali had net cash holdings of more than $73 million.

Year to 30 June	2020	2021
Revenues ($mn)	262.5	373.0
EBIT ($mn)	67.1	127.8
EBIT margin (%)	25.6	34.3
Gross margin (%)	62.7	63.5
Profit before tax ($mn)	60.2	121.2
Profit after tax ($mn)	42.1	84.2
Earnings per share (c)	51.95	104.00
Cash flow per share (c)	88.97	142.11
Dividend (c)	47.5	65
Percentage franked	100	100
Net tangible assets per share ($)	0.90	1.37
Interest cover (times)	9.7	19.4
Return on equity (%)	52.4	88.9
Debt-to-equity ratio (%)	~	~
Current ratio	1.1	1.2

Objective Corporation Limited

ASX code: OCL www.objective.com

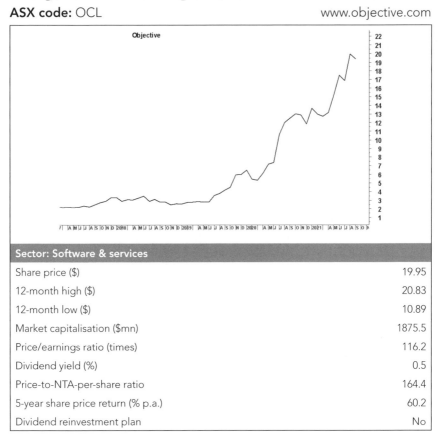

Sector: Software & services	
Share price ($)	19.95
12-month high ($)	20.83
12-month low ($)	10.89
Market capitalisation ($mn)	1875.5
Price/earnings ratio (times)	116.2
Dividend yield (%)	0.5
Price-to-NTA-per-share ratio	164.4
5-year share price return (% p.a.)	60.2
Dividend reinvestment plan	No

Sydney-based Objective, founded in 1987, provides information technology software and services. Its particular specialty is working with federal, state and local governments, as well as government agencies and regulated industries, and it has operations in Australia, New Zealand and the United Kingdom. It operates under many product categories. Objective Enterprise Connect Management (ECM) allows a public or private body to manage all its physical and electronic records. Objective Connect allows organisations to exchange content securely and easily. Objective Keystone helps organisations create and publish new content. Objective Trapeze assists the digitisation process for complex files and documents. Objective Redact removes sensitive information from a document.

Latest business results (June 2021, full year)

In another excellent result, Objective reported double-digit increases in revenues and profits. For reporting purposes the company divides its businesses into four broad segments. The largest of these, Objective Content Solutions — incorporating Objective ECM, Objective Connect and Objective Redact — represents two-thirds of company turnover, and saw revenues up by 13 per cent, thanks to new customers

and a significant expansion of usage. A new division, RegTech S
16 per cent of company income, was based on the July 20?
developer of software for government agencies and reg'
Planning and Building Solutions, achieved 33 per ce
strongly rising customer numbers. A fourth, very
boosted customer numbers, and revenues grew by 4 pei
10 per cent of the total, grew only slightly. However, New .
more than 50 per cent, thanks especially to the iTree acquisitu
about 13 per cent of company income.

Outlook

Objective is a small company working in niche businesses but with a solid re$_t$
and a high level of profitability in its domestic operations. It is working to mo.
businesses, as much as possible, to a subscription model, which will make revenu
and earnings more predictable each year. The company's particular goal is to help
customers streamline the processes of compliance, accountability and governance. Its
products share a common interface, and as the product range grows it is increasingly
able to cross-sell to its existing customer base. It spends heavily on research and
development, and this grew 46 per cent in the June 2021 year to $23 million. It
continues to seek out compatible acquisitions, as well as new markets, and expects
continued solid growth in revenues and profits in the June 2022 year.

Year to 30 June	2020	2021
Revenues ($mn)	70.0	95.1
EBIT ($mn)	13.7	20.7
EBIT margin (%)	19.5	21.8
Profit before tax ($mn)	13.6	20.2
Profit after tax ($mn)	11.0	16.1
Earnings per share (c)	11.84	17.16
Cash flow per share (c)	15.61	22.36
Dividend (c)	7	9
Percentage franked	100	100
Net tangible assets per share ($)	0.19	0.12
Interest cover (times)	160.9	44.0
Return on equity (%)	33.7	39.1
Debt-to-equity ratio (%)	~	~
Current ratio	1.2	1.1

Group Limited

de: OFX   www.ofx.com

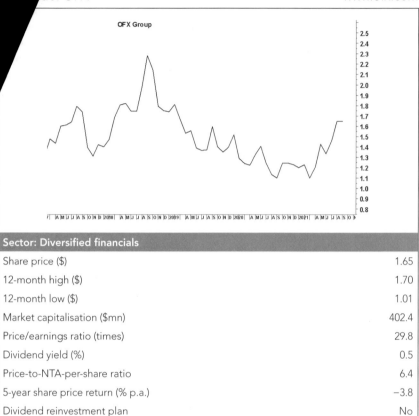

Sector: Diversified financials	
Share price ($)	1.65
12-month high ($)	1.70
12-month low ($)	1.01
Market capitalisation ($mn)	402.4
Price/earnings ratio (times)	29.8
Dividend yield (%)	0.5
Price-to-NTA-per-share ratio	6.4
5-year share price return (% p.a.)	−3.8
Dividend reinvestment plan	No

Sydney-based foreign exchange specialist OFX Group, formerly known as OzForex, was launched in 1998 as a currency information website. It provides international payments services in 55 currencies to more than 190 countries, with offices in Sydney, London, Hong Kong, Singapore, Toronto, Auckland, Dublin and San Francisco.

Latest business results (March 2021, full year)

Profits fell sharply on a small dip in revenues in an environment of economic uncertainty and growing competition, though with a noteworthy recovery in the second half. In particular, the company took a hit of around $10 million to revenues as consumer demand declined, due to sharply reduced foreign travel and immigration. Australian and New Zealand business, which contributes about 50 per cent of company turnover, saw profits well down. European profits, which had risen 20 per cent in the previous year, crashed by more than 40 per cent, with revenues also lower. The very small Asian segment also recorded a drop in revenues and profits. The best result came from North America, which continued its strong growth, including a sparkling 50 per cent jump in profits, after doubling the previous year. North American business now represents about a quarter of company revenues and profits. The total number of the company's active clients fell by 9 per cent to 138 500, but the number of transactions per active client jumped 39 per cent to 10.1, and the total transaction turnover for the year of $25 billion was a little higher than in the previous year.

Outlook

OFX occupies a small position in the huge global foreign currency market. This is a highly competitive business, and much of the company's success derives from developing strong relationships with its clients and from offering them personalised service and more attractive rates than competitors like the big banks. It is also highly dependent on new technologies to help it maintain a cost advantage. Nevertheless, the foreign exchange business appears to offer low barriers to entry, and has been attracting many new entrants, though levels of profitability are low for many of these companies. OFX believes it can maintain its strong North American growth, and a new Dublin office is intended to help build European business. A new strategic alliance with Australian logistics company Wisetech Global is expected to generate $5 million in annual fee and trading income by March 2024. In July 2021 OFX announced a $6.1 million investment in European treasury management software company TreasurUp aimed at boosting its corporate business.

Year to 31 March	2020	2021
Revenues ($mn)	137.2	134.2
EBIT ($mn)	26.6	18.2
EBIT margin (%)	19.4	13.6
Profit before tax ($mn)	26.1	17.3
Profit after tax ($mn)	21.4	13.5
Earnings per share (c)	8.81	5.54
Cash flow per share (c)	13.15	10.36
Dividend (c)	4.7	0.81
Percentage franked	35	0
Net tangible assets per share ($)	0.25	0.26
Interest cover (times)	49.2	20.2
Return on equity (%)	29.4	17.2
Debt-to-equity ratio (%)	~	~

Orica Limited

ASX code: ORI

www.orica.com

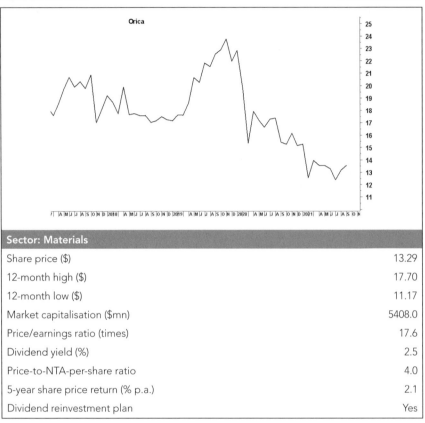

Sector: Materials	
Share price ($)	13.29
12-month high ($)	17.70
12-month low ($)	11.17
Market capitalisation ($mn)	5408.0
Price/earnings ratio (times)	17.6
Dividend yield (%)	2.5
Price-to-NTA-per-share ratio	4.0
5-year share price return (% p.a.)	2.1
Dividend reinvestment plan	Yes

Melbourne-based Orica was founded in 1874 as a supplier of explosives to the Victorian gold mining industry, and for many years it was a subsidiary of Britain's Imperial Chemical Industries. It is today a global leader in commercial explosives for the mining, quarrying, oil and gas, infrastructure and construction sectors. It is also a leading supplier of sodium cyanide for gold extraction. Its Minova business provides support equipment for underground mining and tunnelling operations. It has customers in more than 100 countries, and overseas sales represent more than 70 per cent of total income.

Latest business results (March 2021, half year)

Sales fell and profits crashed as the COVID-19 pandemic curtailed mining activity and souring relations with China hit Australian coal exports. The company was also hurt by a strengthening dollar. The damage was spread across most of the company's reporting segments. The sharpest regional drop in revenues came from North America, down 15 per cent, with profits halving. This region was particularly hard hit by COVID-related restrictions in Mexico and lower coal production in the US. The Europe/Middle East/Africa segment also recorded a double-digit decline in sales, with profits crashing 87 per cent. The Australia/Pacific/Asia segment, representing a third of revenues, saw just a small decline in sales but profits sharply lower, with rising iron ore business unable to offset falling coal-related demand. Latin America saw revenues edge down, but with a sharp drop in profits, as strike action in Chile and social unrest in Peru hurt business. The small Minova business, which in the previous year enjoyed a big jump in profits, this time reported a large drop.

Outlook

With most of its business geared towards the mining industry, Orica's fortunes will rise or fall accordingly. It is wary about the short-term outlook, expecting further foreign exchange losses along with rising depreciation charges and operating costs. In addition, its businesses will continue to be affected by the pandemic and by Australia–China trade issues. In response, it is working on upgrading and rationalising its production facilities, and expects to see a continuing stream of cost efficiencies. Demand from the gold industry represents around 20 per cent of sales, and the company will benefit from any increase in gold activity. It expects considerable synergy benefits and cross-selling opportunities from the $302 million acquisition in 2020 of leading Peruvian industrial explosives manufacturer Exsa. Having achieved some success in turning around its underperforming Minova unit, the company has initiated a sales process for this business.

Year to 30 September	2019	2020
Revenues ($mn)	5878.0	5611.3
EBIT ($mn)	664.8	604.5
EBIT margin (%)	11.3	10.8
Profit before tax ($mn)	555.1	454.9
Profit after tax ($mn)	372.0	299.3
Earnings per share (c)	97.90	75.65
Cash flow per share (c)	170.65	164.45
Dividend (c)	55	33
Percentage franked	9	0
Interest cover (times)	6.1	4.0
Return on equity (%)	12.7	10.0
Half year to 31 March	2020	2021
Revenues ($mn)	2880.3	2623.2
Profit before tax ($mn)	245.6	110.2
Profit after tax ($mn)	165.2	73.4
Earnings per share (c)	42.90	18.90
Dividend (c)	16.5	7.5
Percentage franked	0	0
Net tangible assets per share ($)	4.67	3.36
Debt-to-equity ratio (%)	50.9	63.2
Current ratio	1.4	1.7

Orora Limited

ASX code: ORA   www.ororagroup.com

Sector: Materials	
Share price ($)	3.39
12-month high ($)	3.73
12-month low ($)	2.19
Market capitalisation ($mn)	3017.9
Price/earnings ratio (times)	20.1
Dividend yield (%)	4.1
Price-to-NTA-per-share ratio	8.4
5-year share price return (% p.a.)	5.1
Dividend reinvestment plan	Yes

Melbourne-based Orora was originally a part of packaging giant Amcor. It was demerged in 2013 and listed on the ASX. Today it is a prominent manufacturer of glass bottles, aluminium cans, closures and caps, boxes and cartons, fibre packaging, and packaging materials and supplies. It also provides a wide array of package-related services and has a particular specialty in cardboard recycling and the manufacture of recycled packaging paper. Its Orora Visual business in the US provides customers with visual communication and point-of-purchase display material. The company has manufacturing facilities in Australia, New Zealand and the US.

Latest business results (June 2021, full year)

Revenues edged down — although they rose by nearly 8 per cent on a constant currency basis — and profits were higher, in a good year for Orora. North American operations — responsible for more than 70 per cent of total company turnover — were particularly strong, with a 43 per cent increase in EBIT on a constant currency basis, reflecting the company's efforts to drive down costs, as well as improved trading conditions in the second half. Orora Visual moved from loss to profit. Australasian EBIT grew by just 3 per cent, with stronger volumes in cans and closures, but a decline in glass bottle sales. Orora makes about two-thirds of the Australian wine industry's glass bottles and has been hit by falling exports to China. Despite the growing strength in Orora's North American operations, these were responsible for only 37 per cent of total company EBIT.

Outlook

Orora occupies a strong position for many of its products, with high market shares in Australia. Nevertheless, demand is greatly dependent on economic trends, and the company is vulnerable to any economic slowdown. It has been undertaking a series of measures to reduce costs and stimulate growth, including upgrades for many of its manufacturing facilities. It is boosting its cans production capacity to meet growing demand in Australia and New Zealand, and is also investigating new product moves. A new $25 million bottle plant at Gawler, South Australia, will enable the recycling of some 400 million bottles annually. Orora has expressed a desire to use mergers or acquisitions to expand into new markets in other countries. In the US the company continues to work on boosting profit margins. It is also seeking further bolt-on acquisitions in an effort to build scale in its activities and improve operational efficiency. The company forecasts further profit growth in the June 2022 year, based on continuing strength in its American operations.

Year to 30 June	2020	2021
Revenues ($mn)	3566.2	3538.0
EBIT ($mn)	223.3	249.1
EBIT margin (%)	6.3	7.0
Gross margin (%)	18.3	19.1
Profit before tax ($mn)	172.8	216.3
Profit after tax ($mn)	126.7	156.7
Earnings per share (c)	13.14	16.88
Cash flow per share (c)	26.16	29.83
Dividend (c)	12	14
Percentage franked	16	0
Net tangible assets per share ($)	0.62	0.40
Interest cover (times)	4.4	7.6
Return on equity (%)	9.5	17.4
Debt-to-equity ratio (%)	28.3	58.9
Current ratio	1.3	1.2

Pacific Smiles Group Limited

ASX code: PSQ   investors.pacificsmilesgroup.com.au

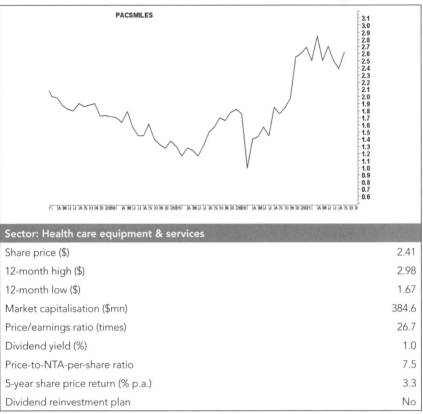

Sector: Health care equipment & services	
Share price ($)	2.41
12-month high ($)	2.98
12-month low ($)	1.67
Market capitalisation ($mn)	384.6
Price/earnings ratio (times)	26.7
Dividend yield (%)	1.0
Price-to-NTA-per-share ratio	7.5
5-year share price return (% p.a.)	3.3
Dividend reinvestment plan	No

Based in Maitland, New South Wales, Pacific Smiles was formally established in 2003 from a group of dental partnerships. Today it provides its dental practices with a wide array of support staff and back-office services that allow the dentists to retain their independence and their clinical autonomy while focusing on their clinical services. It operates under the Pacific Smiles Dental, nib Dental Care and HBF Dental brands. Nearly half its practices are in New South Wales, with others in Victoria, Queensland, Western Australia and Canberra.

Latest business results (June 2021, full year)

Revenues and profits rebounded strongly, having suffered in the previous year when COVID-19 restrictions forced the temporary closure of many of the company's dental practices. It also benefited from the steady rollout of new practices. Total patient fees of $240.8 million were up 29 per cent from June 2020. On a same-centre basis, fees grew by 26 per cent. During the year the company added 15 new centres — 11 in New South Wales, three in Queensland and one in Victoria — bringing the total number of centres at June 2021 to 109, with 467 chairs, up from 383. The company reported that it received $3.1 million in JobKeeper benefits.

Outlook

The Australian market for dental services is worth an estimated $10 billion to $11 billion annually, and is growing steadily. It is a fragmented industry, with around 70 per cent of dentists working in their own private practices or in small partnerships, and some companies, like Pacific Smiles, are now working to consolidate them. Pacific Smiles has a long-term target of 250 centres, 800 dental chairs, an EBITDA margin of at least 15 per cent and a dental industry market share of more than 5 per cent. It finds that as it grows it is able to introduce efficiencies to its practices, boosting business and reducing operating costs, although start-up expenses for new practices can be high. It has entered the Western Australian market through a new 10-year agreement with HBF, the state's largest private health fund. The first three clinics under the agreement have been opened by HBF, and are being operated by Pacific Smiles. In August 2021 the company reported that more than half its clinics were operating under lockdown restrictions and trading on average at just 40 per cent of normal volumes. However, it expected that once conditions stabilised it would begin a steady rollout of some 20 new practices each year.

Year to 30 June	2020	2021
Revenues ($mn)	120.6	153.2
EBIT ($mn)	12.5	21.0
EBIT margin (%)	10.3	13.7
Profit before tax ($mn)	11.8	20.4
Profit after tax ($mn)	8.1	14.0
Earnings per share (c)	5.32	9.02
Cash flow per share (c)	18.48	23.45
Dividend (c)	2.4	2.4
Percentage franked	100	100
Net tangible assets per share ($)	0.17	0.32
Interest cover (times)	18.7	37.3
Return on equity (%)	20.8	28.6
Debt-to-equity ratio (%)	18.2	~
Current ratio	0.8	0.5

Pendal Group Limited

ASX code: PDL   www.pendalgroup.com

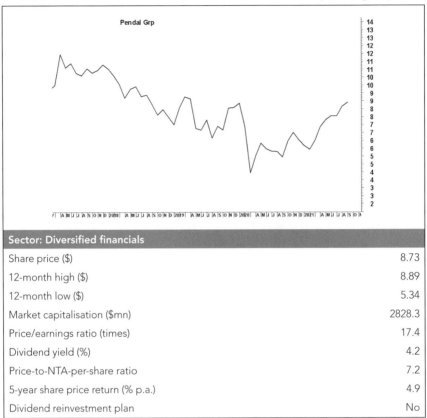

Sector: Diversified financials	
Share price ($)	8.73
12-month high ($)	8.89
12-month low ($)	5.34
Market capitalisation ($mn)	2828.3
Price/earnings ratio (times)	17.4
Dividend yield (%)	4.2
Price-to-NTA-per-share ratio	7.2
5-year share price return (% p.a.)	4.9
Dividend reinvestment plan	No

Sydney-based funds management company Pendal Group started life as part of Ord-BT, an investment banking firm established in 1969. Ord-BT, later renamed as BT Financial Group, was subsequently acquired by Westpac Banking Corporation, which added to it some other funds management businesses, then created BT Investment Management as a new entity to be listed on the ASX. It was later renamed as Pendal Group. Today Pendal actively manages a wide range of investments in Australian equities, listed property and fixed interest, in international fixed interest, in multi-asset portfolios and in alternative investments. Its London-based subsidiary J O Hambro Capital Management, with offices in Singapore and the US, manages international funds. It is acquiring the US investment manager Thompson, Siegel & Walmsley.

Latest business results (March 2021, half year)

Revenues and underlying profits rose, in a good result for the company. Base management fees slipped 2 per cent from the March 2020 half to $234.9 million, but performance fees jumped to $41.1 million, from just $0.6 million a year earlier, with 83 per cent of the company's funds outperforming their benchmarks. Funds under management rose from $86 billion to $101.7 billion, thanks to the strong investment performance and positive market movements. However, a big jump in staff salaries helped generate a 20 per cent increase in operating costs.

Outlook

Pendal is heavily dependent on market activity and investor sentiment. Its business can also be buffeted by its own performance, which helps determine levels of performance fees. In addition, with a majority of its equities funds under management held in foreign currencies it is heavily influenced by currency fluctuations. However, it benefits from moves by Australian investors into overseas equities. It has announced a goal of increasing funds under management by around 50 per cent by September 2025. In particular, it sees great potential in its strong moves into a form of socially responsible investment known as environmental, social and governance (ESG) investing. The company estimates this to be a US$30 trillion market, and its subsidiary Regnan, an ESG specialist, plans a series of socially responsible funds and products that are aligned with the 17 sustainable development goals of the United Nations. Pendal also sees great potential in expanding its reach to American and European clients, and it is building its global distribution team. In addition, it has announced the US$320 million acquisition of US investment manager Thompson, Siegel & Walmsley, which will boost its funds under management by 30 per cent.

Year to 30 September	2019	2020
Revenues ($mn)	491.3	474.8
EBIT ($mn)	200.7	183.2
EBIT margin (%)	40.8	38.6
Profit before tax ($mn)	201.0	181.8
Profit after tax ($mn)	163.5	146.8
Earnings per share (c)	57.57	50.15
Cash flow per share (c)	60.81	55.65
Dividend (c)	45	37
Percentage franked	10	10
Interest cover (times)	~	135.5
Return on equity (%)	18.1	16.3
Half year to 31 March	2020	2021
Revenues ($mn)	243.3	277.0
Profit before tax ($mn)	100.2	106.7
Profit after tax ($mn)	76.6	82.6
Earnings per share (c)	23.70	25.50
Dividend (c)	15	17
Percentage franked	10	10
Net tangible assets per share ($)	1.03	1.21
Debt-to-equity ratio (%)	~	~
Current ratio	1.8	1.8

Perpetual Limited

ASX code: PPT

www.perpetual.com.au

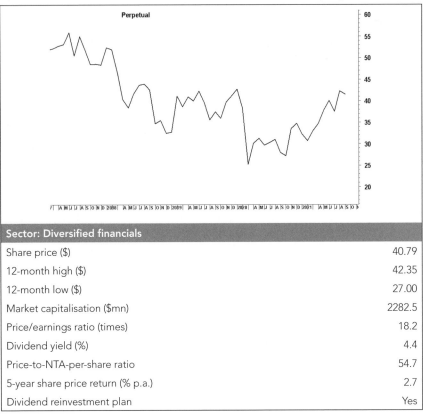

Sector: Diversified financials	
Share price ($)	40.79
12-month high ($)	42.35
12-month low ($)	27.00
Market capitalisation ($mn)	2282.5
Price/earnings ratio (times)	18.2
Dividend yield (%)	4.4
Price-to-NTA-per-share ratio	54.7
5-year share price return (% p.a.)	2.7
Dividend reinvestment plan	Yes

Sydney-based financial services company Perpetual was established in 1886 as Perpetual Trustees. Following two major acquisitions in 2020, Perpetual divides its operations into four broad areas. The largest of these, Perpetual Private, is a specialist boutique financial services business aimed at high-net-worth individuals, and providing its clients with access to tailored financial, tax, legal and estate planning advice. Two asset management divisions offer a range of managed domestic and international investment products to the retail, wholesale and institutional markets. The fourth division, Perpetual Corporate Trust, is a leading provider of corporate trustee and transaction support services to the financial services industry. In August 2021 Perpetual announced the acquisition of boutique wealth advisory firm Jacaranda Financial Planning.

Latest business results (June 2021, full year)

Perpetual has been transformed by its two American acquisitions, the specialist investment firm Trillium Asset Management and a 75 per cent stake in the investment management company Barrow Hanley. Consequently it reported solid gains in revenues and profits, reversing two years of mediocre results. The new Perpetual Asset

Management International division reported revenues of $139 million and an underlying pre-tax profit of $41 million. This included a full year of Trillium and seven months for Barrow Hanley. But the Perpetual Asset Management Australia division saw continuing net outflows from its funds, and revenues and profits were down. At June 2021 the two divisions held a combined $98.3 billion in assets under management. Perpetual Private saw revenues flat for the year but profits higher in line with stronger markets. Perpetual Corporate Trust enjoyed higher revenues and profits, with new clients wins and expanded business with existing clients.

Outlook

Perpetual expects its two American acquisitions to deliver significant long-term growth. It sees particular potential for Trillium, which has a specialty in ethical funds that incorporate environmental, social and governance (ESG) considerations into the investment process. Such funds are growing in popularity, and Perpetual is launching Trillium ESG funds in Australia. In its first year under Perpetual's ownership Trillium recorded the highest net inflows in its history, although Barrow Hanley recorded net outflows. The Perpetual Private division continues to invest in building up its network of advisers, leading to a steady increase in client numbers. The acquisition of Jacaranda Financial Planning — which has a focus on high-net-worth investors and funds under advice of $915 million — is part of this strategy. The well-regarded Perpetual Corporate Trust division continues to grow, and provides the highest profit margins of the company's divisions.

Year to 30 June	2020	2021
Revenues ($mn)	490.5	640.6
Perpetual Private (%)	38	29
Asset management Australia (%)	36	27
Asset management international (%)	0	22
Perpetual Corporate Trust (%)	26	22
EBIT ($mn)	143.4	181.1
EBIT margin (%)	29.2	28.3
Profit before tax ($mn)	139.6	171.2
Profit after tax ($mn)	98.6	124.1
Earnings per share (c)	211.95	223.77
Cash flow per share (c)	281.14	306.59
Dividend (c)	155	180
Percentage franked	100	100
Net tangible assets per share ($)	4.49	0.75
Interest cover (times)	37.5	18.2
Return on equity (%)	15.0	15.8
Debt-to-equity ratio (%)	11.0	20.0
Current ratio	1.3	1.3

Pinnacle Investment Management Group Limited

ASX code: PNI   www.pinnacleinvestment.com

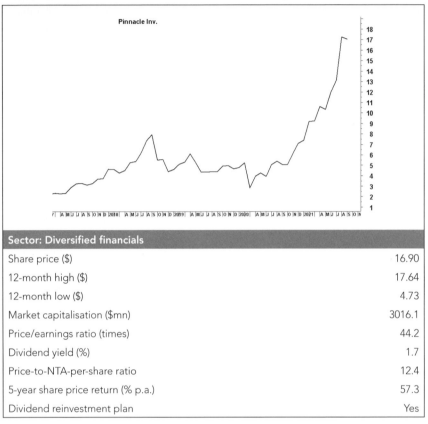

Sector: Diversified financials	
Share price ($)	16.90
12-month high ($)	17.64
12-month low ($)	4.73
Market capitalisation ($mn)	3016.1
Price/earnings ratio (times)	44.2
Dividend yield (%)	1.7
Price-to-NTA-per-share ratio	12.4
5-year share price return (% p.a.)	57.3
Dividend reinvestment plan	Yes

Sydney-based Pinnacle Investment Management started life in 2006 as a boutique funds management company that was majority-owned by Wilson HTM Investment Group. In 2016 it was fully acquired by Wilson Group, with Wilson Group changing its own name to Pinnacle. Today it is a prominent adviser to small funds management groups, providing them with distribution services, business support and responsible entity services, while also holding an equity stake in these companies.

Latest business results (June 2021, full year)

Pinnacle enjoyed an excellent year, with revenues charging ahead and profits more than doubling. At June 2021 the company comprised 16 fund management affiliates, and it held shareholdings in these that ranged from 23.5 per cent to 49.9 per cent. Total revenues during the year for the 16 fund managers of $415.5 million was up from $291.1 million in the previous year. Of this amount, $86.2 million came from performance fees, up from $26.7 million. A particularly strong performance came from Hyperion Asset Management. There were net inflows during the year to the 16 fund manager affiliates of $16.7 billion, and total funds under management reached $89.4 billion at June 2021, up from $58.7 billion a year before.

Outlook

Pinnacle's initial role is to provide its fund manager affiliates with equity, seed capital and working capital. It then allows its managers to focus on investment performance by providing them with marketing and other support services. Pinnacle's own revenues and profits derive from the revenues it receives from its affiliates for its services, together with its share of their profits, and performance is important. It has achieved success with the fund management companies it has chosen to join its group, reporting that 80 per cent of funds with a five-year track record had by June 2021 outperformed their benchmarks during this period. It is seeking to diversify into new asset classes, and views ethical funds as one area with growth potential. Pinnacle has also been steadily boosting its exposure to retail funds, which provide higher margins than institutional funds, and these represent 23 per cent of total funds under management. The company believes its business model could work well overseas, and it has expressed a desire to expand abroad, though the COVID-19 pandemic has forced it to delay any such moves. It is also interested in investing in new affiliates in Australia. Nevertheless, with its business directly tied to trends in global financial markets, Pinnacle could suffer in any prolonged market downturn.

Year to 30 June	2020	2021
Revenues ($mn)	60.4	98.9
EBIT ($mn)	32.8	67.6
EBIT margin (%)	54.4	68.3
Profit before tax ($mn)	32.4	67.0
Profit after tax ($mn)	32.4	67.0
Earnings per share (c)	18.93	38.23
Cash flow per share (c)	19.38	38.76
Dividend (c)	15.4	28.7
Percentage franked	100	100
Net tangible assets per share ($)	1.08	1.37
Interest cover (times)	69.5	125.6
Return on equity (%)	17.7	31.0
Debt-to-equity ratio (%)	7.4	1.6
Current ratio	3.8	8.4

Platinum Asset Management Limited

ASX code: PTM   www.platinum.com.au

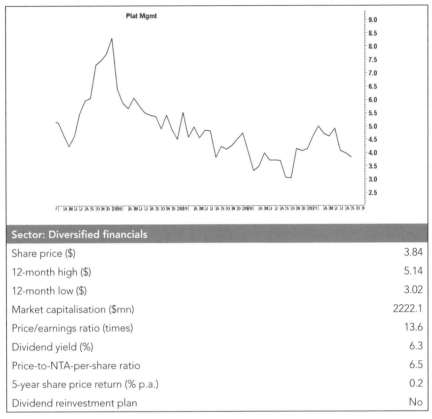

Sector: Diversified financials	
Share price ($)	3.84
12-month high ($)	5.14
12-month low ($)	3.02
Market capitalisation ($mn)	2222.1
Price/earnings ratio (times)	13.6
Dividend yield (%)	6.3
Price-to-NTA-per-share ratio	6.5
5-year share price return (% p.a.)	0.2
Dividend reinvestment plan	No

Sydney funds management company Platinum Asset Management was established in 1994 by former chief executive Kerr Neilson. It has developed a specialty in managing portfolios of international equities. Its primary product is the $8.3 billion Platinum International Fund. Other funds specialise in Europe, Asia, Japan, health care, technology and international brands. Much of the company equity is held by Platinum directors and staff members and by Kerr Neilson and his former wife.

Latest business results (June 2021, full year)

Revenues fell again, reflecting a reduction in both management fees and performance fees, but profits were up. Average funds under management for the year of $23.4 billion were slightly down from the previous year, driving down management fees. Performance fee revenue of $4 million was down from $9.1 million. The wage bill rose, as the company rewarded staff performance. At June 2021 Platinum held funds under management of $23.5 billion, up from $21.4 billion in June 2020, driven mainly by investment returns of $5.5 billion, partially offset by net fund outflows of $2.3 billion.

Outlook

Platinum has gained a degree of renown among Australian investors for an impressive long-term period of outperformance for its international equity funds, thanks to its stock-picking skills, and this has sparked some solid growth in funds under management. However, the more recent performance has been mixed. The company has attributed this to its preference for value stocks, at a time when growth stocks were leading global markets higher. It says that the strong performance of many of its funds in the June 2021 year would normally generate a better funds inflow. However, recent years have seen a growing number of new global fund managers in the Australian market, many with a preference for growth stocks, and the company believes that for the time being these managers will take a significant share of new fund flows. With the continuing rise of exchange-traded funds, the company is exploring the possibility of developing products to target this market. Platinum has noted that investors are increasingly concerned about environmental, social and governance (ESG) issues, and it has recruited a dedicated ESG analyst to help integrate ethical concerns into the company's investment analysis. The company has been working to boost its business with international clients, especially through staff members based in London and a partnership in the US with the financial advisory and distribution services specialist AccessAlpha Worldwide. However, it says the COVID-19 pandemic has severely hampered its ability to develop relations with prospective clients.

Year to 30 June	2020	2021
Revenues ($mn)	285.0	269.2
EBIT ($mn)	219.3	233.9
EBIT margin (%)	77.0	86.9
Profit before tax ($mn)	220.8	234.2
Profit after tax ($mn)	155.6	163.3
Earnings per share (c)	26.76	28.17
Cash flow per share (c)	27.41	28.72
Dividend (c)	24	24
Percentage franked	100	100
Net tangible assets per share ($)	0.55	0.59
Interest cover (times)	~	~
Return on equity (%)	48.6	49.4
Debt-to-equity ratio (%)	~	~
Current ratio	8.7	10.1

Premier Investments Limited

ASX code: PMV   www.premierinvestments.com.au

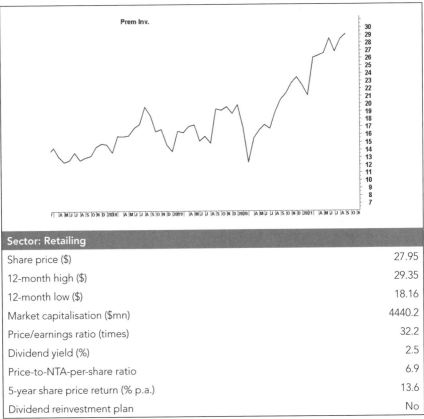

Sector: Retailing	
Share price ($)	27.95
12-month high ($)	29.35
12-month low ($)	18.16
Market capitalisation ($mn)	4440.2
Price/earnings ratio (times)	32.2
Dividend yield (%)	2.5
Price-to-NTA-per-share ratio	6.9
5-year share price return (% p.a.)	13.6
Dividend reinvestment plan	No

Melbourne-based Premier was founded in 1987 and operates as an investment company. Its main holding is a 100 per cent stake in the retailer Just Group, which was founded in 1970. Just Group incorporates the brands Just Jeans, Smiggle, Peter Alexander, Jay Jays, Portmans, Jacqui E and Dotti. Premier also holds 26 per cent of the equity in home appliance specialist Breville Group and a significant equity stake in Myer.

Latest business results (January 2021, half year)

Sales rose and profits soared as Just Group's retail businesses benefited from a pandemic-fuelled burst of consumer spending, which came despite temporary store closures in many regions. The company also benefited from rent reductions and government wage subsidies. The Peter Alexander sleepwear chain was a standout performer, with sales rising by 43 per cent from the January 2020 half and a significant improvement in margins as the company cut back on promotional activity. The five other apparel brands — Just Jeans, Jay Jays, Portmans, Jacqui E and Dotti — delivered a combined 10 per cent growth in sales and some margin improvements, with particular strength for Just Jeans and Jay Jays. Just Group's seventh brand, Smiggle, specialises in colourful school stationery and other products for children, with stores

around the world. It struggled during a period when many stores and s⌐
closed for extended periods, with sales down 26 per cent. In line with other r⌐
Premier saw a surge in online business, with sales up 61 per cent to $157 milli⌐
Premier also received a contribution from Breville Group at the EBIT level of
$16.9 million, up from $13.9 million a year earlier.

Outlook

Despite a volatile retail environment, with store closures continuing during 2021 in
some regions, Premier is optimistic about the short-term outlook. It expects continuing
strong growth in online sales, and plans to expand its distribution capacity during
2022. It has benefited from early decisions to maintain stock at high levels for its stores.
This has been in contrast to some other retailers, who have been hurt by an inability to
get sufficient stock due to COVID-related shipping delays. It has also been able to
negotiate cheaper rents for many stores. After a restructuring of its Smiggle business,
the company believes this division is set for a strong recovery. At January 2021 Premier
held net cash holdings of more than $350 million. Its shareholding in Breville Group,
worth around $1 billion, was on the books for just $268 million.

Year to 25 July*	2019	2020
Revenues ($mn)	1271.0	1216.3
EBIT ($mn)	155.5	209.6
EBIT margin (%)	12.2	17.2
Profit before tax ($mn)	151.7	195.2
Profit after tax ($mn)	106.8	137.8
Earnings per share (c)	67.51	86.89
Cash flow per share (c)	100.35	223.38
Dividend (c)	70	70
Percentage franked	100	100
Interest cover (times)	40.9	14.5
Return on equity (%)	7.9	10.2
Half year to 30 January**	2020	2021
Revenues ($mn)	732.1	784.6
Profit before tax ($mn)	136.8	262.1
Profit after tax ($mn)	99.6	188.2
Earnings per share (c)	62.87	118.50
Dividend (c)	34	34
Percentage franked	100	100
Net tangible assets per share ($)	3.53	4.06
Debt-to-equity ratio (%)	~	~
Current ratio	1.3	1.3

*27 July 2019
**25 January 2020

dicus Limited

www.promed.com.au

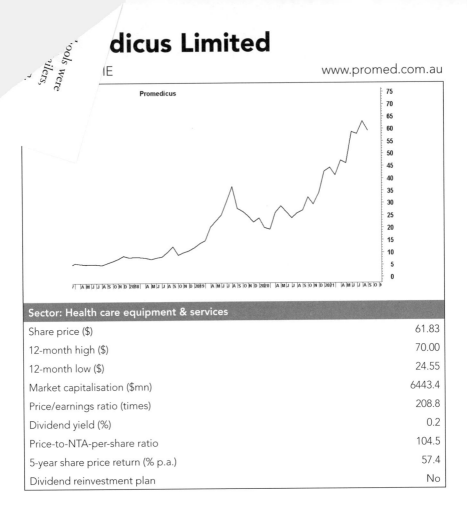

Sector: Health care equipment & services	
Share price ($)	61.83
12-month high ($)	70.00
12-month low ($)	24.55
Market capitalisation ($mn)	6443.4
Price/earnings ratio (times)	208.8
Dividend yield (%)	0.2
Price-to-NTA-per-share ratio	104.5
5-year share price return (% p.a.)	57.4
Dividend reinvestment plan	No

Melbourne-based Pro Medicus, established in 1983, provides software and internet products and services to the medical profession. Its Visage 7.0 medical imaging software provides radiologists and clinicians with advanced visualisation capability for the rapid viewing of medical images. Its Radiology Information Systems (RIS) product provides proprietary medical software for practice management. In Australia it operates the Promedicus.net online network for doctors. It has extensive business operations throughout Australia, Europe and North America, and overseas sales represent around 80 per cent of total turnover.

Latest business results (June 2021, full year)

Pro Medicus enjoyed another year of double-digit revenues and profits growth, with all regions strong. North America represents around three-quarters of total company turnover, and sales and EBIT were up by about 18 per cent as more Visage technology contracts came on stream. Australian sales rose 23 per cent with EBIT up 34 per cent, again due especially to RIS contracts with Healius and I-MED Radiology Network. European sales represent just 6 per cent of total turnover, but they rose 26 per cent, with profits surging nearly eightfold, thanks to a new $10 million, seven-year contract implemented in December 2020 with LMU Klinikum in Germany. A stronger dollar hurt the result, and the company reported that on a constant currency basis its revenues would have been $74 million and the pre-tax profit $47 million.

Outlook

Pro Medicus continues to enjoy some outstanding success in America for its Visage 7 software, which has the speed and functionality to meet the requirements of many different kinds of users. The company is now one of the market leaders in this business, and it is making a substantial investment in research and development activities aimed at new products and enhancements to existing products, including artificial intelligence–based products and cloud-based systems. It also benefits from a new emphasis on telehealth engendered by the COVID-19 pandemic. It has a growing amount of recurring income. During the June 2021 year the company continued to make strong inroads into the American market, with five new contracts. These included a $40 million, seven-year deal with Intermountain Health, the largest health system in Utah, and a $31 million, seven-year deal with the University of California. In June 2021 Pro Medicus signed a contract with Mayo Clinic in the US to work together on the development and commercialisation of artificial intelligence products based on the Visage platform. The company believes its LMU Klinikum contract in Germany will pave the way for further European sales.

Year to 30 June	2020	2021
Revenues ($mn)	56.8	67.9
EBIT ($mn)	29.8	42.7
EBIT margin (%)	52.5	62.9
Profit before tax ($mn)	30.0	42.9
Profit after tax ($mn)	23.1	30.9
Earnings per share (c)	22.21	29.62
Cash flow per share (c)	29.61	36.53
Dividend (c)	12	15
Percentage franked	100	100
Net tangible assets per share ($)	0.40	0.59
Interest cover (times)	~	~
Return on equity (%)	42.2	43.5
Debt-to-equity ratio (%)	~	~
Current ratio	4.8	5.0

PWR Holdings Limited

ASX code: PWH
www.pwr.com.au

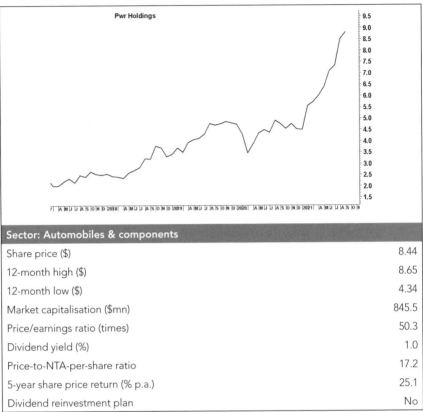

Sector: Automobiles & components	
Share price ($)	8.44
12-month high ($)	8.65
12-month low ($)	4.34
Market capitalisation ($mn)	845.5
Price/earnings ratio (times)	50.3
Dividend yield (%)	1.0
Price-to-NTA-per-share ratio	17.2
5-year share price return (% p.a.)	25.1
Dividend reinvestment plan	No

Based on the Gold Coast, automotive products company PWR got its start in 1987. It specialises in cooling systems, including aluminium radiators, intercoolers and oil coolers. It has a particular specialty in the supply of cooling systems to racing car teams. Other customers include the automotive original equipment manufacturing sector and the automotive after-market sector, along with the aerospace, defence and renewable energy industries. It operates from manufacturing and distribution facilities in Australia and the United States, with a European distribution centre in the United Kingdom. It owns the American cooling products manufacturer C&R Racing. More than 85 per cent of company sales are to customers overseas, mainly in Europe and North America.

Latest business results (June 2021, full year)

Revenues and profits enjoyed double-digit rises, rebounding from the previous year when the COVID-19 pandemic hit business. The result would have been stronger but for unfavourable currency movements. The key was a resumption of motor sport in many parts of the world. This is responsible for more than half the company's annual turnover, and in the prior year much of this activity had been suspended.

Motor sport revenues surged 58 per cent for the company. The automotive aftermarket now contributes 19 per cent of company income, and revenues were up 29 per cent. There was another strong performance from what the company terms emerging technologies, which includes aerospace and defence. Revenues for this sector more than doubled to $8.7 million. PWR North America was especially strong, with revenues up 55 per cent and EBIT soaring fourfold.

Outlook

PWR supplies its cooling systems to most Formula One racing teams, as well as to teams in other motor sports around the world, including Nascar and Indycar. It stands to gain as these sports resume. It also supplies bespoke cooling systems to a range of high-performance automobile companies. It spends heavily on research and development in order to maintain its market-leading position, and it is working to move into other market areas with high growth potential. It believes revenues from these emerging technologies could overtake motor sport revenues by 2024. It sees particular potential in the advance of electric vehicles, and it is working with several electric car manufacturers for the supply of sophisticated cooling technology. Other applications include helicopters, drones and storage batteries for alternative energy systems. PWR is also working with companies involved in the development of hydrogen fuel-cell technology. At June 2021 the company had net cash holdings of more than $11 million.

Year to 30 June	2020	2021
Revenues ($mn)	65.7	79.2
PWR performance products (%)	76	69
PWR North America (%)	24	31
EBIT ($mn)	18.6	22.9
EBIT margin (%)	28.3	28.9
Profit before tax ($mn)	18.2	22.5
Profit after tax ($mn)	13.0	16.8
Earnings per share (c)	13.05	16.78
Cash flow per share (c)	17.75	22.52
Dividend (c)	5.9	8.8
Percentage franked	100	100
Net tangible assets per share ($)	0.39	0.49
Interest cover (times)	49.8	72.4
Return on equity (%)	24.3	28.4
Debt-to-equity ratio (%)	~	~
Current ratio	3.4	2.8

REA Group Limited

ASX code: REA   www.rea-group.com

Rea Group

Sector: Media & entertainment	
Share price ($)	156.02
12-month high ($)	173.11
12-month low ($)	106.69
Market capitalisation ($mn)	20612.9
Price/earnings ratio (times)	64.7
Dividend yield (%)	0.8
Price-to-NTA-per-share ratio	88.6
5-year share price return (% p.a.)	22.4
Dividend reinvestment plan	No

Melbourne-based REA was founded in 1995. Through its websites realestate.com.au and realcommercial.com.au it is a leader in the provision of online real estate advertising services in Australia, with a market share of roughly 60 per cent. It also owns Flatmates.com.au, the residential property data company Hometrack Australia, the short-term co-working property website Spacely and the mortgage broking franchise group Smartline. It has interests in property websites throughout Asia, and has a 20 per cent shareholding in the Move online property marketing company in the US. In June 2021 it completed the acquisition of ASX-listed mortgage broking house Mortgage Choice. News Corp owns more than 60 per cent of REA's equity.

Latest business results (June 2021, full year)

Business rebounded from the downturn of the previous year, with a strong result in a buoyant housing market. More than 90 per cent of income is from domestic property advertising, and revenues rose by 13 per cent, with profits also up. The realestate.com.au property portal attracted 121.9 million visits per month, up 35 per cent from the previous year. The company's commercial and developer revenues rose thanks to new project commencements, which offset a COVID-induced decline in commercial business. The company's mortgage operations saw revenues and profits fall. Asian interests represent about 4 per cent of total turnover, and revenues were down, affected badly by the COVID-19 pandemic, though with profits flat. American business, represented by the company's 20 per cent shareholding in Move, went from loss to profit.

Outlook

REA is heavily geared to trends in the domestic housing market, and it continues to benefit from low interest rates and strong residential sales. However, it is wary about the medium-term outlook, noting that continuing COVID-related lockdowns generate considerable volatility in the housing market, while a general election in 2022 is also expected to have a negative impact. Its $244 million acquisition of Mortgage Choice now gives it more than 5 per cent of the Australian mortgage market, and it plans to build on this business, hoping in the longer term to double its market share. It is also actively working to develop its Asian businesses. It has sold its Malaysian and Thai interests to fast-growing Singaporean company PropertyGuru, in return for an 18 per cent equity stake in PropertyGuru. It has also taken a controlling stake in Elara Technologies, a leading digital real estate venture in India. REA's shareholding in Move, one of the largest real estate websites in the US, has given the company a foothold in the vast American property market.

Year to 30 June	2020	2021
Revenues ($mn)	820.3	927.8
EBIT ($mn)	397.0	481.9
EBIT margin (%)	48.4	51.9
Profit before tax ($mn)	392.3	477.5
Profit after tax ($mn)	268.9	318.0
Earnings per share (c)	204.13	241.06
Cash flow per share (c)	263.82	303.68
Dividend (c)	110	131
Percentage franked	100	100
Net tangible assets per share ($)	1.62	1.76
Interest cover (times)	84.3	109.6
Return on equity (%)	30.4	32.9
Debt-to-equity ratio (%)	12.1	28.7
Current ratio	1.2	2.0

Reece Limited

ASX code: REH

group.reece.com

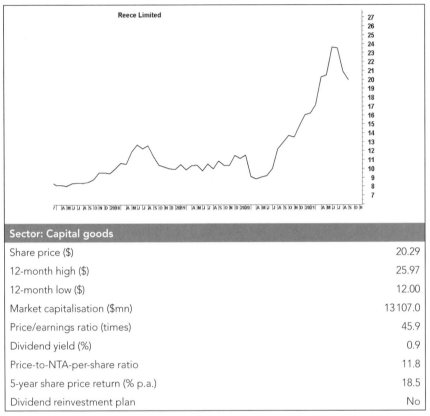

Sector: Capital goods	
Share price ($)	20.29
12-month high ($)	25.97
12-month low ($)	12.00
Market capitalisation ($mn)	13 107.0
Price/earnings ratio (times)	45.9
Dividend yield (%)	0.9
Price-to-NTA-per-share ratio	11.8
5-year share price return (% p.a.)	18.5
Dividend reinvestment plan	No

Melbourne-based plumbing supplies company Reece traces its origins back to 1919, when Harold Reece started selling his products from the back of a truck. It is today one of the country's leading suppliers of plumbing products, with operations also in New Zealand, and it has expanded into related fields. These include a network of businesses in the heating, ventilation, air conditioning and refrigeration sectors, and specialist stores for the landscape and agricultural industries. In 2018 it entered the United States market with the acquisition of Texas plumbing supplies company MORSCO. At June 2021 it operated 642 branches in Australia and New Zealand and 189 in the US.

Latest business results (June 2021, full year)

Sales and profits rose, as the company successfully overcame pandemic-related disruptions to its operations. Australian business represents half of total income, and sales rose 9.2 per cent, thanks especially to a buoyant housing market, with the after-tax profit up 22 per cent. American sales rose 11.4 per cent in local currency though were flat when converted to Australian dollars, with the after-tax profit up 36 per cent in Australian dollars. A massive winter storm in Texas in February 2021 led to widespread property damage and business disruptions, though also boosted demand for plumbing products. In both Australia and the US the company faced the problem of labour shortages and rising costs. Though 50 per cent of company turnover, US operations contributed just 23 per cent of after-tax profit.

Outlook

Reece looks set to benefit from the continuing strength of housing markets in Australia, New Zealand and the US. Nevertheless, it is concerned that rising demand for construction activity is generating price inflation and labour shortages, which may limit growth, with pandemic-related lockdowns a further distraction. It also worries that supply-chain disruptions could lead to shortages of stock, and it has boosted its inventories. It estimates that in the US around half of all projects are now delayed because of a shortage of some items or problems in finding tradespeople. In Australia the company is investing heavily in digital innovation to make business as smooth as possible for its customers, and it also expects to open new branches. However, it is in the US that the company sees its best growth prospects. It operates in 16 states, and Reece is carrying out trials of new branch formats and service concepts, in order to expand business and lower costs. Having reduced its debt levels, it is now also seeking further US acquisitions.

Year to 30 June	2020	2021
Revenues ($mn)	6009.9	6270.7
EBIT ($mn)	410.6	468.1
EBIT margin (%)	6.8	7.5
Gross margin (%)	27.8	28.1
Profit before tax ($mn)	312.5	380.3
Profit after tax ($mn)	229.0	285.6
Earnings per share (c)	39.89	44.21
Cash flow per share (c)	80.37	79.44
Dividend (c)	12	18
Percentage franked	100	100
Net tangible assets per share ($)	1.21	1.71
Interest cover (times)	4.2	5.3
Return on equity (%)	9.7	10.1
Debt-to-equity ratio (%)	27.7	17.5
Current ratio	2.7	2.4

Regis Resources Limited

ASX code: RRL   www.regisresources.com.au

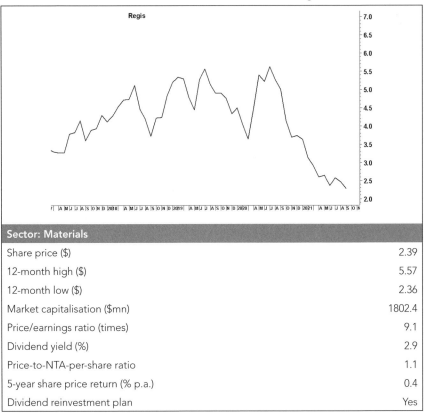

Sector: Materials	
Share price ($)	2.39
12-month high ($)	5.57
12-month low ($)	2.36
Market capitalisation ($mn)	1802.4
Price/earnings ratio (times)	9.1
Dividend yield (%)	2.9
Price-to-NTA-per-share ratio	1.1
5-year share price return (% p.a.)	0.4
Dividend reinvestment plan	Yes

Perth-based Regis Resources is a gold exploration and production company. Its core business is the Duketon Gold Project in the north-eastern goldfields region of Western Australia. Since operations started at Duketon in 2010 the company has been steadily expanding the size of the project and extending mine life. It also owns the McPhillamys Gold Project in western New South Wales, and in April 2021 it acquired a 30 per cent interest in the Tropicana Gold Project in Western Australia.

Latest business results (June 2021, full year)

Revenues rose in line with higher gold production, including the addition of gold from the Tropicana acquisition, but rising costs sent profits down. During the year the company produced 372 870 ounces of gold, including 17 317 ounces from Tropicana, compared to 352 042 ounces in the previous year. It sold 367 285 ounces, up from 353 182 ounces. The average sales price of $2229 per ounce was slightly up from $2200. The average production all-in sustaining cost of $1372 per ounce rose 10 per cent from $1246 in the previous year, as deeper in-pit mining boosted expenses. In addition, there was a 74.5 per cent increase in depreciation and amortisation charges for the year. In the June 2019 year the average cost had been just $1029 per ounce.

Outlook

Regis is set to be revived by its $900 million acquisition of a 30 per cent interest in the Tropicana Gold Project. The other 70 per cent is held by AngloGold Ashanti Australia. This is an operating mine with an estimated life of at least 10 years that provides immediate cash flow to Regis. It is now working with AngloGold Ashanti on studies into the potential for additional underground mines beneath the current pits. The partners are also engaged in exploration activity in the area around the mine. In September 2020 Regis acquired the Ben Hur mineral resource, which will add further life to its Duketon operations. The company's McPhillamys Gold Project in New South Wales contains an estimated 2.02 million ounces of gold, sufficient for a 10-year life, and Regis is in the process of seeking formal regulatory approval for development work to begin. If approval is given, Regis could within several years be producing a total from all its mines of up to 750 000 ounces of gold each year. The company's June 2022 forecast is for production of 460 000 ounces to 515 000 ounces of gold, including up to 135 000 ounces from Tropicana, at an average cost of up to $1135 per ounce.

Year to 30 June	2020	2021
Revenues ($mn)	755.8	819.2
Duketon South operations (%)	73	72
Duketon North operations (%)	27	23
EBIT ($mn)	285.8	214.3
EBIT margin (%)	37.8	26.2
Gross margin (%)	40.2	28.9
Profit before tax ($mn)	284.7	212.4
Profit after tax ($mn)	199.5	146.2
Earnings per share (c)	39.26	26.37
Cash flow per share (c)	60.64	60.06
Dividend (c)	16	7
Percentage franked	100	100
Net tangible assets per share ($)	1.64	2.10
Interest cover (times)	246.8	110.6
Return on equity (%)	25.7	12.1
Debt-to-equity ratio (%)	~	3.2
Current ratio	2.7	2.3

Reliance Worldwide Corporation Limited

ASX code: RWC   www.rwc.com

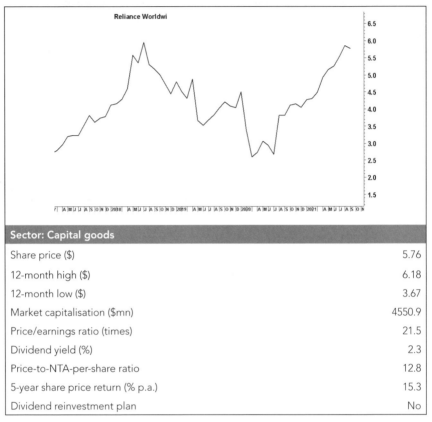

Reliance Worldwi

Sector: Capital goods	
Share price ($)	5.76
12-month high ($)	6.18
12-month low ($)	3.67
Market capitalisation ($mn)	4550.9
Price/earnings ratio (times)	21.5
Dividend yield (%)	2.3
Price-to-NTA-per-share ratio	12.8
5-year share price return (% p.a.)	15.3
Dividend reinvestment plan	No

Melbourne-based engineering firm Reliance dates back to 1949 and the establishment of a small tool shop in Brisbane. It is today a major global manufacturer and distributor of a range of products, particularly for the plumbing and heating industries. Its businesses and brands include SharkBite, Speedfit, HoldRite, CashAcme, StreamLabs and John Guest. In August 2021 it acquired the business interests of LCL, one of Australia's largest producers of copper-based alloys.

Latest business results (June 2021, full year)

Revenues were up and profits surged in an excellent year for Reliance, with all regions reporting growth as consumers around the world chose to invest in upgrading their homes. The result would have been stronger but for the strength of the dollar. North America is the company's largest market, and strong sales continued throughout the year, through both retail and wholesale channels. A severe winter freeze in Texas and surrounding states generated a sudden surge in demand. The company estimates that this emergency added approximately US$42 million to its US sales, on top of already strong demand due to the COVID-19 pandemic. European sales grew 25 per cent on a constant currency basis. Australian business benefited from a strong housing market. Price rises across a range of products helped mitigate the impact of cost inflation, notably for copper, a key component of manufactured brass items.

Outlook

Reliance has achieved great success in meeting surging demand from its customers while at the same time managing the impact of the COVID-19 pandemic on its own operations. It is also benefiting from a cost-reduction program initiated during the June 2021 year that has delivered some $25 million in annual savings, and it is expanding capacity in all its regions. It expects continuing modest growth in North America, with strength in residential demand offsetting non-residential weakness. A strong Australian housing market is also expected to support solid demand for the company's products and European economic recovery is seen as helping to boost sales. Nevertheless, the company saw a notable increase in the cost of some materials during the June 2021 second half, and it has noted that sales are increasingly being constrained by a combination of supply-chain disruptions, raw materials shortages, shipping delays and a shortage of labour in the plumbing trades. Its $37 million acquisition of the business interests of LCL ensure a supply of high-quality brass to support future operations. The company has stated that it is seeking further acquisitions, particularly in the United Kingdom and North America.

Year to 30 June	2020	2021
Revenues ($mn)	1162.4	1340.8
Americas (%)	63	63
Europe/Middle East/Africa (%)	24	25
Asia Pacific (%)	13	12
EBIT ($mn)	189.3	292.9
EBIT margin (%)	16.3	21.8
Gross margin (%)	41.1	44.0
Profit before tax ($mn)	169.3	280.9
Profit after tax ($mn)	130.3	211.9
Earnings per share (c)	16.49	26.82
Cash flow per share (c)	24.34	33.95
Dividend (c)	7	13
Percentage franked	20	20
Net tangible assets per share ($)	0.25	0.45
Interest cover (times)	9.5	24.4
Return on equity (%)	9.2	14.1
Debt-to-equity ratio (%)	21.3	10.9
Current ratio	2.4	2.0

Rio Tinto Limited

ASX code: RIO   www.riotinto.com

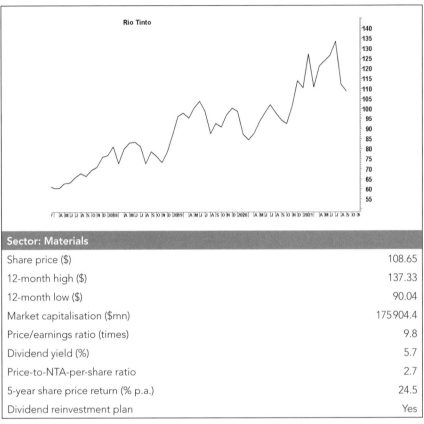

Sector: Materials	
Share price ($)	108.65
12-month high ($)	137.33
12-month low ($)	90.04
Market capitalisation ($mn)	175 904.4
Price/earnings ratio (times)	9.8
Dividend yield (%)	5.7
Price-to-NTA-per-share ratio	2.7
5-year share price return (% p.a.)	24.5
Dividend reinvestment plan	Yes

British-based Rio Tinto, one of the world's largest mining companies, was founded by European investors in 1873 in order to reopen some ancient copper mines on the Tinto River in Spain. It maintains an ASX presence in a dual-listing structure and continues to pay franked dividends to Australian shareholders. Its products include iron ore, copper, gold, industrial minerals, diamonds and aluminium. Subsidiaries include the 86 per cent–owned uranium miner Energy Resources of Australia.

Latest business results (June 2021, half year)

Surging iron ore revenues powered Rio Tinto to a superb result, with strength also in most of the company's other products. Shipments of iron ore during the period actually edged down from June 2020, but a near-doubling of the average realised price generated a sharp increase in revenues and profits. Iron ore represented 69 per cent of total company turnover, and around 75 per cent of the profit. The Aluminium division represented 18 per cent of sales. It too benefited from a big increase in prices, with profits sharply higher, thanks to growing demand as economies in many countries recovered from the impact of COVID-19. Copper was also a significant beneficiary of stronger demand and rising prices. The company's Minerals division, incorporating iron ore pellets and concentrates, titanium dioxide, borates and diamonds, overcame a deteriorating security situation in South Africa — where one of its executives was shot and killed — to post an excellent result. Altogether, 60 per cent of total company sales were to China and a further 17 per cent to the rest of Asia. Note that Rio Tinto reports its results in US dollars. The tables in this book are based on Australian dollar figures and exchange rates supplied by the company.

Outlook

Rio Tinto maintains a substantial portfolio of well-run assets across many countries, and with generally low operating costs, although it has conceded that expenses have been rising at its Western Australian iron ore operations, with some production problems. It must also face the prospect of moves by China to diversify away from Australian producers of iron ore. Rio Tinto forecasts capital expenditure of around US$7.5 billion in each of 2021, 2022 and 2023. A major growth project is the Oyu Tolgoi copper mine development in Mongolia, which is destined eventually to become the world's largest copper mine, although this has been hindered by delays. The company has earmarked US$2.4 billion for the Jadar lithium project in Serbia, aiming to become Europe's largest source of lithium for electric vehicle batteries.

Year to 31 December	2019	2020
Revenues ($mn)	61 664.0	64 577.0
EBIT ($mn)	22 520.9	25 753.6
EBIT margin (%)	36.5	39.9
Profit before tax ($mn)	22 158.0	25 569.6
Profit after tax ($mn)	14 819.0	18 019.0
Earnings per share (c)	909.09	1 114.07
Cash flow per share (c)	1 293.29	1 497.49
Dividend (c)	568.82	613.95
Percentage franked	100	100
Interest cover (times)	62.1	139.9
Return on equity (%)	24.6	30.3
Half year to 30 June	2020	2021
Revenues ($mn)	29 418.0	42 876.0
Profit before tax ($mn)	8 021.0	23 392.0
Profit after tax ($mn)	7 217.0	15 767.0
Earnings per share (c)	446.20	974.40
Dividend (c)	216.47	509.42
Percentage franked	100	100
Net tangible assets per share ($)	32.89	40.54
Debt-to-equity ratio (%)	18.0	~
Current ratio	1.6	2.1

Sandfire Resources Limited

ASX code: SFR   www.sandfire.com.au

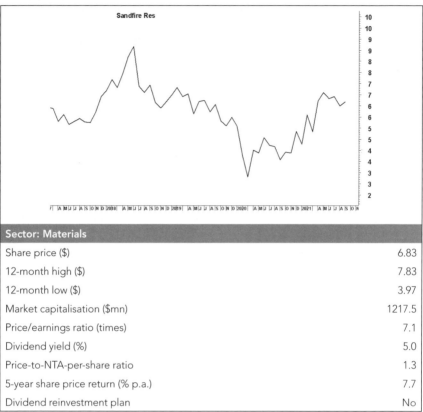

Sector: Materials	
Share price ($)	6.83
12-month high ($)	7.83
12-month low ($)	3.97
Market capitalisation ($mn)	1217.5
Price/earnings ratio (times)	7.1
Dividend yield (%)	5.0
Price-to-NTA-per-share ratio	1.3
5-year share price return (% p.a.)	7.7
Dividend reinvestment plan	No

Perth-based Sandfire Resources dates back to 2004 when geologist Graeme Hutton listed the company on the ASX with a portfolio of exploration projects. In 2009 the company discovered a significant copper and gold resource, and today it is a major copper and gold producer at its DeGrussa mine in Western Australia and also at the nearby Monty mine, which it acquired in 2018. It holds a large interest in the Kalahari Copper Belt of Botswana and has an 87 per cent interest in the Black Butte Copper Project in Montana in the United States.

Latest business results (June 2021, full year)

The continuing strength of international copper prices sent revenues and profits surging. During the year the company produced 70 845 tonnes of copper, down from 72 238 tonnes in the previous year, and 39 459 ounces of gold, down from 42 263 ounces. The average operating cost of US$0.82 per pound was up from US$0.72 per pound in the previous year. Copper contributed 87.3 per cent of the company's revenues, gold 11.4 per cent and silver 1.3 per cent. Work on the company's Botswana holdings contributed an EBIT loss of $18.4 million. Work at Black Butte generated an EBIT loss of $11.1 million.

Outlook

Sandfire is optimistic about the long-term outlook for copper, with strong underlying demand from the construction and industrial sectors and an expected rapid rise in demand from the electric vehicle and the wind and solar energy industries. It sees global demand from clean energy sources rising from 1 million tonnes in 2020 to 5.4 million tonnes in 2030. Meanwhile, supplies are challenged by declining discoveries and reduced mine grades. However, its DeGrussa mine has an estimated life of only several more years. Sandfire's forecast for the June 2022 year is for production of between 64 000 tonnes and 68 000 tonnes of copper and between 30 000 ounces and 34 000 ounces of gold, at an average cost of between US$1.00 and US$1.10 per pound. Sandfire now views its best opportunity for sustained growth as coming from Botswana. It has been granted a mining licence by the Botswana government for its Motheo Copper Project and has begun construction work. It expects production to start in 2023, initially at a rate of around 30 000 tonnes per year, rising subsequently to as much as 60 000 tonnes. It also sees great potential for its Black Butte operations and in August 2020 received a mine operating permit. However, it now faces legal challenges from groups opposed to resource development in the region. In September 2021 Sandfire announced the planned $2.6 billion acquisition of the Minas de Aguas Tenidas copper mine in Spain.

Year to 30 June	2020	2021
Revenues ($mn)	656.8	813.0
EBIT ($mn)	113.8	270.0
EBIT margin (%)	17.3	33.2
Profit before tax ($mn)	111.1	261.0
Profit after tax ($mn)	74.1	171.6
Earnings per share (c)	42.88	96.29
Cash flow per share (c)	159.50	197.18
Dividend (c)	19	34
Percentage franked	100	100
Net tangible assets per share ($)	4.20	5.09
Interest cover (times)	42.5	30.0
Return on equity (%)	11.0	20.7
Debt-to-equity ratio (%)	~	~
Current ratio	5.4	3.5

Schaffer Corporation Limited

ASX code: SFC

www.schaffer.com.au

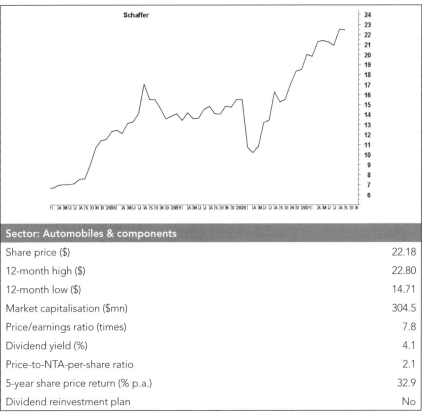

Sector: Automobiles & components	
Share price ($)	22.18
12-month high ($)	22.80
12-month low ($)	14.71
Market capitalisation ($mn)	304.5
Price/earnings ratio (times)	7.8
Dividend yield (%)	4.1
Price-to-NTA-per-share ratio	2.1
5-year share price return (% p.a.)	32.9
Dividend reinvestment plan	No

Perth company Schaffer was founded in 1955 to manufacture sand-lime bricks for the construction industry. Today its Delta Corporation subsidiary produces precast and prestressed concrete floors, beams and wall products, aimed mainly at the Western Australian construction market. However, its primary business now is the manufacture of leather goods, with a particular emphasis on products for the automotive industry, through its 83-per-cent-owned subsidiary Automotive Leather. This business operates from facilities in Australia, China and Slovakia and supplies leading auto makers around the world. A third business for Schaffer is investments and property development, and it owns a growing portfolio of rental and development sites, mainly in Western Australia.

Latest business results (June 2021, full year)

A rebound in demand for automotive leather helped Schaffer to a sparkling result, with sales and profits racing ahead. In the previous year pandemic-related factory closures throughout the global automobile industry had hit this business. Leather revenues rose 27 per cent to $165 million, with the after-tax profit up 38 per cent, thanks to two new contracts and a strong recovery in volumes from existing contracts.

The company's concrete products operation continued to struggle in a challenging Western Australian construction market, with revenues falling a further 7 per cent, although this business moved from loss back into profit. Schaffer's investment and property development portfolio enjoyed a second excellent year, with the after-tax profit jumping 60 per cent. There was an after-tax profit of $1.5 million from the sale of land at the site of a former leather manufacturing facility in North Coogee and $1.9 million in profits from the sale of equities and other investments.

Outlook

Schaffer's core automotive leather goods business is highly dependent on trends in the global car-making sector. It is enjoying a solid recovery, and expects important new contracts with Mercedes and Audi to boost European sales volumes significantly from 2023. The company has invested $3.8 million in new machinery, including three new computer numerical controlled cutting machines. Nevertheless, it has expressed concerns that a worsening global semiconductor chip shortage is increasingly leading to production shutdowns at European auto plants, despite strong global demand for new cars. The company's investment portfolio continues to grow, worth $192 million at June 2021, up 18 per cent from a year earlier. It has started development work on its 34-hectare Jandakot Road land holding, 15 minutes from the Perth CBD, and also expects continuing profits from land sales at its North Coogee site.

Year to 30 June	2020	2021
Revenues ($mn)	155.1	196.0
EBIT ($mn)	40.7	64.4
EBIT margin (%)	26.2	32.9
Gross margin (%)	28.0	33.5
Profit before tax ($mn)	38.5	62.9
Profit after tax ($mn)	23.6	38.8
Earnings per share (c)	171.91	284.88
Cash flow per share (c)	228.80	340.40
Dividend (c)	80	90
Percentage franked	100	100
Net tangible assets per share ($)	8.37	10.32
Interest cover (times)	19.1	42.5
Return on equity (%)	21.3	30.2
Debt-to-equity ratio (%)	14.8	23.1
Current ratio	2.4	2.0

Servcorp Limited

ASX code: SRV

www.servcorp.com.au

Sector: Real estate

Share price ($)	3.40
12-month high ($)	3.77
12-month low ($)	2.26
Market capitalisation ($mn)	329.2
Price/earnings ratio (times)	13.9
Dividend yield (%)	5.3
Price-to-NTA-per-share ratio	1.8
5-year share price return (% p.a.)	−9.8
Dividend reinvestment plan	No

Sydney-based Servcorp was founded in 1978 to provide serviced office space to small businesses. It has expanded to provide advanced corporate infrastructure, including IT and telecommunications services, and office support services. It also offers what it terms virtual offices, providing a prestigious address and a range of services — such as message forwarding and access to meeting rooms — for people or businesses not needing a physical office. About 40 per cent of the company's business is in North Asia, with more than a quarter in Europe and the Middle East. In June 2021 it was operating 125 floors of offices in 43 cities across 21 countries.

Latest business results (June 2021, full year)

The COVID-19 pandemic continued to hit the company, with revenues and profits down and currency fluctuations further contributing to the weakness. The largest market is North Asia, and this business was relatively unscathed, with revenues down and profits actually rising. But the next-largest segment, Europe and the Middle East, experienced a sharp dive in revenues and profits, with particular weakness in France and Kuwait. The Australia/New Zealand/South-East Asia segment also saw a double-digit decline in revenues and profits. The US market reported a particularly sharp decline in revenues, but this largely reflected the company's restructuring of this troubled business, and it recorded a reduced loss from the previous year. During the year the company opened new floors in Manila and closed others in New York and Al Khobar. The total occupancy rate at June 2021 of 72 per cent was up from 69 per cent a year earlier.

Outlook

Servcorp is a world leader in its business, with good market shares and a reputation for quality. However, its activities are being affected by the COVID-19 pandemic, which in the longer term could lead to reduced demand for the company's prestige inner-city office space as increasing numbers of people work from home. In the shorter term, the pandemic has hit demand in some regions and is also obliging the company to negotiate rent relief with its tenants. It has also been obliged to remodel its fashionable co-working spaces in order to facilitate social distancing, though later in 2021 it was reporting a steady increase in demand. In addition, the work-from-home trend could boost demand for the company's virtual offices. After a significant restructuring, Servcorp is seeing a slow turnaround of its poorly performing American operations. It continues to expand, and during the June 2022 year plans new office floors in Macquarie Park, Parramatta, Riyadh and Tokyo.

Year to 30 June	2020	2021
Revenues ($mn)	349.1	269.7
EBIT ($mn)	36.2	29.3
EBIT margin (%)	10.4	10.9
Profit before tax ($mn)	37.5	30.0
Profit after tax ($mn)	30.6	23.6
Earnings per share (c)	31.61	24.38
Cash flow per share (c)	189.09	153.52
Dividend (c)	20	18
Percentage franked	14	0
Net tangible assets per share ($)	2.14	1.93
Interest cover (times)	~	~
Return on equity (%)	13.3	11.2
Debt-to-equity ratio (%)	~	~
Current ratio	0.8	0.9

Seven Group Holdings Limited

ASX code: SVW   www.sevengroup.com.au

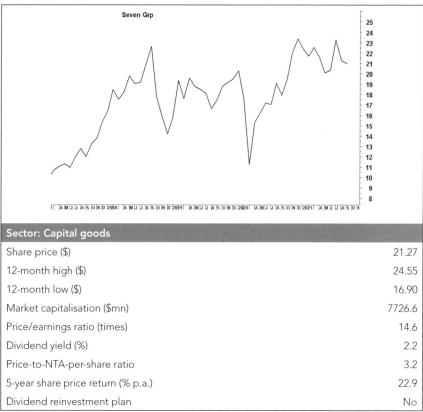

Sector: Capital goods	
Share price ($)	21.27
12-month high ($)	24.55
12-month low ($)	16.90
Market capitalisation ($mn)	7726.6
Price/earnings ratio (times)	14.6
Dividend yield (%)	2.2
Price-to-NTA-per-share ratio	3.2
5-year share price return (% p.a.)	22.9
Dividend reinvestment plan	No

Sydney-based investment company Seven Group Holdings dates back to 1991, when it was formed to manage media interests of the failed Qintex business of Christopher Skase. It has since grown considerably. It owns WesTrac Group, the sole authorised dealer in New South Wales, Western Australia and Australian Capital Territory for Caterpillar construction equipment. It also owns Coates Hire, Australia's largest equipment hire business, and AllightSykes, which supplies lighting towers, generators and pumps. Its SGH Energy business owns a portfolio of oil and gas interests in Australia and the United States. It has a 70 per cent shareholding in building products company Boral and a 30 per cent holding in oil and gas company Beach Energy. It retains a 40 per cent interest in Seven West Media, which manages the Seven Network and West Australian Newspapers. More than half of Seven Group's shares are held by its former chairman Kerry Stokes.

Latest business results (June 2021, full year)

Seven Group achieved a solid result, with single-digit rises in revenues and profit. The key was the company's core holding, WesTrac, which generated around 78 per cent of company income, with underlying EBIT up 8 per cent, thanks to a strong resource sector. The other main pillar of operations, Coates Hire, responsible for nearly 20 per cent of company turnover, was hit by pandemic-related project delays, though cost-cutting initiatives helped the business to a small rise in profits. WesTrac and Coates together contribute about 75 per cent of Seven Group's profits. The investment in Seven West Media delivered a strong rise in profits, but Beach Energy experienced weakness. The company received an initial contribution from its Boral investment.

Outlook

Seven Group is heavily exposed to the resources and construction sectors, through its WesTrac and Coates subsidiaries, and these remain strong. WesTrac expects to benefit as customers expand into gold, lithium, nickel and other minerals. It is also experiencing growing demand for support services. Coates is a beneficiary of an acceleration of large-scale government projects. Seven Group launched a takeover bid for Boral in May 2021. When the offer closed in July 2021 it controlled a majority 70 per cent stake, and it plans to consolidate the company as a new subsidiary. Boral is in the process of a major transformation of its many construction-related businesses, with a medium-term target of up to $250 million in annual benefits. Seven Group expects low single-digit EBIT growth in the June 2022 year, though further COVID-related lockdowns could upset this forecast.

Year to 30 June	2020	2021
Revenues ($mn)	4562.6	4838.7
EBIT ($mn)	737.9	792.1
EBIT margin (%)	16.2	16.4
Profit before tax ($mn)	587.8	629.2
Profit after tax ($mn)	469.6	501.4
Earnings per share (c)	138.53	145.97
Cash flow per share (c)	216.19	221.75
Dividend (c)	42	46
Percentage franked	100	100
Net tangible assets per share ($)	3.62	6.67
Interest cover (times)	4.9	4.9
Return on equity (%)	16.5	14.5
Debt-to-equity ratio (%)	85.0	55.9
Current ratio	2.0	1.0

SG Fleet Group Limited

ASX code: SGF investors.sgfleet.com

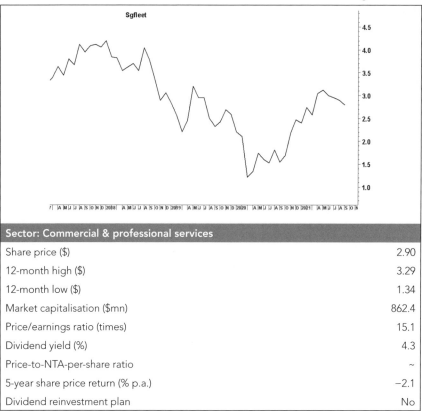

Sector: Commercial & professional services	
Share price ($)	2.90
12-month high ($)	3.29
12-month low ($)	1.34
Market capitalisation ($mn)	862.4
Price/earnings ratio (times)	15.1
Dividend yield (%)	4.3
Price-to-NTA-per-share ratio	~
5-year share price return (% p.a.)	−2.1
Dividend reinvestment plan	No

SG Fleet, based in Sydney, has its roots in the formation in 1986 of Leaseway Transportation, a specialist fleet management company. Leaseway was later sold to the Commonwealth Bank, which in turn sold it in 2004 to a South African company, Super Group, who renamed it FleetAustralia. In 2014 it was listed on the ASX as SG Fleet Group. Today it offers a range of fleet management services in Australia, New Zealand and the United Kingdom. It also provides salary packaging services. It operates under the brand SG Fleet and, in the UK, Fleet Hire. In addition, it operates the nlc vehicle financing business in Australia. South Africa's Super Group continues to hold a 60 per cent equity stake in the company. In 2021 SG Fleet acquired the local operations of European fleet management and vehicle leasing group LeasePlan.

Latest business results (June 2021, full year)

Business rebounded strongly from the previous year, when the COVID-19 pandemic forced a sharp decline in profits. Revenues in Australia were up 4 per cent with underlying EBITDA rising by 17 per cent, thanks to multiple contract extensions and an improved tender win rate. British business represents more than 20 per cent of total company turnover, and revenues rose 15 per cent, with underlying EBITDA surging by 46 per cent as economic activity and vehicle registrations rebounded in the second half. The company's small New Zealand business achieved revenues growth, though with profits largely flat for the year. The company's total fleet size declined from 143 278 vehicles in June 2020 to 138 797 in June 2021.

Outlook

SG Fleet occupies a solid position in a competitive industry. It generates good profit margins, and as it grows it achieves significant economies of scale that boost margins higher. However, its business is influenced to a degree by the state of the economy, and in particular the level of new car sales. Nevertheless, it enjoys a large amount of annuity-style income, with many long-term clients, as it is costly for a car fleet customer to switch providers. It is set to be transformed by the $387 million acquisition, effective from September 2021, of the Australia and New Zealand arm of LeasePlan, which will expand its fleet management and leasing portfolio to some 250 000 vehicles across the two countries. It will allow the company to create additional scale across its operations, including enormous vehicle purchasing power, and it anticipates cost-saving synergies of some $20 million per year within three years of the acquisition.

Year to 30 June	2020	2021
Revenues ($mn)	451.6	481.6
EBIT ($mn)	59.2	83.7
EBIT margin (%)	13.1	17.4
Profit before tax ($mn)	52.4	72.6
Profit after tax ($mn)	36.7	51.6
Earnings per share (c)	14.01	19.15
Cash flow per share (c)	26.33	31.35
Dividend (c)	9.996	12.585
Percentage franked	100	100
Net tangible assets per share ($)	~	~
Interest cover (times)	8.6	7.6
Return on equity (%)	13.3	15.9
Debt-to-equity ratio (%)	5.2	~

Smartgroup Corporation Limited

ASX code: SIQ   www.smartgroup.com.au

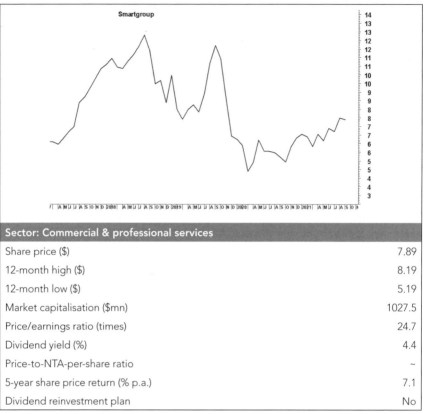

Sector: Commercial & professional services	
Share price ($)	7.89
12-month high ($)	8.19
12-month low ($)	5.19
Market capitalisation ($mn)	1027.5
Price/earnings ratio (times)	24.7
Dividend yield (%)	4.4
Price-to-NTA-per-share ratio	~
5-year share price return (% p.a.)	7.1
Dividend reinvestment plan	No

Sydney-based Smartgroup got its start in 1999 as Smartsalary, a salary packaging specialist. It later branched into other businesses, and has grown significantly, both organically and through acquisition. It is now engaged in salary packaging services, as well as vehicle novated leasing, fleet management, payroll administration, share plan administration and workforce optimisation consulting services.

Latest business results (June 2021, half year)

Revenues edged down but profits bounced back after the COVID-19 pandemic hit business in 2020. Salary packages of 373 500 were up 5 per cent from a year before, thanks in particular to a new health sector client, as well as to organic growth from the existing client base. Vehicle novated lease orders rose strongly, returning to pre-COVID levels, but motor vehicle supply shortages meant that not all orders could be fulfilled in a timely manner. Consequently, novated lease numbers actually fell by 3 per cent. Smartgroup also operates a small fleet management business that represents about 6 per cent of total turnover, and this enjoyed a good period, with a modest increase in fleet vehicle numbers generating a healthy rise in profits.

Outlook

Smartgroup is one of Australia's two largest companies involved in the salary packaging and novated leasing businesses. The other is McMillan Shakespeare. Essentially this business involves taking advantage of complex legislation to provide tax deductions for employees, mainly those working in charities or in the public sector. Smartgroup has grown considerably through a series of acquisitions, and at June 2021 it had around 4000 clients. As it grows it achieves economies of scale, and profit margins increase. It has been achieving success in renewing or extending the contracts of its leading clients. In June 2021 it announced a five-year contract renewal with its largest client, the Department of Defence. It has announced a new strategic plan, named Smart Future, aimed at boosting annual EBITDA by $15 million to $20 million from 2024. This involves spending $5 million to $6 million per year over three years to redesign client and customer portals, migrating to cloud infrastructure and software and investing in business automation and enhanced data analytics capability. The company is also working to boost cross-selling of its various products among existing clients. In addition, it sees a great opportunity among the 1.2 million to 1.5 million employees of its current clients. Though most of these employees own cars, only 66 000 are using novated leases, and Smartgroup has initiated a scheme to target them as potential customers for this business.

Year to 31 December	2019	2020
Revenues ($mn)	249.8	216.3
EBIT ($mn)	91.7	64.2
EBIT margin (%)	36.7	29.7
Profit before tax ($mn)	88.7	61.5
Profit after tax ($mn)	61.4	41.3
Earnings per share (c)	47.58	31.88
Cash flow per share (c)	67.10	51.39
Dividend (c)	43	34.5
Percentage franked	100	100
Interest cover (times)	30.4	23.9
Return on equity (%)	21.6	15.1
Half year to 30 June	2020	2021
Revenues ($mn)	111.4	109.4
Profit before tax ($mn)	33.0	40.2
Profit after tax ($mn)	22.9	27.9
Earnings per share (c)	19.60	20.50
Dividend (c)	17	17.5
Percentage franked	100	100
Net tangible assets per share ($)	~	~
Debt-to-equity ratio (%)	4.8	1.7
Current ratio	1.5	0.9

nic Healthcare Limited

code: SHL   www.sonichealthcare.com

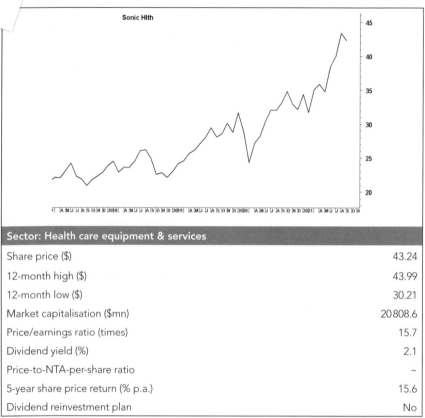

Sector: Health care equipment & services	
Share price ($)	43.24
12-month high ($)	43.99
12-month low ($)	30.21
Market capitalisation ($mn)	20808.6
Price/earnings ratio (times)	15.7
Dividend yield (%)	2.1
Price-to-NTA-per-share ratio	~
5-year share price return (% p.a.)	15.6
Dividend reinvestment plan	No

Sydney-based Sonic Healthcare has its roots in the pathology practice of Douglass Laboratories, which it acquired in 1987. It has since expanded significantly through acquisition and organic growth, and now operates through numerous separate companies. It has become Australia's largest private provider of pathology services and second-largest provider of radiology services. It is also now the world's third-largest pathology services provider, with services to medical practitioners, hospitals, community medical services and their patients in the United States, Germany, Switzerland, Belgium, the United Kingdom and New Zealand. Its Sonic Clinical Services division operates 222 medical centres in Australia, including the Independent Practitioner Network group of medical practices and Sonic HealthPlus occupational health clinics.

Latest business results (June 2021, full year)

Sonic has become a major beneficiary of the COVID-19 pandemic as its laboratories have been called upon to undertake COVID-related testing. Soring revenues and profits would have been even stronger but for the impact of a rising dollar during the year.

Underlying business grew by just 6 per cent, but, due to COVID testing, total revenues jumped 34 per cent on a constant currency basis, with particular strength in Europe and North America, and a major increase in profit margins. Germany has now overtaken Australia as Sonic's second-strongest country, after the US, for its pathology activities. The company's imaging unit was also strong, thanks to investments in new clinics and the acquisition of a majority interest — moving from 40 per cent to 80 per cent — in Melbourne-based Epworth Medical Imaging. The relatively small Sonic Clinical Services business saw revenues decline, largely due to the impact of the pandemic.

Outlook

Sonic saw a slowdown in demand for COVID testing in the second half of the June 2021 year, but strong demand began to revive again with the spread of the Delta variant, and the company expects significant COVID testing revenues to continue into the foreseeable future. It continues to work at building its pathology businesses. It achieved sustained success through its drive to consolidate the once-fragmented Australian pathology industry, and is now doing the same abroad. It has become the market leader in Germany, Switzerland and Britain, and one of the leaders in Belgium and the United States. Thanks to strong profit growth it has made a substantial reduction in its debt levels, and it has declared that it is now seeking further major acquisition opportunities. Its acquisition in September 2021 of Canberra Imaging Group and the opening of five new centres will boost imaging revenues.

Year to 30 June	2020	2021
Revenues ($mn)	6831.8	8754.1
Laboratory — Europe (%)	36	40
Laboratory — USA (%)	27	26
Laboratory — Australia/NZ (%)	23	23
Imaging — Australia (%)	8	7
EBIT ($mn)	803.1	1918.5
EBIT margin (%)	11.8	21.9
Profit before tax ($mn)	695.8	1828.6
Profit after tax ($mn)	527.7	1315.0
Earnings per share (c)	111.15	275.47
Cash flow per share (c)	225.01	409.87
Dividend (c)	85	91
Percentage franked	30	51
Net tangible assets per share ($)	~	~
Interest cover (times)	7.5	21.3
Return on equity (%)	9.6	22.0
Debt-to-equity ratio (%)	35.4	14.2
Current ratio	1.2	1.0

Steadfast Group Limited

ASX code: SDF   www.steadfast.com.au

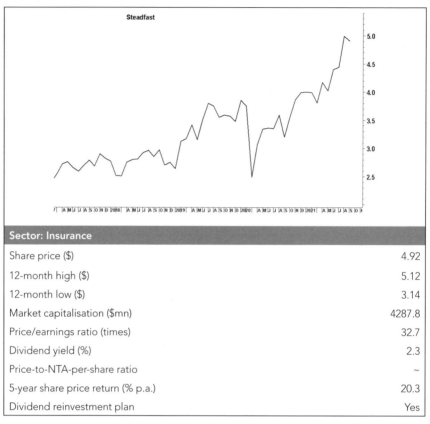

Sector: Insurance	
Share price ($)	4.92
12-month high ($)	5.12
12-month low ($)	3.14
Market capitalisation ($mn)	4287.8
Price/earnings ratio (times)	32.7
Dividend yield (%)	2.3
Price-to-NTA-per-share ratio	~
5-year share price return (% p.a.)	20.3
Dividend reinvestment plan	Yes

Melbourne-based insurance broking firm Steadfast launched in 1996 with the aim of boosting the buying power of small independent general insurance brokers in their dealings with insurers. It has since grown to become the largest insurance broker network and underwriting group in Australasia, with further operations in Asia and Europe. It also manages a range of complementary businesses that include back office services, risk services guidance, work health consultancy, reinsurance and legal advice. It has taken a 60 per cent stake in unisonSteadfast, one of the world's largest networks of general insurance brokers. In August 2021 it acquired insurance broking firm Coverforce.

Latest business results (June 2021, full year)

Steadfast enjoyed a good year, with solid rises in revenues and profits. Its core Steadfast Broking business recorded gross written premium of $9.8 billion, up 18.3 per cent from the previous year, with a particular benefit from price increases implemented during the year as well as from acquisitions. Cost savings helped boost margins. The Steadfast Underwriting Agencies business generated gross written premium of $1.5 billion, up 11.5 per cent, with market share growth and price rises contributing to rising profit margins. At June 2021 Steadfast incorporated a network of 386 brokerages in Australia, 52 in New Zealand and 19 in Singapore. It had equity holdings in 59 of the brokerages.

Outlook

Steadfast is involved in an assortment of initiatives aimed at ensuring long-term growth. Coverforce, which it has acquired for $411.5 million, was one of Australia's largest privately owned insurance brokerages, with a focus on small and medium-sized businesses. It is expected to deliver a substantial boost to business, including significant cost synergies. The company has raised its holding in unisonSteadfast from 40 per cent to a majority 60 per cent. This business encompasses a network of 264 insurance brokerages in 140 countries. Steadfast has also formed a partnership with London-based Howden Group, supporting both Steadfast's British activities and Howden's new Australian operations, which have become a part of the Steadfast network. The company is involved in a series of technology initiatives, including its fast-growing Steadfast Client Trading Platform, and Steadfast Accelerate, which provides automated processes to its network, with significant efficiency gains. Steadfast has a particular expertise in high-margin niche insurance products, with 24 specialist agencies now offering more than 100 niche products. The company's early forecast is for a June 2022 after-tax profit of $159 million to $166 million and earnings per share growth of 10 per cent to 15 per cent.

Year to 30 June	2020	2021
Revenues ($mn)	826.3	899.9
EBIT ($mn)	165.2	205.1
EBIT margin (%)	20.0	22.8
Profit before tax ($mn)	157.0	194.9
Profit after tax ($mn)	108.7	130.7
Earnings per share (c)	12.68	15.06
Cash flow per share (c)	18.99	22.07
Dividend (c)	9.6	11.4
Percentage franked	100	100
Net tangible assets per share ($)	0.01	~
Interest cover (times)	20.2	20.1
Return on equity (%)	10.2	11.5
Debt-to-equity ratio (%)	9.2	39.0
Current ratio	1.2	1.6

Super Retail Group Limited

ASX code: SUL

www.superretailgroup.com.au

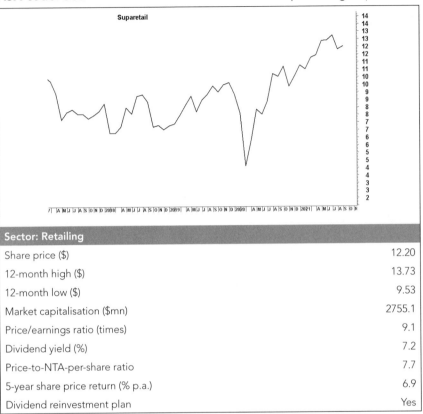

Suparetail

Sector: Retailing	
Share price ($)	12.20
12-month high ($)	13.73
12-month low ($)	9.53
Market capitalisation ($mn)	2755.1
Price/earnings ratio (times)	9.1
Dividend yield (%)	7.2
Price-to-NTA-per-share ratio	7.7
5-year share price return (% p.a.)	6.9
Dividend reinvestment plan	Yes

Specialist retail chain Super Retail Group was established as a mail-order business in 1972 and has its headquarters in Strathpine, Queensland. It now comprises a number of key retail brands, with nearly 700 stores throughout Australia and New Zealand. Supercheap Auto is a retailer of automotive spare parts and related products. Rebel is a prominent sporting goods chain. BCF is a retailer of boating, camping and fishing products. Macpac is an outdoor adventure and activity specialist retailer.

Latest business results (June 2021, full year)

Super Retail enjoyed an excellent year, with strong growth in sales and a surge in profits. The best result came from BCF, with sales up 49 per cent and the pre-tax profit rising nearly sixfold, as domestic tourism and levels of leisure activity rose significantly. There was particularly buoyant demand for camping, caravan, barbecue and water sports equipment. The Macpac division was another beneficiary of the outdoor activity trend, with strong sales of tents, sleeping bags and camping accessories. Supercheap Auto recorded 17 per cent sales growth, with the pre-tax profit up 49 per cent, and solid demand for accessories and car-care products. Rebel benefited from continuing strong sales of home fitness equipment. Total company online sales grew 43 per cent to $416 million.

Outlook

Having restructured its operations, including the 2018 acquisition of Macpac, Super Retail now controls four prominent brands with strong positions in their respective markets. It is working to build these businesses with a variety of strategies. It plans a steady rollout of new stores. It is also boosting its digital capacity, and expects online sales to continue their strong growth. It is increasing its range of higher-margin own-brand and exclusive products at its stores, and is harnessing customer loyalty through the promotion of members' clubs. The company believes that it stands to be a significant beneficiary of a post-pandemic world, as Australian consumers, unable or unwilling to travel abroad, boost spending on domestic leisure and recreation. The company also benefits from rising demand for health and wellbeing products and services. Nevertheless, despite Super Retail's strengths, it operates in a challenging retail environment, with online businesses like Amazon competing for many of its products. With much of its product range imported, it is also vulnerable to both currency fluctuations and supply-chain disruptions. In addition, it reported in August 2021 that lockdowns in several states had forced the temporary closure of many stores, putting a dent in business.

Year to 26 June*	2020	2021
Revenues ($mn)	2825.2	3453.1
Supercheap Auto (%)	39	38
Rebel (%)	37	35
BCF (%)	19	23
Macpac (%)	5	4
EBIT ($mn)	273.4	468.6
EBIT margin (%)	9.7	13.6
Gross margin (%)	45.0	48.0
Profit before tax ($mn)	218.3	427.6
Profit after tax ($mn)	154.1	301.0
Earnings per share (c)	77.98	133.44
Cash flow per share (c)	213.70	266.16
Dividend (c)	19.5	88
Percentage franked	100	100
Net tangible assets per share ($)	0.53	1.59
Interest cover (times)	5.0	11.4
Return on equity (%)	17.1	27.1
Debt-to-equity ratio (%)	~	~
Current ratio	1.1	1.1

*27 June 2020

Supply Network Limited

ASX code: SNL   www.supplynetwork.com.au

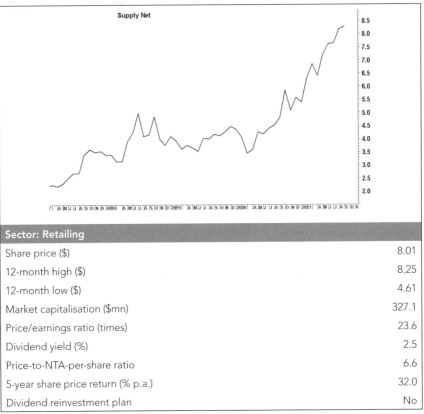

Supply Net

Sector: Retailing	
Share price ($)	8.01
12-month high ($)	8.25
12-month low ($)	4.61
Market capitalisation ($mn)	327.1
Price/earnings ratio (times)	23.6
Dividend yield (%)	2.5
Price-to-NTA-per-share ratio	6.6
5-year share price return (% p.a.)	32.0
Dividend reinvestment plan	No

Sydney-based Supply Network is a supplier of bus and truck parts in the commercial vehicle aftermarket, operating under the brand name Multispares, which was established in 1976. It manages offices, distribution centres and workshops at 18 locations throughout Australia and five in New Zealand.

Latest business results (June 2021, full year)

A rebound in business activities in Australia and New Zealand during the year helped Supply Network to a solid rise in revenues and profits, with strength across all regions of operation. The good result came despite some supply disruptions and other pandemic-related issues, including the closing of state borders, which placed some restrictions on bus and truck travel. In addition, the collapse of inbound tourism greatly curtailed long-distance coach movements. Nevertheless, the company was able to increase its bus-related sales in several important niche categories and the overall bus business held steady. However, in recent years the company has been investing heavily in its truck parts business, and this provided most of the growth. New Zealand revenues — about 19 per cent of the total — grew by 22 per cent, but profits there edged down. The company opened a new branch in Milperra, Sydney, to service the southern Sydney suburbs, and another in Townsville.

Outlook

Supply Network is one of the leaders in the Australian market for the supply of truck and bus parts. With a great diversity of vehicle makes and models, and with a considerable difference in requirements between various regions of the country, the company has established a decentralised management structure with a strong regional focus. Its core activity in recent years has become the supply of truck components, and this now represents more than 80 per cent of total income. Company fleets are the largest customer group, and these are sophisticated buyers of parts with a focus on costs, making this business highly competitive. Independent repair workshops are the next-largest customer group. The company is a beneficiary of the increasing complexity of trucks, which require an ever-growing range of expensive components. It has built up its stock and has added new systems for early identification of stock shortages, but it expects supply disruptions to continue for one to two years. The company has already surpassed its long-term target of $150 million in sales in the June 2022 year, and has launched a new three-year plan, expecting revenue growth of at least 10 per cent in the June 2022 year and with a goal of $200 million in revenues in June 2024.

Year to 30 June	2020	2021
Revenues ($mn)	136.8	162.6
EBIT ($mn)	15.3	21.1
EBIT margin (%)	11.2	13.0
Profit before tax ($mn)	13.6	19.7
Profit after tax ($mn)	9.5	13.8
Earnings per share (c)	23.42	33.91
Cash flow per share (c)	37.36	48.39
Dividend (c)	15.5	20
Percentage franked	100	100
Net tangible assets per share ($)	1.04	1.21
Interest cover (times)	9.0	14.9
Return on equity (%)	23.7	30.2
Debt-to-equity ratio (%)	18.8	7.1
Current ratio	2.4	2.4

›logy One Limited

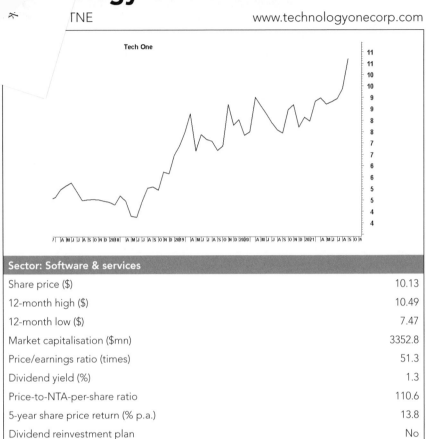

Sector: Software & services	
Share price ($)	10.13
12-month high ($)	10.49
12-month low ($)	7.47
Market capitalisation ($mn)	3352.8
Price/earnings ratio (times)	51.3
Dividend yield (%)	1.3
Price-to-NTA-per-share ratio	110.6
5-year share price return (% p.a.)	13.8
Dividend reinvestment plan	No

Brisbane-based Technology One, founded in 1987, designs, develops, implements and supports a wide range of financial management, accounting and business software. It enjoys particular strength in local government. Its software is also used by educational institutions, including many Australian universities. Other key markets are financial services, central government, and health and community services. It derives revenues not only from the supply of its products but also from annual licence fees. It operates from offices in Australia, New Zealand, Malaysia and the UK. It has opened research and development centres in Indonesia and Vietnam.

Latest business results (March 2021, half year)

Technology One enjoyed an excellent result, with a strong gain in profits. Once again the company enjoyed success in moving its customers onto its Software as a Service (SaaS) cloud platforms. The number of large-scale enterprise SaaS customers rose to 576, up from 475 a year earlier. SaaS annual recurring revenue saw a 41 per cent jump from a year before. Consulting services — essentially the business of implementing the company's software, and representing about 20 per cent of company turnover — saw flat revenues, though with a solid rise in profits. British operations moved from loss to a small profit. There was a noteworthy 5 per cent decline in costs, largely reflecting a big drop in the wage bill. The company maintained its high level of research and development spending, up 14 per cent to $34.6 million.

Outlook

Technology One has become a star among Australian high-tech companies, with growing profits and regular dividend increases. In large part this reflects a strong product line, a solid flow of recurring income, a 99 per cent customer retention rate and a heavy investment in new products and services. It is achieving great success with its SaaS offerings, which put software in the cloud, rather than on the customers' own computers, meaning that the customers always have the latest software versions, and giving them greater flexibility than previously. Among recent successes, a new procurement framework in New Zealand will see more than 20 government agencies there transition to its SaaS products. It also sees considerable growth opportunities in the United Kingdom. Technology One expects that as it achieves increasing economies of scale in its operations its profit margins will continue to expand. It currently receives around $233 million in annual recurring revenues for its SaaS business, and it expects this to grow to more than $500 million by September 2026.

Year to 30 September	2019	2020
Revenues ($mn)	285.0	298.3
EBIT ($mn)	75.8	83.6
EBIT margin (%)	26.6	28.0
Profit before tax ($mn)	76.4	82.5
Profit after tax ($mn)	58.5	62.9
Earnings per share (c)	18.43	19.75
Cash flow per share (c)	20.36	25.60
Dividend (c)	11.93	12.88
Percentage franked	64	60
Interest cover (times)	~	73.2
Return on equity (%)	63.4	50.6
Half year to 31 March	2020	2021
Revenues ($mn)	138.0	144.3
Profit before tax ($mn)	25.9	37.3
Profit after tax ($mn)	19.1	28.2
Earnings per share (c)	5.98	8.80
Dividend (c)	3.47	3.82
Percentage franked	60	60
Net tangible assets per share ($)	0.04	0.09
Debt-to-equity ratio (%)	~	~
Current ratio	0.9	1.0

Virtus Health Limited

ASX code: VRT

www.virtushealth.com.au

Sector: Health care equipment & services	
Share price ($)	6.42
12-month high ($)	7.47
12-month low ($)	3.39
Market capitalisation ($mn)	545.7
Price/earnings ratio (times)	14.2
Dividend yield (%)	3.7
Price-to-NTA-per-share ratio	~
5-year share price return (% p.a.)	0.9
Dividend reinvestment plan	No

Fertility clinic specialist Virtus Health, based in Sydney, was founded in 2002 from the amalgamation of four Sydney IVF (in-vitro fertilisation) practices. It has since joined in partnership with more businesses, and today operates a network of 37 fertility clinics in New South Wales, Victoria, Queensland and Tasmania, and has also expanded abroad, to the United Kingdom, Ireland, Denmark and Singapore. In addition, it has moved into other medical sectors, including the provision of a range of patient diagnostic services and day hospital procedures.

Latest business results (June 2021, full year)

Virtus rebounded strongly from the previous year, when bans on elective surgery and other pandemic-related restrictions had put a dent in its operations. Australia represents about 80 per cent of total income and revenues rose 24 per cent, with EBITDA up 30 per cent. This was largely due to the resumption of elective surgery at many hospitals. However, the company also noted a change in consumer behaviour, with a new focus on home and family during the pandemic appearing to boost demand for the company's reproductive services. Day hospitals performed especially well, with a 41 per cent jump in revenues and a noteworthy increase in non-IVF procedures, which rose to represent 45 per cent of day hospital business. International business was also strong, with each of the four countries reporting double-digit increases in revenues, and with total international EBITDA up 68 per cent. Nevertheless, domestic profit margins remained significantly higher than those abroad.

Outlook

Virtus is well regarded for its fertility services in Australia with high market shares. It expects demand for reproductive services to remain strong. However, the entry to this market of more low-cost service providers has intensified competition, and continuing COVID outbreaks in different parts of the country have led to the deferral of some procedures and rising costs. The company has been engaged in a major restructuring of its day hospitals, leading to improvements in operating efficiency and boosting June 2021 EBITDA by $3.8 million. It continues to work at building its network, with planned new clinic developments. In August 2021 it announced the $45 million acquisition from healthcare provider Healius of the Adora Fertility business and three day hospitals. This delivers four new IVF clinics to Virtus, including its first in Western Australia, and it raises the number of its day hospitals to 10. The company is also expanding capacity at its Danish and British operations. It sees the easing of travel restrictions as boosting Danish business.

Year to 30 June	2020	2021
Revenues ($mn)	258.9	324.6
EBIT ($mn)	33.9	60.2
EBIT margin (%)	13.1	18.6
Profit before tax ($mn)	23.1	51.3
Profit after tax ($mn)	15.2	36.3
Earnings per share (c)	18.98	45.33
Cash flow per share (c)	50.22	75.40
Dividend (c)	12	24
Percentage franked	100	100
Net tangible assets per share ($)	~	~
Interest cover (times)	3.1	6.8
Return on equity (%)	5.5	12.8
Debt-to-equity ratio (%)	47.0	35.6
Current ratio	0.6	0.7

Wesfarmers Limited

ASX code: WES www.wesfarmers.com.au

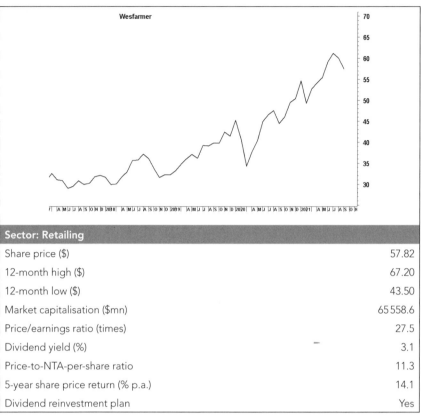

Sector: Retailing	
Share price ($)	57.82
12-month high ($)	67.20
12-month low ($)	43.50
Market capitalisation ($mn)	65 558.6
Price/earnings ratio (times)	27.5
Dividend yield (%)	3.1
Price-to-NTA-per-share ratio	11.3
5-year share price return (% p.a.)	14.1
Dividend reinvestment plan	Yes

Perth-based Wesfarmers, founded in 1914 as a farmers' cooperative, is now a conglomerate with many areas of operation. Having divested itself of its Coles supermarket operations, its primary business now is the Bunnings network of hardware stores. Other retail businesses include the Officeworks, Kmart and Target chains and the Catch online operation. In addition, it produces fertilisers, chemicals and industrial safety products. It has retained a 5 per cent equity stake in Coles, holds 50 per cent of the Flybuys loyalty card business, owns a 25 per cent interest in the ASX-listed BWP property trust — which owns many Bunnings warehouses — and holds half the equity in both the financial services business Gresham Partners and the timber business Wespine Industries. At June 2021 it operated 939 Bunnings, Kmart, Target and Officeworks stores throughout Australia and 73 Bunnings and Kmart stores in New Zealand.

Latest business results (June 2021, full year)

A solid retail performance drove another strong result for Wesfarmers. The core Bunnings operations enjoyed sales growth of 12.4 per cent, or 11.9 per cent on a same-store basis, with pre-tax profit up nearly 20 per cent. The good figures came despite an expenditure of an additional $27 million for COVID-related cleaning, security and protective equipment. The Kmart Group — incorporating Kmart, Target and Catch — achieved 8.3 per cent revenue growth, with profits jumping 69 per cent, though from a relatively low level, and margins remained substantially below those for Bunnings. Officeworks reported single-digit growth in sales and profits. Total group online sales reached $3.3 billion. Among its industrial businesses, the Chemicals, Energy and Fertilisers division recorded higher sales but a dip in profits. The Industrial and Safety division, a supplier of some personal protective equipment, achieved higher sales and profits.

Outlook

Wesfarmers has a variety of strategies for growth, although for the June 2022 year it is concerned about pandemic-related store closures. It also worries that supply shortages and shipping disruptions could affect stock availability. It is optimistic about the long-term outlook for Bunnings, driven by new stores, new sales categories, product innovation and the rollout of a full online offering. It is achieving a satisfying recovery in its Kmart Group, following the conversion of many Target stores to Kmart stores and the closure of others. The company's Covalent Lithium joint venture is set to begin construction of a mine and refinery in Western Australia with the goal of producing 45 000 tonnes annually of lithium hydroxide, for use in lithium batteries, from late 2024. It has made a takeover bid for Australian Pharmaceutical Industries.

Year to 30 June	2020	2021
Revenues ($mn)	30 846.0	33 941.0
Bunnings (%)	49	50
Kmart Group (%)	30	29
Industrials (%)	12	12
Officeworks (%)	9	9
EBIT ($mn)	3 179.0	3 706.0
EBIT margin (%)	10.3	10.9
Profit before tax ($mn)	2 819.0	3 373.0
Profit after tax ($mn)	2 083.0	2 380.0
Earnings per share (c)	184.17	210.43
Cash flow per share (c)	319.27	343.85
Dividend (c)	152	178
Percentage franked	100	100
Net tangible assets per share ($)	4.88	5.13
Interest cover (times)	8.8	11.1
Return on equity (%)	21.6	25.0
Debt-to-equity ratio (%)	~	~
Current ratio	1.1	1.1

PART II
THE TABLES

Table A
Market capitalisation

A company's market capitalisation is determined by multiplying the share price by the number of shares. To be included in this book, a company must be in the All Ordinaries Index, which comprises the 500 largest companies by market capitalisation.

	$mn
BHP	212090.6
Commonwealth Bank	179423.2
Rio Tinto	175904.4
CSL	138103.4
Wesfarmers	65558.6
Fortescue Metals	64315.7
Macquarie	61003.1
Aristocrat Leisure	29392.2
Sonic Healthcare	20808.6
REA	20612.9
Newcrest Mining	20083.5
Brambles	17438.2
ASX	16773.1
Cochlear	15288.1
Reece	13107.0
BlueScope Steel	12422.6
Mineral Resources	10351.1
Medibank Private	9776.7
IDP Education	8478.1
Magellan Financial	8015.3
Seven Group	7726.6
Carsales.com	7142.2
CIMIC	6712.6
Harvey Norman	6653.7
Evolution Mining	6629.6
Pro Medicus	6443.4
ALS	6189.5
Orica	5408.0
JB Hi-Fi	5172.0
Ansell	4613.3
Reliance Worldwide	4550.9
Breville	4522.5
Premier Investments	4440.2
Steadfast	4287.8
ARB	4192.5
Metcash	4150.8
Altium	4100.9
Technology One	3352.8
Orora	3017.9
NIB	3016.5
Pinnacle Investment	3016.1
Pendal	2828.3
IRESS	2795.6
Super Retail	2755.1
CSR	2727.9
Codan	2700.4
Bapcor	2464.1
Beach Energy	2463.8
Dicker Data	2437.6
Perpetual	2282.5
Platinum	2222.1
Credit Corp	2132.6
IPH	2024.3
Objective	1875.5
Elders	1862.4
Regis Resources	1802.4
AUB	1735.1
Collins Foods	1458.8
Costa	1275.2
Hansen Technologies	1227.1
Sandfire Resources	1217.5
Accent	1180.8
Australian Ethical Investment	1176.7
Smartgroup	1027.5
Monadelphous	1001.6
GUD	1000.2
Nick Scali	996.3
McMillan Shakespeare	995.9
Jumbo Interactive	954.8
Integral Diagnostics	885.9
SG Fleet	862.4
PWR	845.5
Data#3	820.7
Bravura Solutions	756.9
GWA	737.3
Money3	730.4
Baby Bunting	690.2
Austal	687.4
Grange Resources	682.8
Adairs	657.7
Infomedia	646.3
Virtus Health	545.7
Beacon Lighting	464.5
OFX	402.4
Pacific Smiles	384.6
Servcorp	329.2
Supply Network	327.1
Michael Hill	326.0
Schaffer	304.5
Clover	269.4
Fiducian	262.5

Table B
Revenues

This list ranks the companies in the book according to their most recent full-year revenues figures (operating income for the banks). The figures include revenues from sales and services, but other revenues — such as interest receipts and investment income — are not generally included.

	$mn
BHP	80 022.4
Rio Tinto	64 577.0
Wesfarmers	33 941.0
Fortescue Metals	29 321.1
Commonwealth Bank	24 156.0
Metcash	14 315.3
CSL	13 130.9
BlueScope Steel	12 872.9
Macquarie	12 774.0
CIMIC	9 004.2
JB Hi-Fi	8 916.1
Sonic Healthcare	8 754.1
Medibank Private	6 910.4
Brambles	6 855.0
Reece	6 270.7
Newcrest Mining	6 021.1
Orica	5 611.3
Seven Group	4 838.7
Harvey Norman	4 438.6
Aristocrat Leisure	4 139.1
Mineral Resources	3 733.6
Orora	3 538.0
Super Retail	3 453.1
Ansell	2 667.0
NIB	2 580.8
CSR	2 122.4
Elders	2 092.6
Dicker Data	1 998.8
Data#3	1 955.2
Evolution Mining	1 864.1
Bapcor	1 761.7
ALS	1 761.4
Monadelphous	1 754.2
Austal	1 572.2
Beach Energy	1 562.0
Cochlear	1 497.6
Reliance Worldwide	1 340.8
Premier Investments	1 216.3
Breville	1 187.7
Costa	1 164.9
Collins Foods	1 065.9
Accent	992.8
ASX	962.3
REA	927.8
Steadfast	899.9

Regis Resources	819.2
Sandfire Resources	813.0
Magellan Financial	665.5
Perpetual	640.6
ARB	623.1
GUD	557.0
Michael Hill	556.5
McMillan Shakespeare	544.2
IRESS	542.6
IDP Education	528.7
Grange Resources	526.3
Adairs	499.8
SG Fleet	481.6
Pendal	474.8
Baby Bunting	468.4
Carsales.com	437.8
Codan	437.0
GWA	405.7
Credit Corp	374.8
Nick Scali	373.0
IPH	359.7
Integral Diagnostics	350.7
Virtus Health	324.6
AUB	313.3
Hansen Technologies	307.7
Technology One	298.3
Beacon Lighting	289.3
Servcorp	269.7
Platinum	269.2
Bravura Solutions	242.3
Altium	237.1
Smartgroup	216.3
Schaffer	196.0
Supply Network	162.6
Pacific Smiles	153.2
Money3	145.1
OFX	134.2
Pinnacle Investment	98.9
Infomedia	97.4
Objective	95.1
Clover	88.3
Jumbo Interactive	83.3
PWR	79.2
Pro Medicus	67.9
Australian Ethical Investment	58.7
Fiducian	58.6

Table C

Year-on-year revenues growth

Companies generally strive for growth, though profit growth is usually of far more significance than a boost in revenues. In fact, it is possible for a company to increase its revenues by all kinds of means — including cutting profit margins or acquiring other companies — and year-on-year revenues growth is of little relevance if other ratios are not also improving. The figures used for this calculation are the latest full-year figures.

	%
Mineral Resources	75.7
Pinnacle Investment	63.9
Fortescue Metals	57.8
Grange Resources	42.8
Nick Scali	42.1
Objective	35.7
ARB	33.9
Perpetual	30.6
Elders	28.7
BHP	28.6
Adairs	28.5
Sonic Healthcare	28.1
Integral Diagnostics	27.3
GUD	27.2
Pacific Smiles	27.1
Schaffer	26.4
Codan	25.6
Virtus Health	25.4
Harvey Norman	25.2
Breville	24.7
Sandfire Resources	23.8
Super Retail	22.2
PWR	20.5
Bapcor	20.4
Data#3	20.4
Accent	19.6
Credit Corp	19.6
Pro Medicus	19.5
Supply Network	18.8
Monadelphous	17.8
Australian Ethical Investment	17.7
Jumbo Interactive	17.1
Money3	17.0
Baby Bunting	15.6
Reliance Worldwide	15.3
Beacon Lighting	15.2
Clover	15.1
BlueScope Steel	14.1
Ansell	14.0
Dicker Data	13.7
REA	13.1
Michael Hill	13.1
Costa	13.0
JB Hi-Fi	12.6
Collins Foods	11.9

Cochlear	10.7
McMillan Shakespeare	10.4
Wesfarmers	10.0
Metcash	9.9
Steadfast	8.9
Regis Resources	8.4
Fiducian	7.2
SG Fleet	6.6
IRESS	6.6
Seven Group	6.1
Newcrest Mining	5.9
Rio Tinto	4.7
Technology One	4.7
NIB	4.4
Reece	4.3
Carsales.com	3.8
Macquarie	3.6
AUB	3.3
CSL	3.0
Infomedia	3.0
Hansen Technologies	2.1
Medibank Private	2.1
GWA	1.8
Commonwealth Bank	1.7
ASX	1.4
Brambles	−0.1
Orora	−0.8
Magellan Financial	−1.1
IPH	−1.6
OFX	−2.2
Altium	−3.4
Pendal	−3.4
ALS	−3.8
Evolution Mining	−4.0
CSR	−4.1
Premier Investments	−4.3
Orica	−4.5
Platinum	−5.5
Aristocrat Leisure	−5.9
Beach Energy	−9.6
IDP Education	−9.9
Bravura Solutions	−11.0
Smartgroup	−13.4
CIMIC	−16.7
Servcorp	−22.8
Austal	−24.6

Table D
EBIT margin

A company's earnings before interest and taxation (EBIT) is sometimes regarded as a better measure of its profitability than the straight pre-tax or post-tax profit figure. EBIT is derived by adding net interest payments (that is, interest payments minus interest receipts) to the pre-tax profit. Different companies choose different methods of financing their operations; by adding back interest payments to their profits, we can help minimise these differences and make comparisons between companies more valid.

The EBIT margin is the EBIT figure as a percentage of annual sales. Clearly a high figure is to be desired, though of course this can be achieved artificially by inflating borrowings (and hence interest payments). And it is noteworthy that efficient companies with strong cashflow, like some of the retailers, can operate most satisfactorily on low margins.

The EBIT margin figure has little relevance for banks, and they have been excluded.

	%
Magellan Financial	88.5
Platinum	86.9
Pinnacle Investment	68.3
Fortescue Metals	67.1
ASX	66.6
Pro Medicus	62.9
REA	51.9
Carsales.com	51.9
Money3	51.7
BHP	49.9
Jumbo Interactive	46.9
Mineral Resources	44.0
Grange Resources	42.7
Rio Tinto	39.9
Newcrest Mining	38.7
Pendal	38.6
Credit Corp	35.2
Nick Scali	34.3
Beach Energy	33.5
Sandfire Resources	33.2
Schaffer	32.9
CSL	31.4
IPH	30.2
Codan	30.0
Smartgroup	29.7
PWR	28.9
AUB	28.8
Fiducian	28.5
Perpetual	28.3
Technology One	28.0
Harvey Norman	27.7
Evolution Mining	27.5
Altium	26.7
Australian Ethical Investment	26.4
Regis Resources	26.2
ARB	24.4
Hansen Technologies	24.3
Steadfast	22.8
McMillan Shakespeare	22.2
Cochlear	22.0
Sonic Healthcare	21.9
Reliance Worldwide	21.8
Objective	21.8
Clover	20.7
Beacon Lighting	20.6
Adairs	20.6
Infomedia	20.5
Virtus Health	18.6
GUD	18.2
SG Fleet	17.4
Premier Investments	17.2
ALS	17.1
Brambles	16.9
GWA	16.9
Bravura Solutions	16.8
Ansell	16.4
Seven Group	16.4
IRESS	15.9
Integral Diagnostics	15.4
Pacific Smiles	13.7
Super Retail	13.6
OFX	13.6
BlueScope Steel	13.4
Michael Hill	13.0
Supply Network	13.0
Accent	12.6
Aristocrat Leisure	12.1
IDP Education	12.1
Breville	11.5
Bapcor	11.4
Wesfarmers	10.9
Servcorp	10.9
Orica	10.8
CSR	10.5
NIB	9.2
Baby Bunting	9.0
Collins Foods	8.5
JB Hi-Fi	8.3
Costa	7.6
Reece	7.5
Medibank Private	7.5
Austal	7.3
Orora	7.0
CIMIC	6.7
Elders	5.1
Dicker Data	4.3
Monadelphous	4.2
Metcash	2.5
Data#3	1.9

Table E
Year-on-year EBIT margin growth

The EBIT (earnings before interest and taxation) margin is one of the measures of a company's efficiency. So a rising margin is much to be desired, as it suggests that a company is achieving success in cutting its costs. This table does not include banks.

	%		%
Michael Hill	354.7	Reece	9.3
BlueScope Steel	167.9	Rio Tinto	9.2
Grange Resources	108.3	McMillan Shakespeare	8.8
Sandfire Resources	91.6	Monadelphous	7.6
Hansen Technologies	91.0	Carsales.com	7.4
Sonic Healthcare	86.4	REA	7.3
NIB	76.5	Fiducian	6.7
Costa	68.8	Wesfarmers	5.9
Mineral Resources	63.6	AUB	5.7
Beacon Lighting	45.9	Technology One	5.4
Cochlear	44.1	Servcorp	4.9
ARB	42.2	Magellan Financial	4.3
Virtus Health	41.8	Brambles	4.2
Premier Investments	40.8	ALS	2.4
Super Retail	40.2	PWR	2.0
Harvey Norman	37.2	Australian Ethical Investment	1.6
Adairs	35.6	CSL	1.6
BHP	34.3	Seven Group	1.2
Reliance Worldwide	34.1	ASX	−0.7
Nick Scali	34.1	IPH	−0.8
SG Fleet	32.5	Integral Diagnostics	−2.5
Pacific Smiles	32.4	GUD	−2.7
Elders	29.8	Bravura Solutions	−2.7
JB Hi-Fi	29.1	Breville	−3.3
Pinnacle Investment	25.6	Perpetual	−3.3
Schaffer	25.3	Orica	−4.7
Fortescue Metals	24.4	Pendal	−5.5
Ansell	23.2	GWA	−6.4
Newcrest Mining	20.4	Collins Foods	−6.8
Pro Medicus	19.7	Dicker Data	−8.1
Codan	17.5	Data#3	−8.2
Austal	16.6	Evolution Mining	−8.8
Supply Network	16.0	CIMIC	−8.8
Medibank Private	15.6	Jumbo Interactive	−10.4
Bapcor	15.2	Altium	−11.2
Steadfast	14.0	Beach Energy	−11.3
Platinum	12.9	Credit Corp	−11.6
Orora	12.4	IRESS	−16.4
Metcash	11.9	Smartgroup	−19.2
Objective	11.5	Infomedia	−24.0
Clover	10.9	OFX	−30.2
CSR	10.8	Regis Resources	−30.8
Accent	10.2	IDP Education	−33.9
Baby Bunting	9.9	Aristocrat Leisure	−51.4
Money3	9.8		

Table F
After-tax profit

This table ranks all the companies according to their most recent full-year after-tax profit.

	$mn
BHP	22 469.7
Rio Tinto	18 019.0
Fortescue Metals	13 546.1
Commonwealth Bank	8 653.0
CSL	3 125.0
Macquarie	3 015.0
Wesfarmers	2 380.0
Newcrest Mining	1 531.6
Sonic Healthcare	1 315.0
BlueScope Steel	1 166.3
Mineral Resources	1 103.0
Harvey Norman	841.4
Brambles	703.9
JB Hi-Fi	506.1
Seven Group	501.4
ASX	480.9
Magellan Financial	412.7
Medibank Private	398.7
CIMIC	371.5
Beach Energy	363.0
Aristocrat Leisure	357.1
Evolution Mining	354.3
Ansell	324.6
REA	318.0
Super Retail	301.0
Orica	299.3
Reece	285.6
Metcash	252.7
Cochlear	236.7
Reliance Worldwide	211.9
Grange Resources	203.2
ALS	185.9
Sandfire Resources	171.6
Platinum	163.3
NIB	161.1
CSR	160.4
Orora	156.7
Carsales.com	152.8
Pendal	146.8
Regis Resources	146.2
Premier Investments	137.8
Steadfast	130.7
Bapcor	130.1
Perpetual	124.1
Elders	122.9

ARB	112.9
Codan	97.3
Breville	91.0
Credit Corp	88.1
Nick Scali	84.2
Austal	81.1
McMillan Shakespeare	79.2
Accent	76.9
IPH	76.2
Pinnacle Investment	67.0
AUB	65.3
GUD	64.0
Adairs	63.7
Technology One	62.9
Costa	60.8
IRESS	59.1
Hansen Technologies	57.3
Dicker Data	57.2
Collins Foods	56.9
SG Fleet	51.6
Monadelphous	47.1
Altium	46.4
Michael Hill	45.3
GWA	42.3
Smartgroup	41.3
IDP Education	39.7
Money3	39.2
Schaffer	38.8
Beacon Lighting	37.6
Virtus Health	36.3
Bravura Solutions	34.6
Integral Diagnostics	31.3
Pro Medicus	30.9
Jumbo Interactive	28.3
Baby Bunting	26.0
Data#3	25.4
Servcorp	23.6
PWR	16.8
Objective	16.1
Infomedia	16.0
Pacific Smiles	14.0
Supply Network	13.8
OFX	13.5
Clover	12.5
Fiducian	12.2
Australian Ethical Investment	11.1

Table G
Year-on-year earnings per share growth

The earnings per share (EPS) figure is a crucial one. It tells you — the shareholder — what your part is of the company's profits, for each of your shares. So investors invariably look for EPS growth in a stock. The year-on-year EPS growth figure is often one of the first ratios that investors look to when evaluating a stock. The figures used for this calculation are the latest full-year figures.

	%
Michael Hill	1381.2
BlueScope Steel	232.8
Mineral Resources	229.7
Grange Resources	162.7
Sonic Healthcare	147.8
Virtus Health	138.8
Sandfire Resources	124.6
Hansen Technologies	117.7
Pinnacle Investment	102.0
Nick Scali	100.2
Fortescue Metals	97.4
ARB	94.9
Costa	87.7
Beacon Lighting	82.7
Adairs	79.5
NIB	78.4
Harvey Norman	72.3
BHP	71.1
Super Retail	71.1
Pacific Smiles	69.5
Schaffer	65.7
Reliance Worldwide	62.6
Altium	61.9
JB Hi-Fi	52.3
Codan	51.3
Objective	45.0
Supply Network	44.8
Ansell	43.9
Elders	40.1
Accent	37.8
SG Fleet	36.6
Cochlear	35.2
Newcrest Mining	33.9
Pro Medicus	33.3
Baby Bunting	33.3
Premier Investments	28.7
PWR	28.6
Monadelphous	28.6
Orora	28.4
Integral Diagnostics	27.1
Bapcor	26.3
Clover	22.8
Rio Tinto	22.5
AUB	21.4
CSR	21.1
Money3	20.3
GUD	19.8
Steadfast	18.7
Commonwealth Bank	18.4
Collins Foods	18.3
Australian Ethical Investment	18.3
REA	18.1
McMillan Shakespeare	17.1
Fiducian	16.4
Breville	14.9
Wesfarmers	14.3
Metcash	13.3
Reece	10.8
Carsales.com	9.1
Medibank Private	8.5
Data#3	7.5
Technology One	7.2
Jumbo Interactive	6.9
Brambles	6.9
Macquarie	6.3
Perpetual	5.6
Seven Group	5.4
Platinum	5.3
CSL	2.3
Dicker Data	1.0
Credit Corp	−0.2
ALS	−1.4
ASX	−3.6
IPH	−3.9
GWA	−5.8
Magellan Financial	−6.8
Austal	−9.7
Pendal	−12.9
Evolution Mining	−12.9
IRESS	−14.8
Bravura Solutions	−14.9
Beach Energy	−21.3
Orica	−22.7
Servcorp	−22.9
Infomedia	−25.1
Regis Resources	−32.8
Smartgroup	−33.0
CIMIC	−36.4
OFX	−37.2
IDP Education	−45.5
Aristocrat Leisure	−52.6

Table H
Return on equity

Shareholders' equity is the company's assets minus its liabilities. It is, in theory, the amount owned by the shareholders of the company. Return on equity is the after-tax profit expressed as a percentage of that equity. Thus, it is the amount of profit that the company managers made for you — the shareholder — from your assets. For many investors it is one of the most important gauges of how well a company is doing. It is one of the requirements for inclusion in this book that all companies have a return on equity of at least 10 per cent in their latest financial year.

	%
Nick Scali	88.9
Fortescue Metals	63.3
Technology One	50.6
Platinum	49.4
CIMIC	49.3
Australian Ethical Investment	49.1
Data#3	46.8
Dicker Data	44.6
Pro Medicus	43.5
JB Hi-Fi	41.9
Adairs	41.8
Magellan Financial	40.5
Mineral Resources	40.3
Objective	39.1
Beacon Lighting	37.8
Codan	35.3
Jumbo Interactive	34.5
REA	32.9
Grange Resources	32.7
BHP	32.6
McMillan Shakespeare	31.8
Pinnacle Investment	31.0
CSL	30.3
Rio Tinto	30.3
Supply Network	30.2
Schaffer	30.2
Fiducian	30.1
Pacific Smiles	28.6
PWR	28.4
Super Retail	27.1
ARB	26.3
Michael Hill	26.1
Baby Bunting	25.9
NIB	25.2
Wesfarmers	25.0
Carsales.com	24.9
Clover	24.3
Harvey Norman	23.0
Sonic Healthcare	22.0
Medibank Private	21.5
Hansen Technologies	21.2
Elders	21.1
Sandfire Resources	20.7
Breville	19.7
GUD	19.3

Metcash	19.2
Brambles	18.6
Accent	18.4
IPH	17.9
Orora	17.4
OFX	17.2
ALS	17.1
BlueScope Steel	16.5
Pendal	16.3
Ansell	15.9
SG Fleet	15.9
Perpetual	15.8
Collins Foods	15.8
Altium	15.3
Cochlear	15.3
Smartgroup	15.1
CSR	14.7
GWA	14.7
Seven Group	14.5
AUB	14.4
Evolution Mining	14.2
Reliance Worldwide	14.1
Macquarie	14.0
Credit Corp	14.0
Aristocrat Leisure	13.4
Money3	13.4
Integral Diagnostics	12.9
ASX	12.9
Bapcor	12.9
Virtus Health	12.8
Beach Energy	12.3
Regis Resources	12.1
Monadelphous	12.1
Newcrest Mining	11.8
IRESS	11.6
Commonwealth Bank	11.5
Steadfast	11.5
Servcorp	11.2
Bravura Solutions	10.8
Austal	10.6
Costa	10.6
Infomedia	10.4
IDP Education	10.3
Premier Investments	10.2
Reece	10.1
Orica	10.0

Table I
Year-on-year return on equity growth

Company managers have a variety of strategies they can use to boost profits. It is much harder to lift the return on equity (ROE). Find a company with a high ROE figure, and one that is growing year by year, and it is possible that you have found a real growth stock. This figure is simply the percentage change in the ROE figure from the previous year to the latest year.

	%
Michael Hill	1310.7
BlueScope Steel	212.6
Virtus Health	132.5
Sonic Healthcare	128.9
Mineral Resources	119.0
Grange Resources	113.5
Hansen Technologies	102.8
Costa	99.7
Sandfire Resources	89.0
Orora	84.0
Pinnacle Investment	75.1
BHP	70.2
Nick Scali	69.7
NIB	68.7
ARB	65.1
Super Retail	59.2
Harvey Norman	58.4
Fortescue Metals	58.2
Beacon Lighting	57.8
Adairs	53.2
Reliance Worldwide	52.6
Altium	41.6
Schaffer	41.4
Ansell	39.7
McMillan Shakespeare	38.3
Pacific Smiles	37.7
JB Hi-Fi	35.5
Accent	34.0
Premier Investments	28.9
Monadelphous	28.6
Supply Network	27.6
Codan	26.9
Brambles	26.7
Newcrest Mining	26.3
Metcash	25.2
Baby Bunting	24.6
Rio Tinto	22.9
Bapcor	22.8
Elders	22.5
CSR	22.2
CIMIC	21.3
SG Fleet	19.2
PWR	16.8
Collins Foods	16.3
Objective	16.1

Wesfarmers	15.8
AUB	13.8
Steadfast	12.7
Commonwealth Bank	11.5
Medibank Private	9.9
REA	8.2
Money3	7.9
Perpetual	5.8
Cochlear	5.5
Reece	4.9
Fiducian	4.8
GUD	4.8
Pro Medicus	3.2
Jumbo Interactive	1.9
Platinum	1.6
Clover	0.2
Australian Ethical Investment	0.1
Integral Diagnostics	−0.1
Macquarie	−0.6
ASX	−1.2
ALS	−1.3
Data#3	−1.6
Breville	−3.0
Credit Corp	−7.1
GWA	−7.4
Pendal	−10.3
Seven Group	−11.9
Evolution Mining	−14.8
CSL	−15.2
Servcorp	−16.0
Austal	−17.5
Magellan Financial	−17.7
IPH	−18.3
Bravura Solutions	−19.0
Technology One	−20.3
Orica	−21.1
IRESS	−24.2
Dicker Data	−28.2
Smartgroup	−30.1
Beach Energy	−30.7
Infomedia	−38.9
OFX	−41.6
Carsales.com	−46.1
Regis Resources	−53.0
IDP Education	−58.6
Aristocrat Leisure	−65.5

Table J
Debt-to-equity ratio

A company's borrowings as a percentage of its shareholders' equity is one of the most common measures of corporate debt. Many investors will be wary of a company with a ratio that is too high. However, a company with a steady business and a regular income flow — such as an electric power company or a large supermarket chain — is generally considered relatively safe with a high level of debt, whereas a small company in a new business field might be thought at risk with even moderate debt levels. Much depends on surrounding circumstances, including the prevailing interest rates. Of course, it is often from borrowing that a company grows, and some investors are not happy buying shares in a company with little or no debt.

There are various ways to calculate the ratio, but for this book the net debt position is used. That is, a company's cash has been deducted from its borrowings. For inclusion in this book no company was allowed a debt-to-equity ratio of more than 70 per cent. Some of the companies had no net debt — their cash position was greater than the amount of their borrowings — and so have been assigned a zero figure in this table. The ratio has no relevance for banks, and they have been excluded.

	%				
Adairs	0.0	Newcrest Mining	0.0	Ansell	13.5
Altium	0.0	Nick Scali	0.0	Sonic Healthcare	14.2
ARB	0.0	Objective	0.0	Accent	15.6
ASX	0.0	OFX	0.0	Bapcor	15.8
Austal	0.0	Pacific Smiles	0.0	Reece	17.5
Australian Ethical Investment	0.0	Pendal	0.0	Evolution Mining	17.8
		Platinum	0.0	Perpetual	20.0
Baby Bunting	0.0	Premier Investments	0.0	Hansen Technologies	22.7
Beacon Lighting	0.0	Pro Medicus	0.0	AUB	22.7
BlueScope Steel	0.0	PWR	0.0	Schaffer	23.1
Bravura Solutions	0.0	Rio Tinto	0.0	Elders	23.5
Breville	0.0	Sandfire Resources	0.0	CIMIC	28.7
Carsales.com	0.0	Servcorp	0.0	REA	28.7
Cochlear	0.0	SG Fleet	0.0	IRESS	31.6
Credit Corp	0.0	Super Retail	0.0	Costa	32.0
CSR	0.0	Technology One	0.0	GWA	34.9
Data#3	0.0	Wesfarmers	0.0	Virtus Health	35.6
Fiducian	0.0	Codan	0.5	GUD	37.7
Fortescue Metals	0.0	Beach Energy	1.5	Steadfast	39.0
Grange Resources	0.0	Pinnacle Investment	1.6	CSL	47.7
IDP Education	0.0	Smartgroup	1.7	Collins Foods	48.4
Infomedia	0.0	NIB	2.6	Aristocrat Leisure	48.9
JB Hi-Fi	0.0	Regis Resources	3.2	Brambles	49.9
Jumbo Interactive	0.0	McMillan Shakespeare	6.8	Dicker Data	51.0
Magellan Financial	0.0	Clover	7.1	Integral Diagnostics	53.6
Medibank Private	0.0	Supply Network	7.1	Seven Group	55.9
Metcash	0.0	Harvey Norman	7.6	Orora	58.9
Michael Hill	0.0	BHP	10.3	Money3	61.1
Mineral Resources	0.0	Reliance Worldwide	10.9	Orica	63.2
Monadelphous	0.0	IPH	12.9	ALS	69.8

Table K
Current ratio

The current ratio is simply the company's current assets divided by its current liabilities. Current assets are cash or assets that can, in theory, be converted quickly into cash. Current liabilities are normally those payable within a year. The current ratio helps measure the ability of a company to repay in a hurry its short-term debt, should the need arise. Banks are not included.

Company	Ratio	Company	Ratio
Platinum	10.1	McMillan Shakespeare	1.7
Pinnacle Investment	8.4	Beach Energy	1.7
Clover	8.0	CSR	1.7
Credit Corp	5.6	GWA	1.7
Pro Medicus	5.0	BHP	1.6
Grange Resources	4.9	ALS	1.6
Infomedia	4.3	Steadfast	1.6
Carsales.com	4.2	Magellan Financial	1.6
Money3	3.8	Costa	1.5
Sandfire Resources	3.5	Harvey Norman	1.5
Cochlear	3.1	Beacon Lighting	1.4
ARB	3.0	Premier Investments	1.3
Newcrest Mining	3.0	Evolution Mining	1.3
Jumbo Interactive	2.9	IRESS	1.3
Fiducian	2.9	Perpetual	1.3
PWR	2.8	Elders	1.2
IPH	2.7	Orora	1.2
GUD	2.7	Baby Bunting	1.2
Aristocrat Leisure	2.6	Nick Scali	1.2
IDP Education	2.5	AUB	1.2
Australian Ethical Investment	2.4	Metcash	1.2
Altium	2.4	Wesfarmers	1.1
Supply Network	2.4	CIMIC	1.1
Reece	2.4	Dicker Data	1.1
CSL	2.4	Codan	1.1
Regis Resources	2.3	ASX	1.1
Fortescue Metals	2.3	Objective	1.1
Breville	2.2	JB Hi-Fi	1.1
Rio Tinto	2.1	Super Retail	1.1
Ansell	2.1	Integral Diagnostics	1.1
Mineral Resources	2.1	Data#3	1.1
Reliance Worldwide	2.0	Technology One	1.0
Schaffer	2.0	Seven Group	1.0
REA	2.0	Sonic Healthcare	1.0
NIB	1.9	Accent	0.9
Monadelphous	1.9	Smartgroup	0.9
Bapcor	1.9	Servcorp	0.9
BlueScope Steel	1.9	Collins Foods	0.8
Bravura Solutions	1.8	Hansen Technologies	0.7
Michael Hill	1.8	Brambles	0.7
Pendal	1.8	Virtus Health	0.7
Medibank Private	1.8	Adairs	0.7
Orica	1.7	Pacific Smiles	0.5
Austal	1.7		

Table L
Price/earnings ratio

The price/earnings ratio (PER) — the current share price divided by the earnings per share figure — is one of the best known of all sharemarket ratios. Essentially it expresses the amount of money investors are ready to pay for each cent or dollar of a company's profits, and it allows you to compare the share prices of different companies of varying sizes and with widely different profits. A high PER suggests the market has a high regard for the company and its growth prospects; a low one may mean that investors are disdainful of the stock. The figures in this table are based on share prices as of 2 September 2021.

Company	PER	Company	PER
Grange Resources	3.4	Monadelphous	21.3
Fortescue Metals	4.7	Hansen Technologies	21.3
Beach Energy	6.8	Reliance Worldwide	21.5
Sandfire Resources	7.1	Fiducian	21.6
Michael Hill	7.2	Clover	21.6
Schaffer	7.8	Bravura Solutions	21.8
Harvey Norman	7.9	Supply Network	23.6
Austal	8.5	Credit Corp	24.2
Regis Resources	9.1	Medibank Private	24.5
Super Retail	9.1	Smartgroup	24.7
Mineral Resources	9.4	Brambles	25.4
BHP	9.4	Collins Foods	25.6
Rio Tinto	9.8	IPH	26.4
JB Hi-Fi	10.2	Baby Bunting	26.4
Adairs	10.3	AUB	26.5
BlueScope Steel	10.6	Pacific Smiles	26.7
Nick Scali	11.8	Wesfarmers	27.5
Beacon Lighting	12.3	Codan	27.9
McMillan Shakespeare	12.6	Integral Diagnostics	28.2
Newcrest Mining	13.1	OFX	29.8
Platinum	13.6	Premier Investments	32.2
Servcorp	13.9	Data#3	32.3
Virtus Health	14.2	Steadfast	32.7
Ansell	14.3	ALS	33.3
Seven Group	14.6	Jumbo Interactive	33.7
Elders	14.9	ASX	34.9
GUD	15.1	ARB	36.7
SG Fleet	15.1	Infomedia	40.4
Accent	15.3	Carsales.com	41.2
Sonic Healthcare	15.7	Dicker Data	41.5
Metcash	16.4	CSL	44.2
CSR	17.0	Pinnacle Investment	44.2
GWA	17.3	IRESS	44.7
Pendal	17.4	Reece	45.9
Orica	17.6	Breville	49.5
Money3	17.6	PWR	50.3
Perpetual	18.2	Technology One	51.3
CIMIC	18.5	Cochlear	64.5
NIB	18.7	REA	64.7
Evolution Mining	18.7	Aristocrat Leisure	82.2
Bapcor	18.9	Altium	88.3
Macquarie	19.3	Australian Ethical Investment	104.7
Magellan Financial	19.4	Objective	116.2
Orora	20.1	Pro Medicus	208.8
Commonwealth Bank	20.7	IDP Education	213.6
Costa	21.0		

Table M
Price-to-NTA-per-share ratio

The NTA-per-share figure expresses the worth of a company's net tangible assets — that is, its assets minus its liabilities and intangible assets — for each share of the company. Intangible assets, such as goodwill or the value of newspaper mastheads, are excluded because it is deemed difficult to place a value on them (though this proposition is debatable), and also because they might not have much worth if separated from the company. The price-to-NTA-per-share ratio relates this figure to the share price.

A ratio of one means that the company is valued exactly according to the value of its assets. A ratio below one suggests that the shares are a bargain, though usually there is a good reason for this. Profits are more important than assets.

In some respects, this is an 'old economy' ratio. For many high-tech companies in the 'new economy' the most important assets are human ones whose worth does not appear on the balance sheet.

Companies with a negative NTA-per-share figure, as a result of having intangible assets valued at more than their net assets, have been omitted from this table.

Grange Resources	0.8	Super Retail	7.7
Beach Energy	0.8	NIB	8.3
Austal	0.9	Orora	8.4
Regis Resources	1.1	Bapcor	8.9
Sandfire Resources	1.3	Nick Scali	8.9
Newcrest Mining	1.5	Magellan Financial	9.1
Harvey Norman	1.8	Bravura Solutions	9.8
Servcorp	1.8	ARB	9.9
Michael Hill	2.0	Infomedia	10.3
BlueScope Steel	2.0	Fiducian	11.2
Schaffer	2.1	Wesfarmers	11.3
Money3	2.4	Cochlear	11.8
Commonwealth Bank	2.5	Reece	11.8
Monadelphous	2.6	Baby Bunting	11.9
CSR	2.6	Pinnacle Investment	12.4
Evolution Mining	2.6	Reliance Worldwide	12.8
Rio Tinto	2.7	ASX	14.3
Fortescue Metals	2.7	Altium	14.7
Macquarie	3.1	Breville	16.3
Seven Group	3.2	Dicker Data	17.2
BHP	3.2	PWR	17.2
Credit Corp	3.2	CSL	18.1
Costa	3.3	JB Hi-Fi	18.7
Mineral Resources	3.3	Data#3	20.3
Orica	4.0	Jumbo Interactive	20.8
Beacon Lighting	4.7	Carsales.com	20.9
Clover	5.0	Accent	21.0
Brambles	5.4	GUD	26.3
Elders	6.2	IDP Education	30.4
Medibank Private	6.3	Codan	35.3
OFX	6.4	Australian Ethical Investment	48.7
Platinum	6.5	Perpetual	54.7
Supply Network	6.6	REA	88.6
Premier Investments	6.9	Pro Medicus	104.5
Pendal	7.2	Technology One	110.6
Ansell	7.3	CIMIC	154.0
McMillan Shakespeare	7.4	Objective	164.4
Pacific Smiles	7.5	AUB	191.2
Metcash	7.5		

Table N
Dividend yield

Many investors buy shares for income, rather than for capital growth. They look for companies that offer a high dividend yield (the dividend expressed as a percentage of the share price). Table N ranks the companies in this book according to their historic dividend yields. Note that the franking credits available from most companies in this book can make the dividend yield substantially higher. The dividend yield changes with the share price. The figures in this table are based on share prices as of 2 September 2021.

	%
Fortescue Metals	17.1
BHP	9.6
Super Retail	7.2
Harvey Norman	6.6
JB Hi-Fi	6.4
Platinum	6.3
Adairs	5.9
Rio Tinto	5.7
GUD	5.4
Michael Hill	5.4
Servcorp	5.3
Nick Scali	5.3
Accent	5.2
Grange Resources	5.1
Mineral Resources	5.0
Sandfire Resources	5.0
Magellan Financial	4.8
McMillan Shakespeare	4.8
GWA	4.5
Perpetual	4.4
Smartgroup	4.4
SG Fleet	4.3
Metcash	4.3
Monadelphous	4.3
Pendal	4.2
Beacon Lighting	4.2
Austal	4.2
Orora	4.1
CSR	4.1
Schaffer	4.1
Virtus Health	3.7
NIB	3.6
Medibank Private	3.6
Commonwealth Bank	3.5
Fiducian	3.2
IRESS	3.2
IPH	3.2
Evolution Mining	3.1
Wesfarmers	3.1
Newcrest Mining	3.0
Regis Resources	2.9
Money3	2.9
Ansell	2.8
Costa	2.8
Data#3	2.8

Bravura Solutions	2.8
Integral Diagnostics	2.8
Macquarie	2.8
CIMIC	2.8
Bapcor	2.8
Baby Bunting	2.6
Infomedia	2.6
ASX	2.6
Premier Investments	2.5
Supply Network	2.5
Orica	2.5
Jumbo Interactive	2.4
AUB	2.4
Dicker Data	2.3
Steadfast	2.3
Credit Corp	2.3
Brambles	2.3
Reliance Worldwide	2.3
Seven Group	2.2
Sonic Healthcare	2.1
Carsales.com	1.9
Beach Energy	1.9
Elders	1.8
Collins Foods	1.8
Codan	1.8
ALS	1.8
Pinnacle Investment	1.7
Hansen Technologies	1.6
Clover	1.5
ARB	1.3
Altium	1.3
Technology One	1.3
BlueScope Steel	1.3
Cochlear	1.1
PWR	1.0
Pacific Smiles	1.0
CSL	1.0
Reece	0.9
REA	0.8
Breville	0.8
Australian Ethical Investment	0.7
Objective	0.5
OFX	0.5
IDP Education	0.3
Pro Medicus	0.2
Aristocrat Leisure	0.2

Table O
Year-on-year dividend growth

Most investors hope for a rising dividend, and this table tells how much each company raised or lowered its dividend in its latest financial year.

	%
Super Retail	351.3
Michael Hill	200.0
Mineral Resources	175.0
BHP	130.3
CSR	130.0
BlueScope Steel	121.4
Adairs	109.1
Newcrest Mining	105.6
Fortescue Metals	103.4
Credit Corp	100.0
Virtus Health	100.0
Harvey Norman	94.4
Pinnacle Investment	86.4
Reliance Worldwide	85.7
McMillan Shakespeare	80.3
Sandfire Resources	78.9
Beacon Lighting	76.0
ARB	72.2
NIB	71.4
Costa	63.6
Cochlear	59.4
GUD	54.1
JB Hi-Fi	51.9
Grange Resources	50.0
Reece	50.0
PWR	49.2
Codan	45.9
Australian Ethical Investment	40.0
Metcash	40.0
Ansell	39.8
Nick Scali	36.8
Baby Bunting	34.3
Integral Diagnostics	31.6
ALS	31.3
Supply Network	29.0
Monadelphous	28.6
Objective	28.6
SG Fleet	25.9
Hansen Technologies	25.0
Money3	25.0
Pro Medicus	25.0
Elders	22.2
Accent	21.6
REA	19.1
Steadfast	18.8

	%
Dicker Data	17.9
Commonwealth Bank	17.4
Wesfarmers	17.1
Fiducian	17.0
Orora	16.7
Perpetual	16.1
Collins Foods	15.0
Bapcor	14.3
Schaffer	12.5
AUB	10.0
Seven Group	9.5
Macquarie	9.3
GWA	8.7
Technology One	8.0
Rio Tinto	7.9
Data#3	7.9
Sonic Healthcare	7.1
Medibank Private	5.8
Clover	5.3
IPH	3.5
Infomedia	3.5
Jumbo Interactive	2.8
Altium	2.6
Carsales.com	1.1
CSL	0.4
Austal	0.0
Beach Energy	0.0
IRESS	0.0
Pacific Smiles	0.0
Platinum	0.0
Premier Investments	0.0
Magellan Financial	−1.7
Brambles	−5.8
ASX	−6.4
Servcorp	−10.0
CIMIC	−15.5
Pendal	−17.8
Smartgroup	−19.8
Bravura Solutions	−21.8
Evolution Mining	−25.0
Breville	−35.4
Orica	−40.0
IDP Education	−51.5
Regis Resources	−56.3
Aristocrat Leisure	−82.1
OFX	−82.8

Table P

Five-year share price return

This table ranks the approximate annual average return to investors from a five-year investment in each of the companies in the book, as of September 2021. It is an accumulated return, based on share price appreciation or depreciation plus dividend payments.

	% p.a.
Australian Ethical Investment	61.7
Objective	60.2
Codan	59.9
Pro Medicus	57.4
Pinnacle Investment	57.3
Jumbo Interactive	52.2
Dicker Data	48.7
IDP Education	45.4
Grange Resources	41.6
Mineral Resources	39.6
Schaffer	32.9
Breville	32.7
Supply Network	32.0
Clover	29.5
Altium	28.3
Data#3	27.8
Elders	26.9
Fortescue Metals	26.1
Aristocrat Leisure	25.4
PWR	25.1
ARB	24.9
Integral Diagnostics	24.9
CSL	24.6
Rio Tinto	24.5
Collins Foods	24.4
Fiducian	24.3
BlueScope Steel	23.9
Infomedia	23.9
Seven Group	22.9
REA	22.4
BHP	21.9
Bravura Solutions	21.8
Money3	20.6
Steadfast	20.3
ALS	20.1
Nick Scali	20.0
Macquarie	19.2
AUB	18.8
Reece	18.5
Magellan Financial	17.3
Beach Energy	16.9
Carsales.com	16.6
Evolution Mining	16.5
Credit Corp	16.4
Metcash	15.9

	% p.a.
Sonic Healthcare	15.6
Reliance Worldwide	15.3
CSR	14.3
Wesfarmers	14.1
ASX	14.0
Baby Bunting	13.8
Technology One	13.8
IPH	13.7
Premier Investments	13.6
Adairs	13.5
JB Hi-Fi	13.4
Ansell	13.0
Cochlear	12.1
NIB	11.4
Commonwealth Bank	11.0
Accent	10.4
Austal	9.8
Medibank Private	9.4
Monadelphous	9.3
Hansen Technologies	8.4
Beacon Lighting	7.7
Sandfire Resources	7.7
IRESS	7.1
Smartgroup	7.1
Super Retail	6.9
Bapcor	6.8
Harvey Norman	6.8
McMillan Shakespeare	6.8
Costa	6.7
GUD	6.1
Orora	5.1
Newcrest Mining	5.0
Brambles	4.9
Pendal	4.9
GWA	4.2
Pacific Smiles	3.3
Perpetual	2.7
Orica	2.1
Virtus Health	0.9
Regis Resources	0.4
Platinum	0.2
CIMIC	−0.9
SG Fleet	−2.1
OFX	−3.8
Michael Hill	−6.8
Servcorp	−9.8

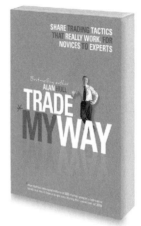

Best-selling author Alan Hull presents the complete sharemarket solution for novices to experts. Whether you're managing your portfolio, trading tactically on the sharemarket or investing in blue chip shares, Alan Hull explains the ins and outs of investing and trading in easy-to-understand and engaging language.

Available in print and e-book formats